DEVELOPMENTAL TRAUMA: THE GAME CHANGER IN THE MENTAL HEALTH PROFESSION

2ND EDITION

Barry K. Weinhold, PhD
Janae B. Weinhold, PhD

PUBLISHED BY:
CICRCL Press
Colorado Springs, Colorado 80918
(719) 445-0565
www.weinholds.org

Second Edition
Copyright © 2018
Barry K. Weinhold, PhD.
Janae B. Weinhold, PhD

Printed in the United States of America
ISBN: 1-882056-23X
ISBN-13: 978-1-882056-23-1

WHAT READERS ARE SAYING
ABOUT THIS BOOK

Developmental Trauma: The Game Changer in the Mental Health Profession skillfully describes how trauma and neglect during the first three years of life can seriously hinder the development of a person's true self and limit a person's skills for relating to others—and it provides essential treatment solutions. A must-read to become a competent trauma-informed professional.

Sandra Felt, LCSW
.... Author, *Beyond the Good-Girl Jail: When You Dare to Live from Your True Self*

"Wow! Clear, strong, and packed with comprehensive powerful information for a new level of mental health knowledge and impact. Get ready!"

Valerie Montgomery, BSW, MA, NCC, LPC, PhD Candidate
Women-Centric Counselor at BeyondBeautiful.net

Developmental Trauma: The Game Changer in Mental Health Profession is a must read for counselors, advocates, and first responders providing services from a trauma informed perspective. The Weinholds present several insightful points that help the reader to ask and understand the question "what happened or didn't happen to you?" Instead of "What's wrong with you?" It is also culturally sensitive and can be adapted for use with any culture. I have found this to be true in working with the Latino community, especially DV, SA and CSA survivors.

Carmen Gutiérrez, MA, PhD Candidate
Bilingual Mental Health Counselor and Advocate,

Developmental Trauma: The Game Changer in the Mental Health Profession, is a must read for every mental health professional and anyone who has lived through developmental trauma. This book has validated not only my professional experience, it has also validated my life experience!

E.K. Wolf, PhD, LPC
Author, *After Incest: From Devastation to Vibrant Aliveness*

Developmental Trauma: The Game Changer in the Mental Health Profession is an excellent primer for mental health practitioners new to the profession and wanting to learn more about human development, trauma, and attachment theory to enhance their professional and clinical skills. It also provides foundational information about developmental trauma, particularly how it correlates with early childhood development, and how it can be healed through process work. Additionally, and significantly, it also describes the evolution in understanding of developmental trauma and its critical role in today's clinical practice.

Michelle M. Morrissey, MA, NCC, LPC

It is my pleasure to recommend the book *Developmental Trauma: The Game Changer in the Mental Health Profession*, as there aren't others in this category. The book provides insight and discussion about the significant impact of developmental trauma, a subject that all levels of behavioral health practitioners need to learn more about. I will highly recommend this overdue book in my trauma-informed care trainings and in the graduate classes I teach.

Debi Grebenik, PhD LCSW
Director, Trauma Training Institute

Developmental Trauma: The Game Changer in the Mental Health Profession is a major theoretical and practical source for understanding the nature of developmental trauma and the path of healing it. Just a few weeks of applying healing interventions covered in this book showed a dramatic improvement in my clients. This rich book is a treasure not only to mental health professionals, but to anyone who is interested in understanding and healing their own developmental trauma.

Elena Glass, MA, LPC NCC

Developmental Trauma: The Game Changer in the Mental Health Profession, is an amazing, genuine book about what is happening with our individual and collective "mental health." The Weinholds have the courage, wisdom, and heart to care enough to write this book, and it has been life changing for me to read and experience it. As a mental health worker, it is time to look beyond a "diagnosis" and help my clients understand what happened to them.

Wendy J. Carter, LCSW
Heart of the Phoenix Counseling and Art, LLC

DEDICATION

We dedicate this book to the students in our *Trauma-Informed Care Certificate Training* courses who were its first readers and critics.

(This page intentionally left blank)

ACKNOWLEDGMENTS

Our heuristic research indicates that developmental trauma is caused by attachment and separation trauma during the first three years of life. We believe its impact is so great that it is blocking human evolution, and therefore must be addressed as a public health issue. This process begins with educating and training behavioral health professionals in a trauma-informed care model that is also attachment-informed and developmental trauma-informed. It is also time to emphasize developmental trauma an integrative healthcare issue.

We applaud the pioneering work of the thousands of behavioral health practitioners who have helped to identify developmental trauma as a clinical reality and are seeking ways to heal it. We particularly honor the efforts of Bessel van der Kolk and his colleagues to add Developmental Trauma Disorder to the DSM-5.

We also acknowledge the many years of research and clinical work by Allen Schore, Dan Siegel, Mary Main, Eric Hesse and Bruce Perry in helping to validate developmental trauma's impact on people's long-term mental and physical health.

A special thanks to Sandra Felt, Valerie Montgomery, Elaine Wolf and Elena Glass for their proofreading, and to Matt Baldanza for his technical support with the final manuscript.

(This page intentionally left blank)

CONTENTS

PART THREE
HEALING DEVELOPMENTAL TRAUMA

INTRODUCTION

THE LAST GAME-CHANGER IN THE MENTAL HEALTH PROFESSION

The last game-changer event in the mental health profession happened in 1980 when PTSD was added to the DSM-III. It was many years later before mental health practitioners realized the game-changing impact that PTSD had on the profession. Now, some 38 years later, developmental trauma (DT) has become the new game-changer.

There are many parallels between the game-changing events of 1980 and what is happening now in the mental health profession. One of these parallels is that many mental health practitioners aren't aware of developmental trauma as a clinical issue nor of the game-change events that it has set in motion. In Chapter Four, we describe the 1980 game-changer event and compare it to the game-change that is happening presently.

There's a difference between PTSD and developmental trauma, and it's an important one. PTSD is caused primarily by event trauma, and developmental trauma is caused by ongoing relational traumas that occur during the first three years of life, particularly in the first year during the parent-child attachment process.

In the mid-80s we began encountering adult clients in our clinical practice who had symptoms of PTSD, but didn't have traumatic events in their past that would account for them. Many of them came to us because they suffered from intractable relationship conflicts that recycled without resolution. These factors forced us to look more deeply at their developmental histories, searching for early traumas that may have happened in their family of origin.

By the early 1990's, we identified what we were seeing in our clients as "developmental trauma." We found their post-traumatic reactions often involved reenactments of caregiver abuse or neglect during the first years of life. Neglect is the most difficult issue to identify because *nothing happened*, so there's nothing to grieve or be angry about.

1

We gradually developed tools to help clients connect the dots between what "happened or didn't happen" to them, but should have, during the first two to three years of life, and the relational issues they were experiencing in their adult relationships. We also began developing new methods for effectively healing developmental traumas.

Because the two of us also were aware of our own developmental traumas and how they appeared during our recurring relational conflicts, we made an important decision. We decided to use our relationship as a "laboratory," as a resource for studying developmental trauma. We learned to connect the dots between our conflicts and the relational template we developed in our first three years of life. We also made healing our own developmental traumas a prerequisite for helping others. This commitment became our life's work.

WHAT DO OTHERS SAY ABOUT DEVELOPMENTAL TRAUMA?

Mental health researchers define it in a variety of ways. Bessel van der Kolk, a leading expert in this field, defines it as "the result of insecure attachments during the first three years causing chronic relational problems, inability to concentrate or regulate feelings, chronic anger, fear and anxiety, self-loathing, aggression, and self-destructive behavior."[1]

Alan Schore, another leading expert at USC and often considered the American father of attachment theory, says that early relational processes can only explain DT, not specific incidents. One of his primary contributions to the field of attachment is the introduction of language from the quantum sciences to help explain the relational dynamics that are at the core of attachment. He uses words such as *attunement, resonance* and *synchrony* to describe the exchange of energy and information that happens in the parent-child relationship.

Schore also uses quantum language to describe mother-infant interactions, and also to describe how therapists attune with their clients via their sensory system and synchronize their right brain to clients' right brains. In the therapist/client shared resonant field of energy, both experience a deep empathic connection that helps heal the relational trauma from their childhood.[2]

Dan Siegel, child psychiatrist at UCLA, defines developmental trauma as the result of attachment failures during the first year of life. He says that developmental trauma impairs the long-term ability of the individual to self-regulate and self-organize. He says it interferes with the ability of an individual to integrate various parts of his/her brain.[3]

Many other practicing clinicians also recognized that event trauma and the symptoms associated with Post-Traumatic Stress Disorder (PTSD) didn't fit with what they were seeing in their clients. Consequently, more and more of them began focusing on the role of adverse childhood experiences as a cause of DT.

WHAT DO WE SAY ABOUT DEVELOPMENTAL TRAUMA?

Our definition of developmental trauma parallels and also goes beyond what we find other developmentalists are saying. We define developmental trauma as *relational* trauma that happened before birth and during the bonding and separation stages of human development. Our definition also includes intentional and unintentional neglect as a causative factor.

Common infant-parent relational traumas involve attachment traumas during pregnancy, birth and the first year of life. These include being unwanted by one or both parents, neglectful or invasive caregiving, early or extended separation from the mother, divorce, surgeries, and growing up in an abusive and neglectful or unstable home environments where there is drug use and violence. Separation trauma that occurs from about eight months to three years, involves punitive and shaming physical and/or emotional discipline practices or a failure to provide proper support for the completion of the separation process. It also can be caused by a lack of appropriate limits by the parents that help the child learn to emotionally regulate themselves.

These relational disconnects create a pattern of developmental trauma that impacts infants' and toddlers' developing brains and nervous systems in ways that disturb their attachment to parents and other early caregivers. These early experiences have far-reaching consequences on people's long-term physical and mental health. They impair not only the individual's capacity for sustained intimacy, but ultimately impact the social/emotional fabric of couple and family relationships, as well as organizations and other large systems.

We recognize that people's natural learning style is to repeat something unfinished in their past until they are able to understand and integrate its meaning into their awareness. Our heuristic research with many clients' relational conflicts revealed the presence of unhealed developmental traumas. Our clinical work helped them connect the dots between their unhealed developmental traumas and the problems they were having in their intimate relationships.

Part II of this book presents a detailed description of our systemic model of human development. This important background information is essential for therapists who are working to identify and heal developmental trauma in themselves and their clients.

DEVELOPMENTAL TRAUMA: A POLITICAL GAME-CHANGER

Developmental trauma is also a political game-changer, having many similarities to the political controversy that surrounded the addition of the PTSD to the DSM-III in 1980. Some of the same factions within the mental health profession that denied the need for PTSD as a diagnostic category in the DSM-III are now denying the importance of developmental trauma and including Developmental Trauma Disorder (DTD) as a diagnostic category in the recently revised Diagnostic and Statistical Manual-V.

The 1980 PTSD diagnostic category emerged from research conducted on Vietnam veterans who were suffering from the long-term effects of combat. The Developmental Trauma Disorder diagnosis emerged from research conducted on children and adults who were suffering from the long-term effects of relational trauma during early childhood. It also includes the demographic research on the long-term effects on physical and mental health of adverse childhood experiences (ACEs). These studies are discussed in later chapters of the book.

In both cases, an influential group of professional therapists and researchers proposed including the new diagnostic category to the members of the American Psychiatric Association (APA) who were revising the current versions of the DSM. In both cases, the writers of the DSM ignored the research results that validated the need for the new diagnostic categories. The crucial difference between these two scenarios was that the PTSD diagnostic category was eventually included in the DSM-III.

The DTD diagnostic category, however, was rejected and is not part of the DSM-5. The APA group involved in revising the DSM-IV refused to accept the research studies involving over 200,000 children and adults and decided to exclude it from the DSM-5. We present the full story of this controversial decision in Chapter Four.

The APA's decision left millions of children and adult clients and their mental health counselors without an official mechanism for identifying, treating and being reimbursed for mental health issues related to developmental trauma. It also leaves a large group of individuals without a framework for understanding why they feel and behave the way they do. This supports a persistent belief that these people are "just crazy."

This situation also created a dilemma for many mental health practitioners. The symptoms they see in their clients call for more sophisticated and more specific clinical protocols, yet they lack an accurate DSM-5 category to diagnose and heal developmental trauma. Some practitioners use existing diagnostic categories such as Reactive Attachment Disorder or the new Childhood PTSD category in the DSM-5. However, these categories exclude adults who are the majority of clients seeking mental health support.

In addition, the wealth of new research findings about attachment and brain development offer exciting new treatment approaches that practitioners are reluctant to use. The research examined the long-term effects of adverse childhood experiences (ACEs) on adult physical and mental health validate the importance of helping people overcome the impact of developmental trauma caused by childhood adversity. Chapter Two offers a more detailed description of this and other related research.

Mental health counselor training programs also do not provide sufficient courses on how to identify and treat the different categories of trauma. Most programs are tied to the American Counseling Association's policies and counselor education programs' CACREP accreditation standards. This core curriculum only contains one course on trauma, Disaster, Trauma, and Crisis Counseling. Meeting CACREP's program standards leaves counselor education programs with no space in the curriculum for trauma-informed care and developmental trauma courses. Even state professional organizations have provided little leadership to help change counselor training programs.

Standard trauma-specific training is almost exclusively designed to treat symptoms of PTSD. While Prolonged Exposure Therapy, EMDR and Cognitive Behavior Therapy have had some success in treating PTSD symptoms caused by event trauma, they are very limited in their ability to heal the long-term relational effects of developmental trauma.

There are other new and more promising intervention tools available, but they are not part of the conventional tool kit used by most therapists. We describe some of these new tools we use with individuals, couples, families, parents and organizations in Part III of this book.

DEVELOPMENTAL TRAUMA: A CONSCIOUSNESS GAME-CHANGER

The word *trauma* has many negative connotations and associations. It's typically considered "bad" and has judgments associated with it that some people use as a negative identity.

We reframe of the concept of trauma, telling our clients that they are good people (identity) who had bad things (experiences) happen to them, and that they need tools and relational support to help them heal from the long-term effects of their experiences. We encourage them to release self-judgments about having unhealed developmental traumas, and use a "tend and befriend" approach that focuses on compassion and empathy.

We also remind clients that the natural learning style of humans is to reenact a childhood trauma until it is understood and integrated into their mind and body. This framework helps redefine their presenting problems as their best effort to repair the long-term effects of hidden and unhealed trauma. We say that they are experiencing a healing in progress, even though it may not feel that way. Whatever clients have been doing is the best they can do, at the moment. An important goal of therapy is helping clients move clients forward in their healing process and helping them learn new ways to understand and heal their traumas.

THE EMERGING SPLIT IN MENTAL HEALTH PRACTICE

Concurrent with the controversy inside the APA about DT, there is also disagreement about the direction of the mental health profession. One part of the mental health field is moving toward is a "corporate model" of mental health care with a strong emphasis on finances and the bottom line. Its strong medical orientation, unfortunately, requires that people must be "sick" before they can get treatment services.

This approach creates a "water wheel" concept of treatment where the client floats into a corporate treatment center, receives a diagnosis and time-limited treatment for their symptoms. Then they are quickly flushed out the front door to fend for themselves.

The corporate model also dictates the use of more impersonal, technical, and mechanical treatment protocols and techniques. This approach doesn't require clinicians to build much of a relationship with their clients, as they are gone very quickly. This is sometimes called the Medical Model of mental health treatment.

Another part of the field is using a developmental/relational approach. It recognizes that clients' problems are primarily the result of developmental trauma and childhood adversity that involve parents and other caregivers. In order to successfully treat these problems and heal the effects of relational trauma, clients must learn how to build and sustain a functional relationship with their therapists.

Therapists need specialized skills to help clients learn new and more effective ways to heal their relational traumas. The relational model of psychotherapy presents a challenge for many therapists, particularly those who have not healed their own relational traumas.

A developmental model of treatment views the client not as someone with symptoms, a disease to cure, or a problem to fix. Rather they are people who had some bad things happen to them that left deep scars on their psyche. This approach is not only more prescriptive and less diagnostic, it is also more humane and compassionate.

A developmental treatment model identifies the incomplete developmental processes that were disrupted during clients' early childhood, and seeks to help clients complete them in present time. The research confirms that using a developmental approach helps clients rewire their brains and reorganize their attachment history.

This moves therapy away from the medical disease model, and towards a "tend and befriend" model of treatment. In this model, the therapeutic relationship becomes a crucible for restoring healthy relationship dynamics.

A DEVELOPMENTAL APPROACH TO MENTAL HEALTH

Most therapists lack a solid grounding in developmental psychology, particularly the importance of pre- and perinatal and early childhood development. We believe they need to understand each stage of development and the essential developmental processes in each. Once they understand the optimal model of human development, therapists find it easier to identify the sources of developmental disruptions and recognize the roots of adult conflicts. These traumas interfere with the completion of the essential developmental processes that disrupts the optimal development of all human systems, starting with the individual. Part II of this book provides you with an overview of early childhood development. Here we also describe Developmental Systems Theory, our meta-theory that presents an optimal model of human development.

BARRY K. WEINHOLD, PHD – JANAE B. WEINHOLD, PHD

PROFESSIONAL SKILLS FOR HEALING
DEVELOPMENTAL TRAUMA

Do you know your own attachment style? This is crucial for avoiding countertransference issues with clients. Research indicates that up to 80-90 percent of the clients who come for psychotherapy have Disorganized Attachment. Statistically, it is very likely that most therapists also have Disorganized Attachment. Understanding and healing your own Disorganized Attachment helps avoid a case of the "blind leading the blind."

Being unaware of your own Disorganized Attachment can have ethical and legal implications for you and for your clients. It creates a professional blind spot that can increase the probability of having grievances filed against you, and can also contribute to burn out.

Our trauma-informed care trainings help participants identify their own unhealed developmental traumas and their attachment history. We also help them avoid "Rescuing" their clients by doing more than half the work, or by trying to work without a clear contract, that is a symptom of a Disorganized Attachment history.

IMPLEMENTING DEVELOPMENTAL TRAUMA HEALING
STRATEGIES IN THE MENTAL HEALTH PROFESSION

Chapter 15 presents a vision of a mental health profession that focuses on healing developmental trauma. This chapter looks at what needs to happen in the next five years, particularly with therapists, to move forward using this developmental perspective. Mental health professionals must become active participants in this game-changing initiative.

Our vision for the future of the mental health profession includes all that's currently known about developmental trauma. In this chapter, we share what trauma-informed care trainings might look like at a national level.

OUR RELATIONSHIP AS A LABORATORY FOR
HEALING DEVELOPMENTAL TRAUMA

Throughout the book we share pieces of our own story about how we've used our relationship as a place to heal our own developmental trauma. We believe that committed, conscious, and cooperative relationships are an excellent place for doing deep healing work. This approach works best for people who have some self-awareness and have skills in navigating "deeper waters," and also the support of caring therapists.

THE IMPORTANCE OF SELF-THERAPY

We believe therapists must work on themselves before working on others. Identifying and healing their own developmental traumas will help them work more effectively with clients in healing their developmental traumas. We emphasize the motto, "Do onto yourself before doing onto others," from the counselor training program that Barry founded at the University of Colorado-Colorado Springs.

We suggest that you take all the self-inventories scattered throughout this book to help you identify any blind spots you might have. These self-assessments can help you locate areas where you might be vulnerable to countertransference. The *Developmental Trauma Inventory* below can help you identify any hidden developmental traumas.

Feel free to also use this and other self-inventories with your clients. The Appendix at the back of the book contains all the self-inventories and self-assessment tools mentioned in this book. We request that you acknowledge us as the authors by retaining our names and copyright marks on all of the self-inventories you use with your clients and others.

SELF-INVENTORY: IDENTIFYING DEVELOPMENTAL TRAUMA

Directions: Read the statements below and use 1–4 to indicate in the blank your self-assessment of each item: 1 = mostly not true, 2 = occasionally true, 3 = usually true and 4 = almost always true.

_____ 1. I have trouble feeling close to the people I care about.

_____ 2. I feel like other people are more in charge of my life than I am.

_____ 3. I seem reluctant to try new things.

_____ 4. I have trouble keeping my weight down.

_____ 5. I am easily bored with what I am doing.

_____ 6. I have trouble accepting help from others even when I need it.

_____ 7. I work best when I am under a lot of pressure.

_____ 8. I have trouble admitting my mistakes.

_____ 9. I tend to forget or not keep agreements I make.

_____ 10. I have trouble handling my time and money effectively.

_____ 11. I use intimidation or manipulation to settle my conflicts.

_____ 12. I feel personally attacked when someone has a conflict with me.

_____ 13. I have a difficult time giving and receiving compliments.

_____ 14. I have a short fuse when I feel frustrated with others or myself.

_____ 15. I tend to blame others for causing the problems I have.

_____ 16. I feel like I have a huge empty place inside of me.

_____ 17. It is hard for me to have positive thoughts about my future.

_____ 18. Inside I feel like a tightly coiled spring.

_____ 19. When I get anxious, I tend to eat or drink too much.

_____ 20. I feel empty and alone.

_____ 21. I tend to question the motives of others.

_____ 22. I feel unloved by others.

_____ 23. I have a hard time defining what I want or need.

_____ 24. When I get into a conflict somebody else gets his or her way.

_____ 25. I tend to overreact to certain people and/or situations that bug me.

_____ 26. I feel like I am on an emotional roller coaster.

_____ 27. I have trouble sticking with any spiritual practices I start.

_____ 28. Important people in my life have abandoned me emotionally or physically.

_____ 29. I have trouble concentrating on what I am doing.

_____ 30. When I think about my childhood, I draw a big blank.

_____ 31. I have trouble experiencing the intimacy I want in my relationships

_____ 32. I have trouble falling asleep and staying asleep.

_____ 33. I tend to "walk on eggs" around certain people or situations.

_____ 34. I avoid places or situations that remind me of experiences from my past.

_____ 35. I have recurring bad dreams about what happened to me in the past.

_____ 36. My thoughts seem to have a life of their own.

_____ 37. I have trouble paying attention to what others are saying.

_____ 38. I tend to avoid situations and people that could cause me conflicts.

_____ 39. I experience big gaps in my memory about my childhood.

_____ 40. I have a hard time knowing what I am feeling inside.

_____ **Total Score**

Interpretation: If your score was between:

40–82   = Some evidence of developmental trauma

83–20   = Moderate evidence of developmental trauma

12–160 = Strong evidence of developmental trauma

Further analysis: Look at the content of items where you scored 3's or 4's for clues to unhealed developmental traumas

(This page intentionally left blank)

PART ONE

AN OVERVIEW OF TRAUMA

(This page intentionally left blank)

CHAPTER ONE

A HISTORY OF TRAUMA

When he first said my diagnosis, I couldn't believe it.
There must be another PTSD than post-traumatic stress
disorder, I thought. I have only heard of war veterans
who have served on the front lines and seen the horrors of
battle being diagnosed with PTSD. I am a Beverly Hills
housewife, not a soldier. I can't have PTSD. Well, I was
wrong. Housewives can get PTSD, too, and yours truly did.

—Taylor Armstrong, *Hiding from Reality: My Story*
of Love, Loss, and Finding the Courage Within

THE ORIGINS OF THE FIELD OF TRAUMATOLOGY

Childhood trauma is a major worldwide public health issue. While the field
of traumatology is now about thirty-five years old, only in the past few years
have we understood that certain memories can be compartmentalized and
stored in different parts of the brain, parts of the mind and body that don't
communicate with each other. This discovery has provoked even more research and prompted the mental health field to change both its theories
about trauma and the way that practitioners treat it.

First a brief look at the history of how the traumatology field evolved.
Trauma was first identified as "shell shock" in veterans after the Civil War
and World War I. After WWI, psychiatrists from all over the world agreed
that a diagnosis of Gross Stress Reaction should be included in the DSM-I.
They also included stress reactions to natural disaster as part of that diagnosis. In 1968, the DSM II came out and, without explanation, omitted the
diagnosis of Gross Stress Reaction.[4]

Interest in the concept waned after World War I, but it was revived during and after WW II. Medical personnel recognized that soldiers who had repeated exposure combat events reacted with symptoms of acute anxiety. They became sensitive to sensory stimuli that reminded them of their original experiences. This syndrome was given a variety of names: traumatic war neurosis, combat fatigue, battle stress and gross stress reaction. After World War II was over, they discovered another type of stress called "the experience of death camp survivors."[5]

Gradually, people recognized that those who experienced civilian disasters had a similar reaction. During this period, research studies focused on two different causes of these anxiety reactions. The first, called the "biological school," posited that stress was a healthy reaction to stressful situations. However, they believed that in some cases, chronic or severe stress could lead to a traumatic neurosis.[6]

The second position, called the "psychological school" emphasized the role of unconscious or repressed memories of early childhood traumas. This led to the formation of defense mechanisms that people used to ward off the repressed memories of early traumas.[7]

Returning Vietnam vets who were exhibiting symptoms of Gross Stress Reaction had no accepted diagnosis for these symptoms. As a result, they could not receive VA benefits or be treated in VA hospitals. Many vets were suffering from acute anxiety, nightmares, a lack of emotional affect and an avoidance of situations that reminded them of the war. Many turned to alcohol and drugs to help them cope with these symptoms. Many committed suicide as a result. Some of the VA psychologists actually thought these vets were psychotic and therefore insane.

As psychiatrists were in the process of updating the DSM III edition to the DSM III-R, mental health professionals hoped that the Gross Stress Reaction would be added back into the revision. Many were calling it "Post Vietnam Syndrome." Dr. Robert Spitzer, a psychiatrist who was highly involved in the revision of the DSM III, told inquiring mental health professionals that there was no plan to add Gross Stress Reaction or anything else like it to the DSM III-R.

At this point, a group of mental health professionals decided to become change agents. They requested a meeting with Dr. Spitzer in which they showed him the VA's records of the many cases they had of returning Vietnam veterans with severe mental stress ailments. They also described their frustration in trying to diagnose and treat veterans.

Spitzer was so moved by this group's presentation that he strongly suggested that a new diagnostic category be added to the DSM III-R. Therefore, in 1980, the DSM III-R added Post Traumatic Stress Disorder to the manual. This new category also included criteria that expanded the definition to include strong emotional reactions to any traumatic event.[8]

As long as men were found to suffer from delayed retrieval of memories related to war atrocities committed by a clearly identifiable enemy, this condition was not a controversial topic and was well documented in psychological literature. PTSD emerged as a clinical disorder primarily from the treatment of Vietnam veterans, who displayed many of the symptoms now described in the Diagnostic and Statistical Manual.

The women's movement of the 1970s paralleled the consciousness-raising that happened in Vietnam veterans' support groups. Women recognized that many of them also had symptoms of combat neurosis. While men were slowly beginning to receive recognition and resources to alleviate their war trauma, many women found their "problem without a name" was anchored in their relationships with Vietnam vets.

This included domestic violence, rape, male domination, and emotional abuse. This awareness actually helped spawn the rise of feminism and an effort to educate society about the existence of post-traumatic stress in women who were in abusive relationships with Vietnam vets and its impact on their lives and their children's lives.[9]

A couple of important things came out of the women's movement. The first was new language to help articulate the impact of dominating and authoritarian male behavior on women, children, and families. The second was a redefinition of rape to include date rape, acquaintance rape, and marital rape.

With the women's movement came the emergence of crisis and domestic violence centers where women and children could get practical, legal, and emotional protection and support for victimization and relational trauma and for symptoms of PTSD.

The children's movement, if it might be called that, began in the 1980s with the emergence of the field of pre- and perinatal psychology. The founding members of this field have continued to build a body of scientific knowledge that supports their premise that humans have consciousness and memory from their very first moment of life.

During the 1990s, the field of traumatology also saw the emergence of many new modalities for treating—not just medicating—the symptoms of trauma. One such tools is Eye Movement Desensitization and Reprocessing (EMDR) that involves moving the eyes side to side while recalling elements of a trauma. It was one of the first trauma reduction tools to be widely used. While it was effective in clearing auditory and visual elements of trauma, initially it did not clear the proprioceptive and relational elements of a trauma.

Thought-Field Therapy (TFT), a body-oriented therapy, worked exceptionally well on clearing trauma related to touch and movement. Emotional Freedom Therapy (EFT), also a body-oriented therapy, involves specific patterns of tapping on the body's energy meridians. Much of the early research on these new technologies was conducted with veterans of the Vietnam War, who helped build a solid research base for their effectiveness in treating symptoms of PTSD.

PTSD: A SOCIAL & POLITICAL GAME-CHANGER

Adding PTSD to the DSM-IV-R became a social, political and mental health game-changer, causing massive ripples of change throughout many social and political systems. It changed the way that psychiatric research was structured and funded. The education of psychiatrists and mental health professionals had to be revised, and new textbooks had to be written. It also affected domestic relationships.

When women and girls began revealing delayed recall of traumatic memories related to sexual assault and domestic violence in the mid-1970s, this information was considered unbelievable and initially considered highly controversial. Investigations regarding the prevalence of domestic violence, which grew out of the women's movement, validated the existence of post-traumatic stress in women who survived domestic battery, incest, street rape, acquaintance rape, date rape, and rape in their marriage.

It became clear to many investigators during the women's movement that their subordinate position was maintained and enforced by the hidden violence of men. When female victims began seeking justice against their alleged perpetrators, however, the issue came out of the closet and moved from science into politics.[10]

The issue of delayed recall of memories involving childhood trauma, particularly sexual abuse, became a political issue during the 1990s. The idea of unscrupulous therapists deliberately planting sexual abuse memories in clients became one of the most heated debates in psychology and psychiatry. It was labelled "The False Memory Syndrome."

Proponents of these political issues dismissed a century of clinical observation and scientific investigations from battlefields, emergency rooms, and psychiatric wards and labeled delayed recall of traumatic memories as "false memories." They attributed the delayed recall to "memory implantations" by unscrupulous therapists.

This sudden shift in attitude regarding delayed retrieval of memory illustrates how society reacts when scientific discoveries conflict with established values and beliefs that support the cultural denial of a problem. Psychology and psychiatry have traditionally been vulnerable in such instances and often were pressured into giving up the pursuit of science and, instead, conformed to the prevailing societal attitudes. The cultural denial about the impact of trauma is reflected in the shortage of available treatment programs and of academically based training in effective treatments. The impact of this attack was also visible in the ferocity with which the "false memory" debate was pursued in both courtrooms and in academic psychiatry and psychology programs.

During the debate, researchers from the field of traumatology presented extensive evidence proving the correlation of post-traumatic stress reactions with child abuse and domestic violence, and demonstrating that PTSD is more than shell shock or combat trauma or "false memories."

OUR DISCOVERY OF DEVELOPMENTAL TRAUMA

After our marriage in 1984, we began having relational conflicts that triggered emotional dysregulation and disrupted our intimacy. This was a primary factor in deciding to convert our relationship as a laboratory to study conflict. Here we learned to identify the underlying developmental factors that were disrupting our relationship. We also discovered unhealed developmental trauma from the first three years of our lives as its primary cause.

We both had severe adverse childhood experiences, particularly in the first year of life. Barry suffered from emotional and physical neglect and abandonment because his mother had post-partum depression during the first few months after his birth. She was unable to function as a mother. She went back to work when Barry was a week old and left him with a series of baby sitters. This abandonment made it difficult for him to trust and affected his attachment with his mother. Barry weighed six pounds at birth and by four weeks his weight had dropped to five pounds. He was a classic "failure to thrive" baby."

When Barry was eight weeks old, his mother also almost drowned him during a bath. His dad intervened and Barry went to live with his grandmother and aunt. His early caregivers were nurturing women who did their best to care for him, and probably saved his life.

When he was ten months old, while with his parents, he fell down a flight of stairs in his walker. His mother failed to close the gate at the top of the stairs. After this incident, his grandmother allowed his parents to move into a house she owned. His mother continued to work and they hired a Mennonite girl to take care of him. During the first year of his life, Barry had four primary mother figures. While this helped him survive, it left him with confused insecure attachments, and made it difficult for him to bond with women in his adult relationships.

Barry also came to fear his mother, creating the foundation for the Disorganized Attachment Style. When Janae behaved in any way that reminded him of his scary mother, he would withdraw and go into protective mode. He did outpatient "reparenting" therapy as an adult that helped him heal some of his fears stemming from his early abandonment and multiple attachment figures.

Janae's early trauma began with a difficult birth where she almost died. Her mother was anesthetized and she was born with the umbilical cord wrapped around her neck, causing a forceps birth. Then she was kept in a nursery and separated from her mother for over a week.

Her mother had a shock reaction when she discovered she was pregnant again when Janae was about three months old. Janae's mother went to the hospital for the birth of her sister when Janae was eleven months old, and she was left with her grandmother for over a week. Her grandmother was a cold, mean-hearted person who left Janae to cry in a crib upstairs. During this period, Janae had an acute despair reaction often called going into the "black hole." This event causing a bonding break with her mother that she was never able to fully repair.

When Janae returned home after this, she refused to re-bond with her mother, rejecting all her efforts to reunite. Janae became anxious, defiant and counterdependent. After her sister's birth, her mother became overwhelmed from having two children so close in age, which caused her to increasingly dissociate.

In order to make herself feel more secure, Janae gradually became her mother's "little helper." When she received praise for growing up so fast and becoming so capable, she became her mother's caretaker. Janae became proficient in organizing the physical environment around herself and her mother, with the hope that this would make her mother more stable and be more emotionally present.

The year that Janae was thirteen, her mother had a series of deaths. She lost both her parents, an aunt who was like a mother to her, and a close first cousin. Janae's father also betrayed her during an extended family conflict. The accumulated loss and betrayal sent her into a spiraling depression. She eventually committed suicide by carbon monoxide poisoning, and took Janae's 5-year old brother with her.

Because Janae never had a secure attachment to her mother, she got triggered any time she felt Barry withdrawing from her. She kept expecting him to abandon her and tested him a lot to make sure his love was real and that she could count on him.

We eventually recognized the serious limitations that our histories created in having authentic intimacy. We both had Disorganized Attachment histories with our mothers, and our trauma patterns matched perfectly in ways that were able to trigger all of our fears and frailties.

We realized that we needed to work cooperatively to heal these wounds if we were going to function effectively as intimate partners, as professional colleagues, and as mental health practitioners. Learning the underlying attachment and relational issues helped us become more compassionate towards each other, except when we got triggered by a memory of early childhood trauma. Our periodic episodes of conflict and disconnect were opportunities for growth and healing. This motivated us to consciously convert our relationship into a "laboratory" to do healing work, and to build trust with each other. While there were times when this path was painful, we did learn to trust. Resolving conflicts became a primary resource for deepening our relationship and clearing the trauma we each brought to it.

SHARING WITH CLIENTS AND STUDENTS
FROM OUR RELATIONAL LABORATORY

As we began to share what we learned in our relational laboratory with our clients and students, we found that much of it was helpful to others. Sometime during the mid-eighties, we began attracting couple clients who reported relational conflicts with similar symptoms: emotional dysregulation, getting triggered, hypervigilance, and trust and intimacy issues.

When we asked about traumatic events during early childhood that might be causing these symptoms, clients typically could not remember any.

Since we were already tuned into our own attachment history, we recognized that the trauma we had experienced was relational trauma from our parents who neglected our needs.

After the PTSD diagnostic category was added to the DSM-III in 1980, we and many other therapists began using it to describe the symptoms we were seeing in our clients, particularly with a history of childhood trauma. We eventually realized, however, the diagnostic criteria weren't a good fit for many clients, and not a good fit for those who suffered emotional abuse and neglect.

By the mid-90's, we identified what we were seeing in our clients and ourselves as "developmental trauma." Then we began looking for ways to help our clients based what we were learning from them and in our personal laboratory.

We defined *developmental trauma* as a form of subtle, but chronic, relational trauma that causes developmental delays during the bonding and separations stages in the first three years of life. We saw the long-term effects of unrecognized and unhealed developmental trauma as the major causes of delayed and distorted development in all human systems: individuals, couples, families, groups/organizations, nation–states, and the entire human race. The individual is seen as a "fractal" that gets replicated in all larger human systems.

Ultimately, we identified the sources of developmental or relational trauma as:

- Mothers with Disorganized Attachment that cause chronic disconnects and misattunement between the mother and child.
- Early, forced and or repeated separations between the mother and child.
- Emotionally or physically absent fathers.
- Parents, particularly mothers, with neurological, physical or mental illness anchored in depression, grief or unresolved loss and trauma. These parents often developed symptoms similar to the Borderline Personality Disorder and the Narcissistic Personality Disorder.
- Traumatic experiences during the prenatal and perinatal periods of development, or during the birth process.

We saw ourselves and our clients displaying some of the following symptoms of this unhealed trauma:

- Low self-esteem, often masked by acting superior.
- Needy, clingy or pseudo-independent behavior.

- Inability to deal with stress and adversity, and poor resiliency skills.
- Lack of self-control or trying to control others in order to feel in control.
- Inability to develop and sustain friendships. Finding fault with things others said or did.
- Alienation from and opposition to parents, caregivers, and other authority figures. A distrust of people in authority.
- Antisocial attitudes and behaviors. Use of drugs and alcohol to self-medicate.
- Aggression and violence when triggered by memories of early abuse or neglect.
- Difficulty in experiencing genuine trust, intimacy, and affection. Testing others to see if they are safe to be close to.
- Negative, hopeless, pessimistic view of self, family and society.
- Lack of empathy, compassion and remorse, with a cynical view of life.
- Repetition of the cycle of maltreatment and attachment disorders when they parented their own children.

In children and adolescents, we saw:

- Behavioral and academic problems at school.
- Speech and language problems.
- Incessant chatter and repetitive questions.
- Difficulties learning and diagnoses of ADD or ADHD.
- Executive function issues and disorganized behavior.
- Anxiety or panic attacks.
- Depression, apathy & general moodiness.
- Susceptibility to chronic illnesses.
- Obsession with food: hording, gorging, refusing to eat, eating strange things and hiding food.

From this we developed a series of working hypotheses:

- Early childhood emotional/psychological trauma is a primary predictor of future mental, emotional, learning and physical problems.
- Trauma creates an ongoing level of stress that is not beneficial, and has profound impact in not only shaping the developing brain, but also social, emotional and physical development of the individual.
- Emotional trauma is linked to attachment issues, particularly a Disorganized Attachment history.
- Emotional trauma is more likely to be caused by neglect (depression, grief, and trauma) rather than by abuse.

- It is not possible to separate mental and physical health.
- Solid sociological research evidence shows that social and life-style factors profoundly influence both the cause and cure of mental and emotional disability.

This led us to develop the following standards of practice:

- Young children depend on primary caretakers for brain regulation and development. Therefore, treating the parent is often the most efficient way to treat the child.
- Brain change is facilitated by the exchange of information and energy during physical and emotional relationship experiences. Therefore, therapeutic relationships provide the major resource for creating changes in brain function and behavior.
- The quality of the therapeutic relationship determines the success of therapy.
- Physical and emotional experiences in a relationship happen mostly through nonverbal communication, including eye contact, facial expression, tone of voice, posture, touch, intensity and timing or pace. In order to be able to follow the client's process, therapists must pay close attention to these cues, not just the verbal content of clients.
- Therapists must consciously engage in nonverbal, right-brain-to-right-brain processes that evoke the reparatory changes in their clients. This allows therapists to follow clients' process, moment by moment. This also requires therapists to follow their own physical and emotional experiences and conscious reflections, as well as those of the client. This requires consistent practice on the part of the therapist who wants to help heal traumas in his/her clients.
- Less is more. Avoid directing the client's process and simply learn to follow it, looking for opportunities to intervene, remembering that the shared field between you is doing the "real work."
- Trying to speed up clients' healing process slows it down.
- Ask clients' permission before using a therapeutic intervention. This allows them to set the pace of their therapeutic process.
- Use tools that help clients get to the core impact of their developmental traumas as quickly as possible.

OUR OWN DEVELOPMENTAL THEORY & CLINICAL MODEL

Eventually, we created *Developmental Systems Theory* (DST), a paradigm based on the principles we discovered in our "laboratory." We eventually created our own clinical approach for healing developmental trauma that Janae describes in her book, *LOVEvolution: A Heart-Centered Approach for Healing Developmental Trauma*.[11]

(This page intentionally left blank)

CHAPTER TWO

TRAUMA-INFORMED CARE TRAINING

*Many individuals who seek treatment in behavioral health
settings have histories of trauma in their lives; either they
don't draw connections between the trauma and their
presenting problems, or they avoid the topic altogether.*

—*TIP 57: SAMSHA's Manual on TIT*

WHAT IS TRAUMA-INFORMED CARE?

Trauma-informed care is a growing trend in the mental health profession.
The Substance Abuse and Mental Health Services Administration (SAM-
HSA), a branch of the U.S. Department of Health and Human Services, is a
leader in promoting the adoption of trauma-informed care in the behavioral
healthcare field. SAMHSA defines trauma-informed care as:

*"This model emphasizes the need for behavioral health practitio-
ners and organizations to recognize the prevalence of trauma and its
pervasive impact on the lives of the people they serve and to develop
trauma-sensitive or trauma-responsive services. It provides key information to help behavioral health practitioners and program administrators become trauma aware and trauma informed, improve
screening and assessment processes, and use science-informed intervention strategies across settings. Trauma-informed services may also
include trauma-specific services and may involve trauma specialists
(individuals with advanced training and education to provide specific treatment interventions to address traumatic stress reactions).
TIC anticipates the role that trauma can play across the continuum*

of care-actively establishing integrated and/or collaborative processes to address the needs of traumatized individuals and communities."[12]

TRAUMA-INFORMED INTERVENTION PRINCIPLES AND STRATEGIES

A TIC approach begins with clients' first contact with an agency or private practice. The primary goal of the agency is to create a safe place for clients to get help for the effects of their traumas and to avoid practices that could be re-traumatize the client. This requires all personnel in an agency or private practice to get trained in Trauma-Informed Care, including receptionists, intake personnel, direct service staff, supervisors, administrators, peer support specialists, and board members. Any agency that wishes to be Trauma-Informed needs to review and revise its policies, procedures and practices.

SAMHSA'S TRADITIONAL MODEL OF TRAUMA-INFORMED CARE

SAMHSA approach to trauma-informed behavioral health care shifts the focus away from "What's wrong with this person?" to a more holistic view of "What happened (or didn't happen) to this person?"

While symptoms may prompt a person to seek the assistance of a physician or mental health counselor, implementing a trauma-informed approach to treatment creates a place of safety and mutual respect where a person's whole history can be considered. This enables trauma survivors and providers to work together to find the best avenues for healing and wellness. A program, organization, or system that is trauma-informed follows SAMHSA's four "R's:"

- **Realizes** the widespread impact of trauma and understands potential paths for recovery.
- **Recognizes** the signs and symptoms of trauma in clients, families, staff, and others involved with the system.
- **Responds** by fully integrating knowledge about trauma into policies, procedures, and practices.
- Actively **avoids Re-traumatizing** clients.[13]

In addition, the National Council on Behavior Health (NCBH) is also promoting trauma-informed care. Other groups such as the National Child Traumatic Stress Network (NCTS) are providing resources in the form of mini-grants, articles and multi-media courses to educate both professionals and non-professionals on the standards of trauma-informed care. Here is what they say on their website:

> "A trauma-informed child-and family-service system is one in which all parties involved recognize and respond to the impact of traumatic stress on those who have contact with the system including children, caregivers, and service providers. Programs and agencies within such a system infuse and sustain trauma awareness, knowledge, and skills into their organizational cultures, practices, and policies. They act in collaboration with all those who are involved with the child, using the best available science, to facilitate and support the recovery and resiliency of the child and family." [14]

NCTS also describes a trauma-informed perspective service system programs, agencies, and service providers in the following way:

(1) routinely screen for trauma exposure and related symptoms;
(2) use culturally appropriate evidence-based assessment and treatment for traumatic stress and associated mental health symptoms; and
(3) make resources available to children, families, and providers on trauma exposure, its impact, and treatment.

NCTS also includes the following:

(4) engage in efforts to strengthen the resilience and protective factors of children and families impacted by and vulnerable to trauma;
(5) address parent and caregiver trauma and its impact on the family system;
(6) emphasize continuity of care and collaboration across child-service systems;
(7) maintain an environment of care for staff that addresses, minimizes, and treats secondary traumatic stress, and that increases staff resilience. [15]

Another national player is the National Technical Assistance for Children's Mental Health at Georgetown University. They provide resources on their website to help educate the general public on traumas-informed care. [16]

The Child Welfare Information Gateway that is part of the federal Department of Health & Human Services also provides information to the general public about trauma-informed care. [17] Initiatives are being started at the state level, through the efforts of the National Association of State Mental Health Program Directors. They have a website called *The National Center for Trauma Informed Care*. As of December 2017, all 50 states now have active trauma-informed care initiatives, and some of them like Texas and Wisconsin have statewide initiatives.

This effort at the national and state levels is also supported by the dedicated efforts of people like Dan Siegel, Bessel van der Kolk, Allen Schore, and Bruce Perry to inform professionals and the general public about the need for trauma-informed care. Our own efforts locally in Colorado Springs are aimed at helping to create a trauma-informed mental health service delivery system and a trauma-informed community.

THE IMPORTANCE OF TRAUMA-INFORMED CARE TRAINING

While SAMHSA has made great progress in their national campaign for trauma-informed care, its focus is primarily on addressing a category of trauma we call Event Trauma. We have identified three other categories of trauma—Developmental Trauma, Inherited Trauma, and Complicated Trauma—that we think behavioral healthcare practitioners should also be informed about. SAMHSA's *TIP 57 Manual* contains only one page on complex or developmental trauma. The charts below describe our four categories of trauma.

Table 2-1. Four Categories of Trauma

1. Event Trauma	2. Developmental Trauma
Happens later in life	Happens during childhood, involves witnessing or experiencing multiple adverse interpersonal events involving caretaker(s) for at least one year
Caused by a single or acute event that leaves a lasting imprint on the central nervous system.	The result of multiple experiences of chronic and acute relational traumas that involve abandonment, abuse or neglect by adult caregivers and leave a lasting imprint on the central nervous system.
No residue of shame-based emotions and perceptions; no impact on the sense of Self	Leaves a residue of shame-based emotions and perceptions and impacts the sense of Self
Is not developmentally sensitive and does not impair long-term social and emotional development.	People have problems regulating their emotions, have problems with impulse control and unpredictable behaviors, and experience suspicion, distrust, problems with intimacy that result in social isolation.

1. Event Trauma	2. Developmental Trauma
People typically remember these traumatizing events and experience flashbacks and re-experiencing when exposed to triggers that remind them of the original event.	People typically do not remember these early relational experiences, but they show up later as social and emotional triggers in close adult relationships.
People learn to avoid re-experiencing the triggers related to the original event by avoiding situations that remind them of it.	People learn to avoid re-experiencing the triggers from these relational traumas by avoiding situations or people that might trigger memories of these traumas.
Can be the cause of self-medicating addictions that help clients cope with symptoms of Post-Traumatic Stress Disorder (PTSD).	Can cause self-medicating addictions that help them cope with symptoms of Developmental Trauma Disorder (DTD).
People with PTSD display flashbacks, nightmares, ad severe anxiety, and uncontrollable thoughts about the event.	Children with DTD display pervasive, complex, often extreme, and sometimes contradictory patterns of emotional and physiological dysregulation, including self-hatred. Their moods and feelings include rage, aggressiveness, deep sadness, fear, withdrawal, detachment and flatness, and dissociation—and when upset, they are unable to either calm themselves down or describe what they are feeling.

Table 2-2. Four Categories of Trauma (part 2)

3. Inherited/Epigenetic Trauma	4. Complicated Trauma
Unresolved traumatic experiences in ancestors' past left molecular scars that adhere to our DNA	Vicarious or secondary trauma
Our DNA remains the same but the scars form an imprint that influences our psychology and behavior	Unresolved trauma
Recognizes the intergenerational impact of trauma	Can be a combination of event, developmental, Inherited/epigenetic, or moral injury trauma

3. Inherited/Epigenetic Trauma	4. Complicated Trauma
The principles of epigenetics also recognize that the impact of trauma gene applies not only traumas and weaknesses but also strengths and resiliencies	Complicated to identify
New research shows that these alterations can be reversed in enriched, low-stress environments	Complicated to treat and heal

You can see there are distinct differences between these four categories of trauma, differences that have yet to be recognized by most behavioral healthcare professionals. We believe these differences are important from both practitioner and ethical perspectives.

The past decade has seen a reemergence of the importance of identifying and treating the short-term and long-term effects of trauma. Trauma-Informed Care training recognizes that trauma can pervasively affect an individual's wellbeing, including long-term physical and mental health.

The emphasis in this growing trend, however, is primarily on Event Trauma, not childhood or Developmental Trauma. In addition, we now know that all forms of trauma including Event Trauma and Developmental Trauma are linked to physical health, psychological stress, quality of life, mental illnesses, and substance abuse.

Counselors with primary treatment responsibilities need to understand how to recognize the symptoms of developmental trauma and also how to treat it. Most training programs do not adequately prepare new professionals for this. Even veteran professionals lack the training they need to properly identify and treat these four categories of trauma.

This creates high risk situations in which clients can be misdiagnosed, their symptoms not properly identified and treated, or both. This places mental health practitioners at risk for being charged with malpractice, and subject to countertransference and job burnout.

Most of the current trauma-informed care trainings and trauma courses in universities focus primarily on understanding and treating Event Trauma. SAMHSA's manual, *Treatment Improvement Protocol* or *TIP 57 Manual for Professionals*, devotes about 99 percent on identifying and treating clients who have experienced Event Trauma of some kind.[18]

Granted that some of the symptoms of PTSD, the standard diagnosis criteria for Event Trauma, are similar to those of Developmental Trauma. (See Table 2-3 below for a comparison).

Table 2-3. PTSD Diagnosis vs. Developmental Trauma Diagnosis

PTSD Diagnosis Criteria	DTD Diagnosis Criteria
Happens later in life as a single event	Happens during childhood, involves witnessing or experiencing multiple adverse interpersonal events involving caretaker(s) for at least one year
The person experienced, witnessed or was confronted with an event or events that involved actual or threatened death or serious injury, or a threat to the physical integrity of self or others. *Vicarious traumatization* occurs when a person witnesses the serious injury or death of others.	Seven major diagnostic criteria: • Affective and physiological dysregulation. • Attentional and behavioral dysregulation. • Self and relational dysregulation. • Chronically altered perception and expectations. • At least two posttraumatic symptoms. • Functional impairment- at least two of the following areas: academic, family, peers, legal, and health. • Duration of disorder is at least 6 months.
The person has intense fear, helplessness, or horror.	Can directly affect subsequent development, which if not addressed, can distort the development of the individual for the rest of his/her life span.
The person has clinically significant distress and impairment in social, occupational, or other important areas of functioning.	Can affect digestion, appetite, sleep, the immune system, and temperature regulation. Mostly the effects are experienced in the upper chest and the disorders connected to that are of the body.
Can be categorized as acute, delayed, chronic, or intermittent/recurrent.	Can cause auto-immune disorders because the heightened awareness of perceived threats eventually depletes the immune system.

PTSD Diagnosis Criteria	DTD Diagnosis Criteria
Identified by the standard clinical symptoms of PTSD: • *Re-experiencing* the traumatic event • *Avoidance* of things that remind one of the traumatic event or a general numbing reaction • *Hyperarousal* symptoms	Affects speech areas of the brain, blocking the ability to talk about a traumatic state while in it. Because the connections between the amygdala and the language areas of the pre-frontal cortex are not well developed it is difficult to use talk therapy to heal developmental traumas.
Can be the cause of self-medicating addictions that help clients cope with symptoms of Post-Traumatic Stress Disorder (PTSD).	Can cause emotion, sensation, perception and thought to be dissociated into separate fragments. People ignore what is going on in their body.
People with PTSD display flashbacks, nightmares, ad severe anxiety, and uncontrollable thoughts about the event.	Can impair processing in one or more sensory systems, if any of those sensory systems were involved in the early trauma experiences. People have distortions in their sensory awareness as a result.
	Typical symptoms include dissociation, rejection of help from others, intense levels of affect, oppositionalism, impulsivity, distrust, flashbacks, nightmares, attentional problems, physical aggression, psychosomatic disturbances, medical illnesses, school difficulties, depression, self-hatred, and self-injurious behaviors.
	Causes dysregulation in the attentional system. This can look like AD/HD but it isn't. This causes people to wall off their memory of traumatic events that tends to blunt their natural curiosity and exploratory behaviors.
	Causes internal fragmentation that leads to internal disorganization of the Self and prevents an integration of sensory, cognitive, emotional and behavioral experiences. The person builds compartments to hold these experiences and to construct their life to protect this compartmentalized memory.

PTSD Diagnosis Criteria	DTD Diagnosis Criteria
	Causes fragmentation of emotional awareness. people to disconnect from their own feelings, so they may not even know they are having an emotional experience. This inhibits their ability to self-regulate their feeling states.
	Impacts people's Internal Working Model, causing them to see the world as a place that causes hurt and pain. They tend to expect continuing traumatic experiences.

If the focus is on identifying the effects of Event Trauma rather than Developmental Trauma, it is easy to miss seeing its obvious signs and symptoms of Relational Trauma. Consequently, those with symptoms of Developmental trauma alone who come for counseling can be easily misdiagnosed as having symptoms of PTSD caused by Event Trauma.

When we first began treating adult clients, many of them had symptoms of PTSD, but lacked a history of Event Trauma or childhood abuse that could account for the severity of their adult symptoms. This motivated us to look deeper into their histories, and what we found was surprising.

In most cases, the long-term effects of developmental trauma came more from neglect rather than abuse. Unless you know what questions to ask, even a seasoned therapist could easily overlook these symptoms. In neglect, nothing happened. So, there is nothing to grieve or feel angry or resentful about. Understanding this helped us recognize the long-term impact of developmental trauma.

We also began to look at addictions, and reenactment and re-experiencing behaviors through a developmental lens. What we saw, from a developmental standpoint, were mostly symptoms of early childhood trauma that occurred during the first three years of life.

We summarized our findings in two books, *Breaking Free of the Codependency Trap*[19] and *The Flight From Intimacy*.[20] In these two books, we mapped out an optimal model of development during the first three years of life. This helped us identify the impact of developmental trauma from a developmental perspective.

Even though we had ample evidence from our clinical research, it was the epidemiological research released in 1995 through the ACE studies that confirmed our findings: adverse childhood experiences have a long-lasting impact on the physical and mental health of adults. We summarize this research below, which has been replicated and validated in over 80 follow-up studies.

THE ACE STUDY: THE LONG-TERM EFFECTS OF ADVERSE CHILDHOOD EXPERIENCES ON PHYSICAL & MENTAL HEALTH[21]

Dr. Vincent Felitti of Kaiser Permanente and Dr. Robert Anda of the Centers for Disease Control designed and conducted an initial phase of the ACE (Adverse Childhood Experiences) Study. It was conducted at Kaiser Permanente from 1995 to 1997 by more than 17,000 participants from the San Diego Area.

They were given a standardized physical examination and asked to fill out a confidential survey that contained 10 questions about childhood maltreatment and family dysfunction, as well as items detailing their current health status and behaviors. This information was combined with the results of their physical examination to form the baseline data for the study. Here is the ACE Questionnaire used in this epidemiological research:

Prior to your 18th birthday:

- Did a parent or other adult in the household often or very often... Swear at you, insult you, put you down, or humiliate you? or Act in a way that made you afraid that you might be physically hurt?
  No___ If Yes, enter 1 ___

- Did a parent or other adult in the household often or very often... Push, grab, slap, or throw something at you? or Ever hit you so hard that you had marks or were injured?
  No___ If Yes, enter 1 ___

- Did an adult or a person at least 5 years older than you ever... Touch or fondle you or have you touch their body in a sexual way? or Attempt or actually have oral, anal, or vaginal intercourse with you?
  No___ If Yes, enter 1 ___

- Did you often or very often feel that ... No one in your family loved you or thought you were important or special? or Your family didn't

look out for each other, feel close to each other, or support each other?
No___ If Yes, enter 1 ___

- Did you often or very often feel that ... You didn't have enough to eat, had to wear dirty clothes, and had no one to protect you? or Your parents were too drunk or high to take care of you or take you to the doctor if you needed it?
  No___ If Yes, enter 1 ___

- Were your parents ever separated or divorced?
  No___ If Yes, enter 1 ___

- Was your mother or stepmother: Often or very often pushed, grabbed, slapped, or had something thrown at her? or Sometimes, often, or very often kicked, bitten, hit with a fist, or hit with something hard? or Ever repeatedly hit over at least a few minutes or threatened with a gun or knife?
  No___ If Yes, enter 1 ___

- Did you live with anyone who was a problem drinker or alcoholic, or who used street drugs?
  No___ If Yes, enter 1 ___

- Was a household member depressed or mentally ill, or did a household member attempt suicide?
  No___ If Yes, enter 1 ___

- Did a household member go to prison?
  No___ If Yes, enter 1 ___

Now add up your "Yes" answers: This is your ACE Score.

The researchers in this study found that childhood abuse, neglect, and exposure to other traumatic stressors, which they termed "adverse childhood experiences" (ACEs) were very common. Almost two-thirds of the study participants reported at least one ACE, and more than one of five reported three or more ACEs. The short-and long-term outcomes of these childhood exposures include a multitude of adult health and social problems.

The ACE score assesses the total number of adverse childhood experiences. The study showed that the higher the number of ACE experiences, the higher the risk of later developing adult health problems. That is, the more ACE's a person has, the higher the probability of having adult physical and mental health problems.

Since the original study, over 80 other ACE related studies have been done with similar results. According to the original findings, adults who had four or more "yes's" to the ACE questions are, in general, twice as likely to have heart disease, when compared to people whose ACE score was zero. Adult women with five or more "yes's" are at least four times as likely to have depression as those with no ACE "yeses."

Dr. Rob Anda, epidemiologist and co-developer of the original ACE study shared this about his work. "Just the sheer scale of the suffering—it was really disturbing to me," Anda remembers. "I actually ... I remember being in my study and I wept."

A major follow-up study was conducted by the CDC in 2009 with 26,229 randomly selected adults living in five different states.[22] They found that almost 60 percent of the respondents had at least one ACE and about 9 percent had five or more ACEs. Most of the results were very similar to the original results. However, one, new finding emerged showing that people with six or more ACEs lived about 20 years less than those with no ACEs.

Here is a summary of the results of the ACE related studies:

Adverse Childhood Experiences Are Linked to Numerous Measures of Poor Mental and Physical Health:

I. Social Functioning
   a. High perceived stress
   b. Relationship problems
   c. Married to an alcoholic
   d. Difficulty with job

II. Mental Health
   a. Anxiety
   b. Depression
   c. Poor anger control
   d. Panic reactions
   e. Sleep disturbances
   f. Memory disturbances
   g. Hallucinations

III. Sexual Health
   a. Age of first intercourse
   b. Unintended pregnancy
   c. Teen pregnancy
   d. Teen paternity

    e. Fetal death

    f. Sexual dissatisfaction

IV. Risk Factors for Common Diseases

    a. Obesity

    b. Promiscuity

    c. Alcoholism

    d. Smoking

    e. Illicit drugs

f. IV drugs

    g. High perceived risk of HIV

    h. Multiple somatic symptoms

    V. Prevalent Diseases

    a. Ischemic heart disease

    b. Chronic lung disease

    c. Liver disease

    d. Cancer

    e. Skeletal fractures

    f. Sexually transmitted infections

LIMITATIONS OF THE ACE STUDIES

These results are very important because they show correlations between the effects of adverse childhood experiences, not only on adult mental health, but also on adult physical health as well. This research supports the movement toward an integrated model of physical and behavioral health services. However, we see some important limitations in this research, including the following:

- This is correlational research, which means an association does not necessarily mean that one thing causes the other thing. This has been the biggest criticism of this research, particularly by the medical community. However, there have been other similar non-correlational, longitudinal studies that came to very similar conclusions.

- Without further interviews, it is impossible to determine whether or not those reported having ACEs actually healed the adverse experiences they had as a child. There was no attempt to determine what they did to try to heal from the effects of the ACEs. Naturally, if they did, the long-term effects would likely be diminished. It would be interesting to find out through further interviews of the subjects in these studies whether or not they did seek counseling or in other ways attempted to heal their wounds from adverse childhood experiences.

- The results were based solely on the subject's recall of adverse childhood experiences. We know from our clinical work with adults that many of them do not remember what happened to them in the first 3-years of their life where most developmental trauma occurs. This is particularly true of childhood neglect. This might indicate the results under-report the severity of their early childhood adverse experiences. Many of the reported ACEs may actually have happened later in childhood when cognitive memory was better developed.

- The 10 original questions focused mostly on experiences of childhood abuse. Little can be determined from the study's questions about the long-term effects of neglect, which we find more impactful than the long-term effects of abuse as a cause of developmental trauma.

- There was no attempt to determine if there were factors in the subjects' life that caused them to be resilient. However, recently this factor has been studied and some of the results suggest that this is an important factor that needs more research.

- The "Yes-No" form of the questions makes it impossible to know what a "yes" answer really means. It does not address the frequency of the adverse childhood experience. Did it happen once or twice or was in a series of adverse experiences? Obviously, if this were a repeated experience, it would likely have more long-term impact than if it only happened once or twice

Even though there are these limitations cited above to these studies, they are having a significant impact on the awareness of the general public about the long-term effects on physical health of adverse childhood experiences. This impact is similar to the impact that second-hand smoke research findings had on the general public in the stop smoking campaign. Most of that research was correlational, but it influenced public opinion and led to the U. S. government declaring that smoking was harmful to your health.

Our clinical research indicates that developmental traumas are caused mostly by neglect rather than abuse during the first three years of a child's life. Please utilize the several tools we developed to assess the long-term effects of neglect. One is the *Childhood Adverse Neglect Inventory* contained in the Appendix at the end of this book to help you determine the long-term effects of ACEs due to early childhood neglect. The other is the *Two Lists Writing Exercise*, also found in the Appendix.

THE TRAUMA CONTINUUM

We first summarized our research on developmental trauma in our textbook, *Conflict Resolution: The Partnership Way.*[23] This book describes how intractable interpersonal conflicts in adult relationships are often anchored invisible and unhealed developmental shocks, traumas, or stresses. All three states are the result of relational disconnects that occur during the first three years of life. We also show how the Adrenal Stress Response (ASR) activates freeze, flight, and fight reactions during a conflict, and how each of these responses involves different parts of the brain and the central nervous system.

In order to understand this complex information, we placed the Adrenal Stress Responses of freeze, flight, fight and freeze on a continuum. Our Trauma Continuum identifies the part of the brain, the part of the central nervous system, the time orientation, and the behaviors that are characteristic of each.

Table 2-4 below presents an overview of the trauma continuum. It begins with common behavioral symptoms and then identifies the parts of the brain that are active, the parts of the autonomic nervous system that are involved, and the internal orientation to time and intervention approaches for each.

Table 2-4. The Trauma Continuum[24]

	SHOCK	TRAUMA	STRESS
Behavioral symptoms	• Whitening of the skin. • Staring, reduced blinking. • Sudden flattening of affect. • Amnesia of events. • Lack of affect in describing a charged situation. • Paralyzed speech. • Cold limbs. • Agoraphobia. • Need to stand far away from others to feel safe. • Unresponsiveness. • Bulging eyes. • Flaccid muscles.	• Reddening of the skin. • Rapid eye blinking. • Edgy laughter. • Fidgeting. • Profuse sweating in social situations. • Compulsive talking. • Hypervigilance. • Emotional outbursts. • Exaggerated startle response with long duration. • Sudden heat in body. • Darting eyes. • Over-responsiveness. • Tense muscles. • Difficulty sleeping.	• Active, engaged but edgy and anxious. • Strained facial expressions. • Lack of consistent eye contact. • Talks louder. • Difficulty relaxing.

	SHOCK	TRAUMA	STRESS
Brain part involved	Brain stem, reptilian brain, ectoderm tissue	Limbic brain, mesoderm tissue	Neocortex. Endoderm tissue
Autonomic nervous system part involved	Parasympathetic nervous system	Sympathetic nervous system	Social engagement system
Orientation to time	Dissociated	Past & present events entwined and confused	In present time
Interventions	*Goal: Help re-embody after dissociation* • Avoid analysis, catharsis, and looking into the past or future. • Focus on present time. • Track the urge to withdraw. •Explore empowering options for restoring sense of Self. • Encourage the expression of feelings. • Use nurturing, comforting, and protective language to hold clients in a "therapeutic embrace" while they return to their bodies.	*Goal: Interrupting adrenaline cycle* • Bring body, emotions, and thought into present time. • Develop both/and thinking by holding dualities, opposites, and paradoxes. • Learn to process intense emotional experiences by feeling, witnessing, and surviving the emotions. • Transform traumatic emotional experiences into narrative memories. • Use nurturing, comforting, and protective language to hold clients in a "therapeutic embrace" while they move through the trauma. • Quiet, focusing, stilling awareness practices such as journaling and walking. • Time in nature.	*Goal: Communicating with clients to help them stay socially and emotionally engaged in present time* • Develop bodily awareness of unconscious and involuntary internal biological states. • Develop conscious and voluntary control of internal biological states.

	SHOCK	TRAUMA	STRESS
Interventions *(cont.)*		• Identify the fear behind the trauma reaction. • Develop comfort with eye contact. • Create clear personal boundaries.	

DISTINCTIONS BETWEEN DEVELOPMENTAL SHOCK, TRAUMA, AND STRESS

We discovered through our work with the Trauma Continuum each state requires specific therapeutic interventions. One set works best with developmental shock, a second with developmental trauma, and a third set for developmental stress.

Once we created the Trauma Continuum, we realized how few clinicians understood the difference between these distinct psychophysical states. We also realized that many use interventions that are not only inappropriate, but can cause harm.

Healing developmental shock, trauma or stress requires tools that specifically focus on visual, auditory and emotional, sensory memories, on relational components, on emotions, on the beliefs about the Self, and on body memories. These distinct interventions support clients in gradually moving deeper into layers of memories storing unhealed developmental shock, trauma, and stress. Effective therapists follow their clients' process while simultaneously following their own, identifying both their conscious and unconscious cues, working carefully at the edge between these two realities, while also monitoring sensory and behavioral cues. This same context gets applied to the treatment of developmental shock, trauma, or stress.

For a more extensive description of how to heal developmental shock, trauma and stress, see Janae's book, *LOVEvolution: A Heart-Centered Approach for Healing Developmental Trauma.*[25]

UNIQUE ASPECTS OF OUR TRAUMA-INFORMED CERTIFICATE TRAINING

Our trauma-informed care model, which follows many of SAMHSA's core principles, includes the following:

- It is Developmental Trauma-Informed.

- It is Attachment-Informed.
- We focus on identifying adverse childhood experiences that are caused by often ignored neglect as well as abuse.
- We share our own simple to use trauma-specific interventions.
- We include information about the Trauma Continuum, which recognizes shock, trauma & stress as unique states,
- We use a broader context for becoming "Trauma-Informed" that is important from both practical and ethical perspectives,
- We encourage clinicians to heal their own trauma histories, and implement our motto of "Do unto ourselves before doing unto others."
- We emphasize clinicians & practitioners as the primary intervention "tool" for helping clients and organizations overcome histories containing Developmental Trauma.
- We help participants recognize and organize "disorganized" systems where people are struggling with Disorganized Attachment, unresolved Adverse Childhood Experiences, and other forms of Developmental Trauma.
- We present integrative healthcare models that support clients' and organizations' mental, emotional and physical health.
- Our constructivistic trainings involve participants in the learning experience.
- We identify the therapist as the primary therapeutic "tool," whose task is to create a safe and stable treatment environment.
- We focus on identifying hidden relational traumas that include neglect and abuse.
- We emphasize both personal development and professional skill development.
- We encourage participants to "Do onto themselves before doing onto others."
- We believe that it is critical for therapists to continually work on healing their own developmental traumas. This includes getting good supervision to help prevent countertransference issues from interfering with their effectiveness.

CHAPTER THREE

BECOMING DEVELOPMENTAL
TRAUMA-INFORMED

*By developing a contaminated, stigmatized identity, the child
victim takes the evil of the abuser into herself and thereby
preserves her primary attachments to her parents. Because
the inner sense of badness preserves a relationship, it is not
readily given up even after the abuse has stopped; rather, it
becomes a stable part of the child's personality structure.*

—Judith Lewis Herman, *Trauma and Recovery*

TRAUMA AS DEFINED IN THE
TRAUMATOLOGY LITERATURE

There is an enormous body of literature in the field of traumatology. Unfortunately, it doesn't really discriminate between event trauma and relationally based developmental trauma, nor does it discriminate between shock, trauma and stress or between chronic and acute trauma.

A *trauma* has traditionally been defined as any experience that overwhelms the psyche and the body's nervous system and creates lasting changes in its hormonal stress response.[26] Traumas connect cellular intelligence, and the three-part nervous system (sympathetic, parasympathetic, and Social Engagement Systems) with the heart and right brain. Traumas create heightened biological sensitivities to auditory, visual, sensory, and movement stimuli and relational cues such as facial expressions, voice tone, and body language.[27]

Most research on the causes of trauma focuses on extreme or acute events such as accidents, murder, wars, natural catastrophes, human-made ecological disasters, and physical and sexual child abuse. Most traumatologists recognize that exposure to event trauma, particularly repeated exposure to similar kinds of events, cause symptoms of post-traumatic stress, create developmental delays, and contribute to degenerative illnesses.

Most of the current traumatology research has yet to study the long-term effects of developmental shock, trauma, or stress because they are outside the traditional definitions of trauma. Our approach goes beyond this traditional trauma paradigm.

WHAT CAUSES DEVELOPMENTAL TRAUMA?

The literature in the field of traumatology is slowly containing more and more information about developmental trauma. We define *developmental trauma* as a form of chronic relational trauma that changes the structure and function of a child's developing brain and nervous system. These structural and functional changes cause developmental delays during the bonding and separations stages. These changes to the brain and nervous system have long-term health consequences. Developmental trauma, by our definition, is primarily the result of Disorganized Attachment (DA) that disturbs mother-child dynamics during the first year of life.

Mothers who have DA typically have a history of relational or developmental trauma during the first year of their own lives, and involve physical and/or emotional abuse, and neglect. This makes it difficult for them to attach securely to their own infants, and helps to perpetuate an intergenerational pattern of the Disorganized Attachment history.

When mothers dissociate or show facial expressions or behaviors to their infants that make them appear scary or dangerous, infants' feel afraid and withdraw. Their brain stems automatically activate a protective reaction that help them quickly retreat from their "scary mother."

A second brain signal comes simultaneously from the mammalian part of infants' brains. This ancient mammalian wiring fires unconsciously telling the child to run to the mother for safety. When children experience these two conflicting signals from different parts of their brains, they fragment psychologically and dissociate. When infants both need and fear their attachment figure at the same time, they face an *irresolvable* paradox: the mother becomes both the source of protection and the source of alarm.

These two conflicting messages short-circuit an infant's brain and nervous system. This short-circuit is visible in their eyes as a "freeze" or shock reaction. The child's body stops moving, and they lose their ability to communicate.

The Adrenal Stress Response causes their blood to be pulled from their hands and feet and into their core. Their skin color turns white, and their eyes bulge and stop blinking. When the conflicting signals from the brain to both flee and to attach are sufficiently intense, they actually dissociate. Living with a "scary mother" becomes an experience of chronic adrenal stress, and may be a primary contributing factor to the onset of chronic and degenerative diseases in adulthood.[28] We write about the attachment process in more detail in Part II of this book.

DEVELOPMENTAL TRAUMA AND DISORGANIZED ATTACHMENT

Mary Main and her research colleagues at UC-Berkeley first identified Disorganized Attachment. She used the Strange Situation Protocol (SSP) research instrument to examine the quality of parent-child relationships. Main saw children in research settings who displayed bizarre and unpredictable kinds of behavior when they were separated and then reunited with their mothers.

Main was unable to explain their puzzling behavior until she developed the *Adult Attachment Interview* (AAI), an instrument for identifying mothers' patterns of attachment. This instrument showed that children with DA had mothers with a DA history. Main's subsequent research with mothers and infants indicated a high correlation between *mothers with DA* and children with DA, and with its intergenerational transmission.

Based on Main's findings and our own heuristic research, we believe that this intergenerational transmission of DA is the primary cause of developmental trauma. We also believe that the long-term impact of unrecognized and unhealed developmental trauma is the major cause of delayed development in all human systems: individuals, couples, families, groups/organizations, nation–states, and the human race itself. We write about this extensively in our textbook for counselors, *Conflict Resolution: The Partnership Way.*[29]

Subtle relational, developmental trauma is so pervasive in Western society that it has become virtually invisible. Two of our goals in writing this book are to make the world more aware of the effects of this form of chronic relational trauma, and to provide tools for healing it with the hope of helping humanity evolve.

TRAUMA AND BRAIN FUNCTION[30]

New discoveries from brain research are overturning the concept of the brain as a fixed and inaccessible organ. No longer seen as a self-contained unit with a preset, unchangeable structure set at birth, the brain is now recognized as a flexible, malleable instrument capable of adapting to a broad range of physical, emotional, cognitive, and environmental stimuli over the lifespan.

According to Allan Schore, "The human cerebral cortex adds about 70% of its final DNA content after birth."[31] A new area of brain research focuses on prenatal development and the treatment of post-traumatic stress symptoms. From this new area of research, the correlation between childhood trauma and subsequent disturbances or social behavior and violence is gradually becoming accepted.[32]

Developmental trauma particularly registers in the limbic or mammalian brain. It activates the sympathetic nervous system, which stimulates the production of adrenal hormones and causes the fight/flight response, hypervigilance, and hyperactivity. It creates more aggressive, physical behavior and conflict that can lead to adrenal fatigue and exhaustion contributing to cellular breakdown and disease.

Physically the symptoms include reddening or flushing of the skin, darting eyes and rapid eye blinking, edgy laughter, and hypervigilance designed to prevent exposure to the triggers of stressful or intimate conflicts. Other symptoms include over-responding to stressful situations and hyperactivity, an exaggerated startle reflex, tense muscles, and regressive states that cause confusion between past and present realities.

Addictions or compulsive behaviors such as sleeping, eating, working, exercising, smoking, drinking, shopping, gambling, and sex are ways that people avoid encountering the emotions they repressed from previous unrecognized and unhealed traumatic experiences. This is usually a defense against falling into a shock reaction and dissociation. Our developmental definition of an addiction is a "ritualized, compulsive, comfort-seeking behavior."

Developmental trauma, as described in our trauma continuum, is stored primarily in the limbic or mammalian brain, which processes and stores memories related to our relationships and emotions. Structurally, it contains the hypothalamus, the amygdala, and the hippocampus. Early emotional memories are stored in the amygdala as pictures, symbols, or icons rather than narrative language. Severe traumas from wars, famines, forced migrations, natural catastrophes, and other collective traumas such as global catastrophes, for example, are also symbolically stored in the amygdala as a form of genetic or race memory that is now known as inherited or epigenetic trauma.

Trauma disrupts the circuitry between the hypothalamus, the amygdala, the hippocampus and the pre-frontal cortex of the brain. This prevents people with severe trauma from developing empathy, compassion and other positive behaviors. Trauma also disrupts the circuitry to the corpus callosum, a structure found in mammalian brains that connects the left hemisphere's cognitive function with the right hemisphere's emotional, relational and symbolic functions. Short circuits in the corpus callosum can impair not only a person's ability to recognize his or her feelings, but also the ability to express them. This impairment creates *alexithymia*, or the lack of words to express feelings.[33]

THE BIOCHEMISTRY OF TRAUMA[34]

Our research on the biochemical aspects of both shock and trauma revealed that virtually all human experience is dictated and regulated by the production and release of hormones and other chemicals such as peptides, proteins, and neurotransmitters. From a biochemical perspective, it is clear that the body has a very specific response program it uses to cope with perceived danger, one that can be tracked and monitored.

Developmental trauma, whether it is acute or chronic, represents the midpoint of the developmental shock/trauma/ stress continuum and causes a full mobilization of the body at a biochemical level. The hypothalamus, pituitary, and adrenal glands all secrete specialized hormones such as epinephrine, nor-epinephrine, cortisol, and cortisone that are responsible for this mobilization.

They coordinate the function of the body's organs to generate a protection response. The blood vessels constrict in the digestive tract and force the blood to the arms and legs for fighting or fleeing. In the protection mode, all growth-related functions in the body temporarily stop and if they do not go back on line, due to chronic hypervigilance, can eventually compromise the body's physical survival because of reduced reserves of vital energy.

CORTISOL, THE FEAR HORMONE

Cortisol, also known as the "fear hormone," is responsible for aggression, hyperarousal, and anxiety. It is associated with depression, addictions, a weakened immune response, obesity, diabetes, osteoporosis, and a suppressed libido. Excessive amounts of cortisol can cause adrenal fatigue and exhaustion that have a global impact on physical health. Some researchers associate long-term adrenal stress with clogged arteries, heart disease, high blood pressure, and the breakdown of muscles, bones and joints.[35, 36]

Developmental trauma causes excess amounts of these hormones to be released into the body, and is considered as a major factor in causing chronic and degenerative diseases. Cortisol and its related hormones are also responsible for the flight reactions and the hypervigilant behavior commonly associated with trauma.

The rapid-fire biochemical processes that occur after being triggered create an internal feeling of collapse often described as "shattering." This psychobiological experience involves the breakdown of psychological defenses, more commonly known as a "nervous breakdown," as the brain shifts from the more complex and sophisticated neocortex part of the brain, to the limbic brain and eventually to the cerebellum and old brain.

During this process, people to confuse past events with present-time events, and encounter dissociated memory and split-off feelings and beliefs related to past events involving shock and trauma. This psychological collapse also overwhelms the SES and sympathetic parts of the autonomic nervous system, activates the Adrenal Stress Response, and contributes to the re-experiencing component of PTSD.[37]

During life crisis experiences, small amounts of cortisol from the adrenal glands provide a quick burst of energy to ensure survival, heighten memory, boost immunity, lower sensitivity to pain, and help maintain the biological homeostasis of the body. Although cortisol is a critical part of the body's response to stress, it was designed only for short-term use. Once the crisis is over, the body's natural relaxation response allows the blood pressure, heart rate, digestive functioning, and hormonal levels to return to their normal state.

The most important part of the biochemical experience of trauma, however, is the experience of escalated or chronic emotional states. When people are unable to re-regulate themselves emotionally, they respond in one of several ways. Cortisol may drive them to act out "fight" responses by becoming aggressive or hyperactive, or to act out "flight" responses and by avoiding the feelings connected to any unhealed traumas.

It may be difficult to believe, but virtually all of this dramatic internal biochemical activity is invisible to other people. With training, however, it becomes possible to recognize these subtle physiological and behavioral symptoms.

These include changes that are associated with shock and trauma—the size of the pupils in the eyes, skin color, and in the ability to communicate. More severe responses to trauma can include explosive behaviors such as emotional outbursts and crying. Implosive behaviors such as vomiting and fainting are symptoms of shock rather than trauma.

Trauma-informed care is a vital part of the movement to integrate the behavioral and physical health services. We believe it is impossible to separate these two realms, and both physical and behavioral care professionals need training to help them recognize the interconnectedness. For this reason, our training in trauma-informed care focuses on the integration of the mental and the physical aspects of healing developmental trauma.

RESEARCH ON THE LONG-TERM EFFECTS OF CHILDHOOD TRAUMA

Bessel van der Kolk, and others[38] described the following long-term effects of childhood trauma:

- Generalized hyperarousal and difficulty in modulating arousal
- Aggression against self and others
- Inability to modulate sexual impulses
- Problems with social attachments – excessive dependence or isolation
- Alterations in neurobiological processes involved in stimulus discrimination
- Problems with attention and concentration
- Dissociation
- Somatization
- Conditioned fear responses to trauma related stimuli
- Loss of trust, hope, and a sense of personal identity
- Social avoidance or loss of meaningful attachments
- Lack of participation in preparing for the future

Cole and Putnam[39] proposed that children who are traumatized by abuse, developmental delays, and loss of self-regulatory processes have profound and tragic problems with self-definition, including:

- Disturbances of the sense of Self such as a sense of separateness, loss of autobiographical memories, and disturbances of body image;

- Poorly modulated affect and impulse control, including aggression against self and others; and
- Insecurity in relationships, characterized by distrust, suspiciousness, lack of intimacy, aggression and isolation.

They concluded that:

- The lack or loss of self-regulation is possibly the most far reaching effect of psychological trauma in both children and adults. Affect dysregulation makes people vulnerable to engage in a variety of pathological attempts at self-regulation, such as self-mutilation, eating disorders, and all forms of substance abuse.
- In addition, children exposed to trauma have been shown consistently to have increased vulnerability to infections, including the common cold virus, respiratory infections, Epstein Barr, hepatitis B, Herpes simplex and cytomegalovirus. Antibodies to these viral infections have been shown consistently to rise with stress. Scaer hypothesized that "exposure to high levels of chronic stress may increase susceptibility to infectious diseases due to immune suppression."[40]

Children form an internal-working-model of themselves, other people and of the world around them during their first year through their primary attachment relationships. Their self-perception and worldviews get distorted by violence, hostility and fear. Insecurely attached children lack protection in their most important relationships. If exposed to trauma, their limited coping abilities are more likely to be completely overwhelmed by stress. Coping alone, with few options or resources, children respond with hyperarousal or dissociation

Two predominant adaptive response patterns to extreme threat occur along 1) the hyperarousal continuum (fight or flight) and 2) the dissociative continuum (freezing, numbness and surrender). Dissociation is a defense against fear or pain. It allows children to escape mentally from frightening or painful things that are happening to them. Each of these response patterns activates a unique combination of neural systems.

However, if clinicians fail to look through a trauma lens to conceptualize client presenting problems as correlated with current or past trauma, they may fail to see that trauma victims, young and old, organize much of their lives around repetitive patterns of reliving and warding off traumatic memories, reminders, and affects.[41] This leads to misdiagnoses and poor outcomes. Therapists who use a trauma lens ask different questions. Instead of asking the client, "What is the matter with you?" they need to ask, "What happened to you?" or "What didn't happen to you?" This is how to begin work with a new client.

THE IMPACT OF DEVELOPMENTAL TRAUMA ON YOUNG CHILDREN

Violato and Russell[42] conducted a Canadian meta-analysis of 88 published research studies on the effects of non-maternal care on the development of infants and young children. They found that infants and young children, particularly boys, who spend more than 20 hours a week away from their mothers, experience impaired social–emotional development, behavioral development, and maternal attachment. Their study found no support for the belief that high quality childcare is an acceptable substitute for parental care.

Most American women, unfortunately, are returning to work relatively soon after giving birth. National estimates from U. S. Census data reveal that among first-time mothers employed and giving birth between 1996 and 2000, 60% had returned to work by 3 months after delivery.[43]

Schore is very clear that early disruptions in the mother–infant relationship cause long-lasting emotional dysregulation. Although short-term episodes of emotional dysregulation are not problematic, prolonged negative states are toxic for infants. Although infants possess some capacity to modulate low-intensity negative affect states, these states continue to escalate in intensity, frequency and duration.[44]

The cultural lack of awareness about social and emotional needs of young children contributes to what we believe is widespread cultural neglect. This has serious implications for our national policy of federal and state support for childcare that clearly encourage new mothers to return to work as quickly as possible.

The countries in Western, Central, and Eastern Europe have universal parental and maternal leave policies that are much more supportive of infants and families. Their maternity leave periods average around 10 months[45] and they typically provide some form of wage replacement or income supplement for both parents.[46]

Other research on the impact of developmental trauma indicates that many 2- to 4-year-old children, who are not exposed to extreme adversities involving maltreatment or deprivation, are stressed because of their social experiences in childcare facilities.[47] Children this age show a rise in cortisol levels when they are enrolled in full-time childcare, but not on the days when they are at home.

We find the interpretation of this research interesting as it focuses on the stressful nature of peer relationships during this period of development, as though these interactions might be the primary cause of the children's elevated cortisol levels.

We interpret this information children's stressful experiences in childcare facilities as caused too much time away from the mother, too many different adult caregivers in the childcare facility, caregiving by emotionally unsupportive adults, and too few adults caring for too many children.

This same research study indicated that long hours in childcare facilities strain children's sympathetic and parasympathetic nervous systems. Over the course of the day, cortisol levels climb, and they were the greatest in the children least skilled in social interactions, particularly those rejected by peers or rated as less socially competent and not able to regulate their emotions.

This same study indicated that facilities where adults provided sensitive, responsive, and individualized care, children had little or no evidence of childcare-induced cortisol elevations. We interpret this finding as an indication that childcare environments that provide care equivalent to that provided by children's mothers does not stress them emotionally.

The findings of this study about the impact of childcare on children's development contradict those of the Canadian meta-analysis. This kind of confusion among experts makes it even more difficult for parents of infants to make decisions about when new mothers should return to work. These questions, which involve delicate choices between the social and emotional needs of the infant and the larger needs of the couple and family, are never easy.

JANAE'S EXPERIENCES WORKING WITH CHILDCARE PROVIDERS

Unfortunately, childcare professionals and early childhood educators are only just beginning to understand the importance of children's social and emotional needs. I (Janae) began training people working in these fields in the late 1990s and found that the biggest obstacle to upgrading the profession was the impaired social, emotional, and mental health of the providers and educators themselves. While there were childcare providers who attended my presentations, workshops, and trainings and implemented some of my suggestions, many still showed tremendous resistance to changing how they cared for young children.

DEVELOPMENTAL TRAUMA: THE GAME CHANGER
IN THE MENTAL HEALTH PROFESSION

My biggest complaint about the childcare and early childhood profession is their insistence on using time-out practices to isolate very young children when they become emotionally dysregulated. This is absolutely the worst thing they could do for the child and is, in my opinion, a primary cause of elevated cortisol levels in preschool age children. It is particularly bad for those between the ages of 2 and 4.

Asking a child who is energetically disconnected from caring adults to re-regulate themselves is not only impossible for most young children, I believe it is also highly unethical. I developed a set of time-in practices that I handed out at my presentations and posted on our website. While some saw the logic in this practice, many ignored the principle.

I finally concluded that adults use time-outs as a way to re-regulate themselves and to separate themselves from the children who trigger them in some way. Once I discovered this, I began encouraging stressed childcare providers to create backup support within their facility so that they could take a time-out from the children and the stressful environment and calm themselves. During our discussions, some were able to recognize how their personal stress increased the children's levels of stress and actually made the problem worse.

The "custodial" model of childcare so popular a generation back, which focused on the physical care of children, has gradually changed into an "educational" model that focuses on brain development and emphasizes cognitive learning skills. The emerging "social and emotional" model is, in our opinion, too confrontive to many in the field as it asks them to look at *why* they treat children the way they do.

This self-reflection requires that they examine the experiences of their own early childhood and look for correlations between their personal issues with children who trigger them, and their unrecognized and unhealed developmental shock, trauma, and stress from the past. Most are still unwilling to take this step.

Parents and professionals also lack awareness about children's social and emotional needs during custody hearings and in the establishment of visitation rights when parents' divorce. Much needs to be done to inform those who are making these decisions of the impact of their decisions on the children.

(This page intentionally left blank)

CHAPTER FOUR

WHY DEVELOPMENTAL TRAUMA
IS A GAME CHANGER

*In my early professional years, I was asking the question: How
can I treat, or cure, or change this person? Now I would phrase
the question in this way: How can I provide a relationship,
which this person may use for his own personal growth?*

—Carl R. Rogers

RESEARCH FROM OUR RELATIONAL LABORATORY

When we first began our heuristic research on developmental trauma, it was
a very personal experience that began in our relational laboratory. Our research happened in a tight circle of collaborators that included our clients
and our students. It gradually expanded to include the readers of our books
and people who visited our website.

While we were researching and writing our textbook, *Healing Developmental Trauma: A Systems Approach to Counseling Individuals, Couples
and Families,*[48] we discovered other researchers who had been working on
parallel paths. They also were researching and writing about developmental
trauma. It was comforting to find ourselves part of this larger community
of mental health practitioners who were focused on developmental trauma.

Our assumptions about the growing acceptance of attachment and de-
velopmental trauma were shaken, however, when we received our March/
April 2010 issue of the *Psychotherapy Networker* magazine, and read Dr.
Mary Sykes Wylie's hard-hitting article, "The Long Shadow of Trauma."[49]

This article described a struggle within the mental health community
regarding the validity of childhood trauma, specifically developmental trauma, that had polarized the profession into two factions—one seeing devel-

opmental trauma as insignificant, the other seeing it as life-changing and game-changing. Here's a summary of Wylie's article.

DEVELOPMENTAL TRAUMA EMERGES IN THE CHILD TRAUMA RESEARCH

Dr. Wylie's article described in great detail the long-term efforts of Dr. Bessel van der Kolk and many of his colleagues to make changes related to the PTSD diagnosis in both the DSM-IVR and the DSM-5 editions. Van der Kolk's clinical work indicated that the criteria for a diagnosis of PTSD did not fit the child clients he and his colleagues were treating.

So, van der Kolk and his colleague Joseph Spinazzola organized a complex trauma task force. Between 2002 and 2003, they conducted a survey (via clinician reports) of 1,700 children receiving trauma-focused treatment at 38 different centers across the country. They found more evidence of what two decades of research had already revealed: nearly 80 percent of the surveyed kids had been exposed to multiple and/or prolonged interpersonal trauma, and of those, less than a 25 percent met the diagnostic criteria for PTSD.

These children showed pervasive, complex, often extreme, and sometimes contradictory patterns of emotional and physiological dysregulation. Their moods and feelings could be all over the place—rage, aggressiveness, deep sadness, fear, withdrawal, detachment and flatness, and dissociation—and when upset, they could neither calm themselves down nor describe what they were feeling.

To soothe themselves, they'd engage in chronic masturbation, rocking, or self-harming activities (biting, cutting, burning, and hitting themselves, pulling their hair out, picking at their skin until it bled). They often had physical problems—sleep disturbances, headaches, bad digestion, and unexplained pain, oversensitivity to touch or sound— as well as difficulties with language processing and fine-motor coordination.

They were clingy and dependent, even with the person who abused them. They often loathed themselves, felt defective and worthless, and distrusted other people. Not surprisingly, they couldn't concentrate, performed poorly in school, and made few, if any, friends. "These kids have serious problems with affect regulation, dissociation, attention, concentration, risk-taking, aggression, impulse control, and self-image—they hate themselves," says van der Kolk. "But they don't have PTSD."[50]

Wylie's article went on to talk about New York University researcher, Marylene Cloitre, also discovered that *emotional* abuse and neglect—the absence, failure, or distortion of the child's relationship to a primary care-giver—was as traumatic, if not more, than actual physical abuse. The concept of *relationship trauma* had begun to emerge in researchers' thinking.

"The severity of a particular trauma—assault, accident, whatever—determined PTSD symptoms," van der Kolk said, "but the child's relationship to the abuser determined everything else—anger, suicidality, self-injury, disturbed relationships, tendency to be re-victimized." At the heart of emotional abuse or neglect is a failure of parental attachment and attunement, not to mention overt hostility, worse in its way than physical abuse because it does such a number on the developing brain and nervous system of a child.

Children who experience relationship trauma are left with a bone-deep sense that "something is very wrong with the way I am." Many other researchers began to recognize these kinds of deep wounds in their clients. The core emotion connected with these experiences is shame. What particularly distinguished this new "trauma syndrome" from garden-variety PTSD was the immense damage done to a chronically abused child's budding sense of personal identity and coherent selfhood.

DEVELOPMENTAL TRAUMA: THE GAME CHANGER

We found Wylie's recount of the emergence of developmental trauma riveting. In it she describes how this new complex trauma syndrome spurred van der Kolk and his collaborators to push their agenda even harder to change the DSM.

In 2005, the complex trauma task force, which he chaired, began working in earnest on constructing a new diagnosis, called Developmental Trauma Disorder (DTD), which, they hoped, would capture the multifaceted reality experienced by chronically abused children and adolescents—with an emphasis on developmental and attachment issues.

Finally, in January 2009, the committee submitted to the DSM Trauma, PTSD, and Dissociative Disorders Sub-Work Group. They proposed elaborate criteria (DSM-speak for symptom list) for DTD. Their list included exposure to prolonged trauma, causing pervasive impairments of psychobiological dysregulation (of emotions and bodily functions, of awareness and sensations, of attention and behavior, of their sense of self and their relationships). They also included at least two symptoms of standard PTSD, and multiple functional impairments (with school, family, peer group, the law, health, and jobs or job training).

They also requested support for a field trial to develop accurate assessment tools, test the criteria, and address still-unanswered questions. With their proposal, they included supporting evidence from 130 research papers representing 100,000 children.

The DSM committee's response to the complex trauma task force was that it had "inundated" them with too much data, but not the right kind: they needed to submit *other* kinds of data concerning 17 issues, including possible genetic transmission, environmental risk factors, temperamental antecedents, bio-markers, familial patterns, and treatment response. van der Kolk noted that almost none of these 17 issues are known about any currently existing psychiatric diagnosis.

After a two-week, night-and-day, largely sleepless extravaganza of work, the National Child Traumatic Stress Network task force resubmitted the proposal. It included an even bigger barrage of supporting materials, including combined data on 20,000 traumatized children gathered from various sources—among them, 4,500 children from the NCTSN, 7,000 from the Illinois child welfare system, and almost 2,000 collected by Julian Ford from a juvenile justice center.

Participating Chicago NCTSN director, Bradley Stolbach, did the preliminary analysis, which convincingly showed that kids suffering from long-term trauma are indeed different from those suffering single-incidence trauma. In addition to the data on these 20,000 children, they analyzed and submitted more than 300 research articles. They also enclosed a joint letter from the National Association of State Mental Health Directors, representing 53 states, urging DSM to adopt the new diagnosis. Says van der Kolk, "I'd guess that we gave DSM more documentation supporting DTD than ever before provided for any other psychiatric diagnosis."[51]

DIAGNOSTIC CRITERIA FOR DEVELOPMENTAL TRAUMA DISORDER[52]

Here are the diagnostic criteria for the DTD diagnostic category that the NCTSN task force submitted to the APA, along with the research findings to support their proposal:

Major diagnostic criteria for DTD: There are seven major diagnostic criteria for DTD.

- Witnessing or experiencing multiple adverse interpersonal events involving caretaker(s) for at least one year.

- Affective and physiological dysregulation.
- Attentional and behavioral dysregulation.
- Self and relational dysregulation.
- Chronically altered perception and expectations.
- At least two posttraumatic symptoms.
- Functional impairment- at least two of the following areas: academic, family, peers, legal, and health.
- Duration of disorder is at least 6 months.

The NCTSN task force also listed the effects of developmental trauma disorder, along with the research findings to support them.

Developmental effects: DTD can directly affect subsequent development, which if not addressed, can distort the development of the individual for the rest of his/her life span.

Somatic effects: Trauma can affect digestion, appetite, sleep, the immune system, and temperature regulation. Mostly the effects are experienced in the upper chest and the disorders connected to that part of the body.

Autoimmune effects: DTD can cause autoimmune disorders because the heightened awareness of perceived threats eventually depletes the immune system.

Speech and language: Speech areas of the brain are affected blocking the ability to talk about a traumatic state while in it. Because the connections between the amygdala and the language areas of the pre-frontal cortex are not well developed it is difficult to use talk therapy to heal developmental traumas.

Dissociation: In a trauma state, emotion, sensation, perception and thought are dissociated into separate fragments. This causes people to ignore what is going on in their body. Instead, they are not present a lot of times. This is highly relevant to academic achievement, the ability to learn from past experiences and to plan for the future.

Sensory Systems: DTD can impair processing in one or more sensory systems, if any of those sensory systems were involved in the early trauma experiences. People have distortions in their sensory awareness as a result.

Attentional system: DTD also dysregulates the attentional system. This can look like ADHD but it isn't. This causes people to wall off their memory of traumatic events that tends to blunt their natural curiosity and exploratory behaviors.

Fragmentation/disorganization: Object relations theory says that whatever is communicated to the traumatized child as being off limits for the caregiver will become off limits to the child's Self. This fragmentation of the developing Self leads to internal disorganization and prevents the integration of sensory, cognitive, emotional and behavioral experiences. The child learns to build compartments to hold these experiences and that is how they then have to construct their lives.

Fragmentation of emotional awareness: Traumatized people become disconnected from their own feelings. Consequently, they may not even know they are having an emotional experience. This inhibits their ability to re-regulate their feeling states.

The human face: A traumatized person usually locks in on the caregiver's face and they are trapped by what they think the face is conveying to them. Here lies the cause of future avoidance of eye contact and physical closeness.

Internal Working Model: Traumatized people develop an Internal Working Model of the world as a place that causes hurt and pain. As a result, they tend to expect continuing traumatic experiences.

Symptomatic presentation of DTD: The typical symptoms include dissociation, rejection of help from others, intense levels of affect, oppositionalism, impulsivity, distrust, flashbacks, nightmares, attentional problems, physical aggression, psychosomatic disturbances, medical illnesses, school difficulties, depression, self-hatred, and self-injurious behaviors.

THE DEVELOPMENTAL TRAUMA DISORDER DIAGNOSTIC CATEGORY PROPOSAL GETS REJECTED

Wylie's article also describes the outcome of this gargantuan effort to add the DTD diagnostic category to the DSM-5. In June 2013, she says, the APA issued the DSM-5 edition without including the DTD diagnostic category. In his denial letter, the DSM subcommittee chair Matthew Friedman, executive director of the National Center for PTSD, highlighted the issues.

He wrote that "the consensus is that it is unlikely that DTD can be included in the main part of *DSM-5* in its present form because of the current lack of evidence in support of the diagnosis and the lack of prospective testing of your proposed diagnostic criteria."[53]

The DSM trauma subgroup didn't necessarily refute the reams of supporting data they had receive, they just didn't think any of it was relevant. They agreed that the data cited by the DTD task force showed that chronically abused children had more symptoms than others, but they were still not impressed. They did not believe abused children were inappropriately diagnosed or treated under the current system, or that this new diagnosis was required to fill a "missing diagnostic niche."

The DSM subcommittee members consisted primarily of epidemiologists and other researchers who worked in university psychiatry settings rather than with real people in clinics. Chair Matthew Friedman also said, "the consensus is that it is unlikely that DTD can be included in the main part of *DSM-5* in its present form because of the current lack of evidence in support of the diagnosis and the lack of prospective testing of your proposed diagnostic criteria."

Yes, they agreed that the data cited by the DTD task force showed that chronically abused children had more symptoms than others, but so what? That didn't mean they were inappropriately diagnosed or treated under the current system, or that this new diagnosis was required to fill a "missing diagnostic niche." There was just no consensus in the child trauma field that DTD would be clinically useful.

Furthermore, Friedman's response also said there were no "published accounts about children with this disorder" and "no research had been performed using the particular, specific criteria," nor "studies on differential responses to treatment." In any case, there was only "scant evidence" that interpersonal trauma (i.e., family-based trauma) has a unique influence apart from non-interpersonal trauma. Nor was there much evidence that chronic childhood abuse disrupted children's development, which was "more clinical intuition than a research-based fact."

Finally, what seemed to make the DSM subgroup figuratively recoil in horror was the sheer *muchness* of the diagnosis. "The range of symptoms covered in the proposed criteria is too broad, ...it would supersede not only PTSD, it would supersede all internalizing and externalizing disorders that appeared following interpersonal trauma and poor rearing. Nearly any problem that followed childhood mistreatment would have to receive this new diagnosis." They found it "most worrisome" that the proposed DTD symptoms were so similar to those of borderline personality disorder.

According to Wylie, the complex trauma group responded with a polite, but barbed, rebuttal. They were hardly addressing a "diagnostic niche,"

63

they replied but a substantial proportion of the one million children who are confirmed every year to be abused and neglected, plus the half-million living in foster care. There was also a great deal of consensus, thank you very much, from thousands of clinicians who treat chronically traumatized children—if the DSM subgroup liked, the NCTSN task force estimated that it could assemble a petition to DSM in favor of such a diagnosis signed by 10,000 clinicians.

Were DTD to be included, its supporters believe it would be a *game changer*. Just as the creation of PTSD "transformed the health care system for individuals exposed to traumatic stress and led to an explosion of specialized research and practice," said psychologist Bradley Stolbach, "the inclusion of [DTD] in *DSM-5*… will be a powerful catalyst for transformation of the systems that serve children."

By the time we finished Wylie's article, it was clear to us that the DSM subgroups perceived the DTD diagnosis as a *political threat* because it could change the structure of the established order. Adding this new diagnostic category might ripple through the country's behavioral healthcare system and literally "move the cheese" of the whole structure: practitioners, researchers, educators, and textbook publishers. This fear wasn't an idle fantasy of the DSM committee, as they were all well aware that the introduction of PTSD to the DSM-III in 1980 had done exactly this. So, the DTD effort was a case of too much, too fast for the status-quo members of the American Psychiatric Association.

DEVELOPMENTAL TRAUMA AND THE EMOTIONAL REVOLUTION

Most mental health practitioners who are working in the trenches don't pay much attention to the academicians and tradition-keepers. They are too connected to the needs and lives of their clients, and simply want to be more skilled, more ethical and more capable of reducing their clients' suffering. Emotionally attuned and heart-connected, they focus on how to help clients rather than diagnosing them.

Allan Schore and other neuropsychologists and therapists, say that psychotherapy has been undergoing an "emotional revolution," for the past 15 years.[54] It seems to be sweeping away all that came before it, and changing the game.

During the '60s and '70s, a behavioral model dominated psychology, then in the '80s and '90s it was cognitive models. Schore believes that "affect and psychobiological processes are now taking center stage." The intense, research-driven interdisciplinary study of emotion, psychobiology, development, and relationship (attachment theory—front and center) are now transforming both neuroscience and psychotherapy.

In the world of psychotherapy, few models of human development have attracted more acceptance and respect in recent years than the role that early bonding experiences play in adult psychological well-being.

University of Rochester professor Richard M. Ryan says that researchers and practitioners now recognize the limits of exclusively cognitive approaches for understanding the initiation and regulation of human behavior. More practically, cognitive interventions that do not address motivation and emotion are increasingly proving to be short-lived in their efficacy, and limited in the problems to which they can be applied." The emotional revolution, Ryan says, is "long overdue."[55]

This revolution is helping to break through the age-old divide between mind and body. For the first time in history, science is helping both researchers and practitioners bring the mind, brain, body and spirit together in one whole and complete human organism. Of course, therapists like this revolution because it has the potential to enormously raise the prestige of psychotherapy. The therapist, through the art of a certain specialized form of relationship and attuned connection, isn't just helping people feel better, but deeply changing and reorganizing the physical function and structure of clients' brains as well.

DEVELOPMENTAL TRAUMA: DISAGREEMENTS BETWEEN THE EXPERTS

Given the magnitude of the emotional revolution, it's difficult to imagine that there might be "experts" who would openly challenge and even dispute the developmental paradigm and the massive amounts of research validating the importance of attachment.

A confrontation between Jerome Kagan and Dan Siegel at the March 2010 Psychotherapy Networker Conference revealed the presence of another fault line in the mental health profession. According the description of this confrontation in the March/April 2011 *Psychotherapy Networker* magazine, this fault line had polarized into two groups—true believers in attachment and its doubters.[56]

Five hundred people sat in a packed workshop during the Psychotherapy Networker conference, listening to eminent developmental psychologist and researcher Jerome Kagan present on his four decades of research. Midway through his discussion of the clinical relevance of inborn temperament, he attempted to clarify a question related to an earlier, seemingly disparaging, comment he'd made about attachment theory. He clarified his position by saying, "I'm glad that attachment theory is dead, I never thought it would go anywhere."

A moment of stunned silence became a low hum, as people shifted in their seats and murmured. Whatever their imperfect understanding of the voluminous research literature of attachment theory, most therapists in the room believed that the early emotional attunement of a mother/caregiver (or lack of it) profoundly affects the child's psychological development. So, when Kagan delivered his offhand rebuke, he raised fundamental questions about the research findings that most therapists there considered not just theory, but well-established fact.

Suddenly, child psychiatrist, brain researcher, and staunch attachment theory proponent, Daniel Siegel, jumped out of his seat and leapt into the stunned silence following Kagan's bombshell. Siegel looked for a floor microphone to respond, and, finding none, strode up the center aisle and bounded onto the stage.

A startled Kagan looked on as the entire ballroom audience sat dumbfounded. Siegel, the morning's conference keynote speaker, asked for a microphone and announced: "I can't let this audience listen to your argument without hearing the other side. Have you actually *read* the attachment research?" he demanded of Kagan.

The two proceeded to have a heated, impromptu debate that later became the talk of the conference. Part of the buzz was because two stars—Jerome Kagan, arguably the most revered developmental psychologist in the world, and Daniel Siegel—openly disagreed. Each had an impressive resume and passionately held convictions on the age-old question about human development: which counts more—nature or nurture?

Beyond the drama of the debate, two things stood out in their spontaneous encounter. First was the surprise that a discussion of research findings could generate such emotional fervor at a psychotherapy conference and, second that the majority of the audience felt shocked that there could even *be* a debate about the role of early experience in human development.

DEVELOPMENTAL TRAUMA CHANGES
THE GAME IN CLINICAL PRACTICE

Prominent mental health researchers and practitioners such as Dan Siegel, Bessel van der Kolk and Bruce Perry openly share about how their work with attachment theory has changed and transformed them. They say that their discovery of developmental trauma, and their clinical work with adults and children suffering from abuse, neglect and relational trauma has changed them and the way that they practice psychotherapy. Their research and clinical practice experiences moved them away from the traditional medical model in which they were trained, and towards a more integrated, humanizing, relational, heartful model of helping traumatized clients.

They each discovered that it's one thing to create a theory that explains the long-term impact of people's attachment experiences. It is quite another to develop therapeutic models that help clients get beyond developmental trauma's limitations. But this is what they have done, and they openly talk about how they have personally and professionally changed their games.

The two of us also were confronted with the challenge of merging theory with clinical practice, which led to the creation of our *Developmental Systems Theory* and our developmental clinical model. Janae describes both in detail in her book, *LOVEvolution: A Heart-Centered Approach for Healing Developmental Trauma.*[57]

Attachment theorist John Bowlby believed that therapists could provide what the parents hadn't—a safe, dependable, empathetic, and attuned presence. This attuned presence enabled the client to do some of the "growing up" he/she couldn't afford to do in the unsafe early environment.

Attachment theory suggests that the most important aspect of a clinical relationship is the therapist's capacity for emotional *attunement*—the ability to hear, see, sense, interpret, and respond to the client's verbal and nonverbal cues in a way that communicates to the client that he/she is genuinely seen, felt, and understood. Attachment research emphasizes the psychobiological core of attunement between mother and child—the continual, subtle, body-based, interactive exchange of looks, vocalizations, body language, eye contact, and speech.

Client-therapist attunement—or "interpersonal neurobiology," as Daniel Siegel calls it, is really a highly complex, supremely delicate, interpersonal dance between two biological/psychological systems. This shared field of energy between the therapist and the client contains elements that replicate the healthy attachments between parent and child, or between husband and wife, or friend and friend. If this happens, therapy is effective in healing developmental trauma.

The idea that therapists should establish a close, empathic bond with clients—provide "unconditional positive regard" and a "corrective emotional experience" for clients—is old hat to psychodynamic therapists. At a time when brief, technical, pragmatic, medical-model therapies had become the norm, attachment research offered genuine scientific validation for using emotion-focused approaches that integrate infant and early childhood experiences. While attachment theory in itself didn't provide an accompanying toolbox of tactics and techniques, it did offer a new therapeutic approach, justifying deep, soul-felt work that offers clients a genuinely chance for a new beginning.

Of the core group of therapists influenced by attachment theory during the late 1980s and early '90s, Daniel Siegel's work has particularly helped therapists integrate both attachment theory and neuroscience into their clinical work. When Siegel, trained as a child psychiatrist, describes his discovery of attachment theory it sounds like a conversion story.

A student of Mary Main and Erik Hesse, Siegel believes that adults who have therapy or other reparative life experiences can learn to create a reflective, coherent, and emotionally rich story about their own childhoods. No matter how neglectful, abusive, or inadequate, he found that people could "earn" the emotional security they'd missed and then learn to create healthy relationships with their own children. "I loved the way attachment research showed that fate (having less-than-perfect parents) isn't necessarily destiny," says Siegel. He adds, "If you can make sense of your life story, you can change it."[58]

THE DEVELOPMENTAL FAULT LINE AND A FORK IN THE ROAD

The developmental fault line that surfaced during the confrontation between Jerome Kagan and Dan Siegel at the Psychotherapy Networker Conference in 2010 now looks more like a fork in the road. DSM panelist, Matthew Friedman's commented that, "the consensus is that it is unlikely that DTD can be included in the main part of *DSM-5* in its present form because of the current lack of evidence in support of the diagnosis and the lack of prospective testing of your proposed diagnostic criteria." This represents a position held by one faction of mental health professionals, one that Jerome Kagan and others support.

A group at the other end of the spectrum—including John Bowlby's followers, Dan Siegel, Allen Schore, Bessel van der Kolk—say just the opposite: "You need presence, you need mirroring, you need someone out there who knows what you see, so you can know what you know, and speak what you speak," said van der Kolk. Then he quoted attachment pioneer, John Bowlby, "What cannot be communicated to the mother by the child cannot be communicated to the self of the child."' If a child doesn't get this sense of "*presence*" from a trusted adult, she can't connect with her own felt inner experience and, ultimately, can't develop a sense of her own authentic self.

The more traditional group seems to want to pull the profession towards a more rigid, centralized and medical model of therapy. Its message sometimes sounds like this.

> *"This is the disease. This is its name. This is what causes it. This is the drug that treats it. This is the vaccine that prevents it.*
> *"This is how accurate diagnosis is done. These are the tests. These are the possible results and what they mean.*
> *"These are the data and the statistics. They are correct. There can be no argument about them.*
> *"This is life. These are the components of life. All change and improvement result from our management of the components.*
> *"This is the path. It is governed by truth which science reveals. Walk the path. We will inform you when you stray. We will report new improvements.*

While these statements may be a bit exaggerated, they do capture a certain rigidity and lack of emotional sensitivity that seeps out when people in this group speak. Professionals who work in large mental health care facilities say that they increasingly feel the influence of this group in their work settings. Often, they say, management requests that they exclusively use the evidence-based "alphabet" treatment protocols. Since the implementation of Obamacare, large mental health facilities now have so many clients that practitioners are carrying high caseloads and working more hours than ever before. This has encouraged more standardized and dehumanized treatment approaches.

Private practitioners have more freedom in determining what treatment protocols to use with their clients. Those who take third-party payments from Medicare, Medicaid or insurance companies have oversight and some monitoring of their treatment choices. Those with the most freedom to follow their clients' developmental journeys take no insurance, participate in no groups and negotiate all payment directly with clients.

This last group also not only doesn't diagnose clients, many have stopped using the DSM altogether. This group includes practitioners such as Dan Siegel and Bruce Perry, director of the Child Trauma Academy in Houston, Texas. Both have moved away from the medical model and towards a systemic, integrated model of care, and for good reason, according to van der Kolk.

THE SHORTCOMINGS OF CONVENTIONAL TRAUMA TREATMENTS

van der Kolk takes particular issue with two of the most widely used trauma-specific techniques: cognitive behavioral therapy and exposure therapy. Exposure therapy involves confronting patients over and over with what most haunts them, until they become desensitized to it. Van der Kolk places the technique "among the worst possible treatments" for trauma."[59]

It works less than half the time, he says, and even then does not provide true relief, as desensitization is not the same as healing. He holds a similar view of cognitive behavioral therapy, or CBT, which seeks to alter behavior through a kind of Socratic dialogue that helps patients recognize the maladaptive connections between their thoughts and their emotions. "Trauma has nothing whatsoever to do with cognition," says van der Kolk. "It has to do with your body being reset to interpret the world as a dangerous place."

That reset begins in the deep recesses of the brain with its most primitive structures, regions that, he says, no cognitive therapy can access. "It's not something you can talk yourself out of." His view places him on the fringes of the psychiatric mainstream.

It's not the first time van der Kolk has been placed there. In the early 1990s, he was a lead defender of repressed-memory therapy, which Harvard psychologist, Richard McNally, later called "the worst catastrophe to befall the mental-health field since the lobotomy era." van der Kolk also served as an expert witness in a string of high-profile sexual-abuse cases that centered on the recovery of repressed memories. He testified that it was possible—common, even—for victims of extreme or repeated sexual trauma to suppress all memory of that trauma and then recall it years later in therapy.

He'd seen plenty of such examples in his own patients, he said, and could cite additional cases from the medical literature going back at least 100 years.

In the 1980s and '90s, people from all over the country filed scores of legal cases accusing parents, priests and day care workers of horrific sex crimes, which they claimed to have only just remembered with the help of a therapist.

As a result of his outspoken efforts to defend therapists who were accused of "planting false memories," he lost his faculty position at Harvard and had his clinic there closed. van der Kolk eventually changed the game for himself by building a network of like-minded researchers, body therapists and loyal friends from his Harvard days. The group converged around an idea that was powerful in its simplicity. The way to treat psychological trauma was not through the mind but through the body.

In so many cases, it was patients' bodies that had been grossly violated, and it was their bodies that had failed them. Their legs had not run quickly enough, arms had not pushed powerfully enough, voices had not screamed loudly enough to evade disaster. And it was their bodies that now crumpled under the slightest of stresses. They dove for cover with every car alarm or saw every stranger as an assailant in waiting.

How could their minds possibly be healed if they found the bodies that encased those minds so intolerable? "The single most important issue for traumatized people is to find a sense of safety in their own bodies," van der Kolk says. "Unfortunately, most psychiatrists pay no attention whatsoever to sensate experiences. They simply do not agree that it matters."

When frontline mental health troops—overwhelmed and underpaid social workers and therapists serving in poor communities hear about this new diagnosis—they respond with a collective "At last!" But none of this is in people's purview—the connection between these vast social problems and the way we raise our kids isn't being made.[60]

WHAT IS WRONG WITH THIS PICTURE?

At the same time that the DTD diagnostic category was rejected by the APA, SAMHSA proclaims in its trauma-informed care literature that 90 percent of all clients who go for treatment at public mental health centers are suffering from the effects of trauma.

Only twenty-seven of the fifty states have implemented statewide trauma-informed initiatives. So most mental health centers are not yet trauma-informed, meaning that most clients don't get the appropriate treatment for their presenting issues.

SAMHSA also provides free resources and support to help states launch trauma-informed initiatives. In addition, The National Council on Behavioral Health highly recommends that all behavioral health agencies become trauma-informed. The National Association of State Mental Health Program Directors also have recommended that all state mental health programs become trauma-informed. So, the trend is growing, but not nearly fast enough to meet the needs of the people now enrolled in Obamacare, Medicare and Medicaid.

DEVELOPMENTAL TRAUMA: THE NEXT STEPS

Though temporarily stymied, the NCTSN task force is by no means defeated. van der Kolk's Trauma Center has raised sufficient funds to conduct a Developmental Trauma Disorder field trial, and has enlisted five additional sites to help conduct the required research. Van der Kolk is still optimistic. He said shortly after the APA announced their decision, "We're still going ahead full throttle."

He is calling for a massive public crusade against child maltreatment similar to the model of the anti-smoking campaign begun by Surgeon General C. Everett Koop in 1982. He said, "We need someone important in public life to have the courage to stand up and take a very visible stand on something like this—it has a huge impact on both science and society."[61]

Our online course *Freaked Out: How Hidden Developmental Trauma Can Disrupt Your Life and Relationships*, and our website, www.freakedoutnomore.info are designed to help the general public connect the dots between their adverse childhood experiences and their adult physical and mental health problems. These resources are designed to help many people understand the long-term effects of hidden developmental trauma.

PART TWO

AN OVERVIEW OF
DEVELOPMENTAL PSYCHOLOGY

(This page intentionally left blank)

CHAPTER FIVE

BECOMING ATTACHMENT INFORMED

You cannot predict the outcome of human development.
All you can do is like a farmer and create the
conditions under which it will begin to flourish.

—Ken Robinson

WHAT DID YOU LEARN IN COLLEGE ABOUT HUMAN DEVELOPMENT?

If you ever studied developmental psychology, you probably heard the names Sigmund Freud, Jean Piaget, Eric Erikson, and Donald Winnicott. It is less likely you know about the work of attachment researchers such as John Bowlby, Mary Ainsworth, Mary Main, Erik Hesse and Margaret Mahler, as their work is less known.

ALL DEVELOPMENT IS CONTINUOUS

A foundational concept of developmental psychology is that human development is continuous throughout the lifespan. If a psychological task isn't completed in early childhood, a child's physical development does not stop, it continues. Any trauma, unmet need, incomplete psychological developmental process, or unresolved conflict creates a "hole" in the unfolding long-term development. A child with fewer of these "holes" is more resilient, and able to tolerate stress and adversity later in life.

Unmet needs and incomplete developmental processes continue to re-cycle and press for completion at every transition in our subsequent development. They are most obvious during our most intimate relationship conflicts with partners, children, friends, and coworkers. These incomplete developmental processes not only recycle in our close relationships, they also contribute to collective conflicts in larger systems such as neighborhoods, communities, nations and our global family.

Humans, fortunately, have many built-in defense mechanisms to help them survive. Unfortunately, these same defense systems divert their life energy from their efforts to individuate and become self-actualized. Our ability to make sense out of our early childhood experiences and understand how they affect us over our lifespan ultimately determines our effectiveness as a person, a therapist, a partner, a colleague and parent.

A SUMMARY OF THE RESEARCH ON ATTACHMENT

Please be aware there is an extensive research body of knowledge on this topic. We recommend that you look more deeply into some of the studies that focus on working with the children or adults you have as clients.

Early attachment relationships provide an infant with protection against danger and uncertainty of many kinds. Attachment according to Dan Siegel "…is an inborn system in the brain that evolves in ways that influence and organize motivational, emotional and memory processes with respect to significant care giving figures."[62]

The attachment system motivates an infant to seek proximity to parents (and other primary caregivers) and to establish communication with them. At the most basic evolutionary level, this behavioral system improves the chances of the infant's survival."[63]

There are two broad categories of attachment: secure and insecure. They can also be classified as *Organized* and *Disorganized*, a more useful attachment framework. Generally, the more secure and organized a person's attachment style, the more resilient they are. In addition, the more resilient a person is, the more that they are able to cope with upsetting and emotionally dysregulating experiences.

Mary Ainsworth's original research on attachment using the *Strange Situation Protocol* indicated that about 70 percent of infants had secure attachment, and 30 percent insecure.[64] The insecure category was 15 percent avoidant and 15 percent ambivalent. Mary Main's more recent research revealed a third category of attachment, Disorganized Attachment.[65]

The strange and sometimes bizarre behavior she saw in children she identified as "D-type" led her to examine the attachment histories of these children's mothers using the *Adult Attachment Interview*,[66] an instrument that she created for identifying adult attachment history. Her research on the Disorganized Attachment revealed that the mothers of children with D-type attachment typically were dismissing or preoccupied in the way that they parented their children.

Jay Belsky drew upon the findings of other researchers who used the Adult Attachment Interview and the Strange Situation Protocol to study the intergenerational transmission of attachment. He concluded that the process of intergenerational transmission happens through parent-child interactions.[67] He also identified three contributing factors: (a) the quality of parenting experienced by the child is a strong predictor of attachment style; (b) attachment security or insecurity established during infancy is relatively stable over time; and (c) attachment style experienced in adulthood shapes subsequent parenting behavior, and thereby facilitates security/insecurity in her offspring.

WHY MENTAL HEALTH PRACTITIONERS NEED TO IDENTIFY THEIR OWN ATTACHMENT

Mental health practitioners are ethically required to "do no harm." Because the client-therapist relationship is at the core of effective and ethical psychotherapy, it is extremely important for mental health practitioners to know and understand their own attachment history. It is critical for them to have made sense out of their childhood experiences and to have cleared the trauma associated with them.

Research by Mary Main and Erik Hesse indicates that up to 80 or 90% of psychotherapy clients' have Disorganized Attachment. Because of the disturbed relationship dynamics associated with Disorganized Attachment, there is a high probability of mental health practitioners also having DA. This means that there is considerable risk of therapists having countertransference issues. From an attachment perspective, this mirroring phenomenon makes it virtually impossible for practitioners to uphold the "no harm" ethic in their professional work with clients. The best options are good training and good supervision.

DO YOU KNOW YOUR ATTACHMENT STRATEGY?

The research of Mary Main and Erik Hesse indicates that between 80 and 90 percent of the clients who come for therapy have Disorganized Attachment.[68] Their research findings suggest that mental health professionals are likely to also have DA. We encourage you to read more about Main and Hesse's attachment research at UC- Berkeley.

We believe that it's important to clear the adverse experiences that anchor behaviors associated with your own attachment strategy. The good news is that the relational distortions related to DA can be cleared quite effectively with the right kind of support, including individual therapy and good clinical supervision.

The self-inventory below will help you identify your attachment history, particularly the disorganized/dissociative version. If you have a high score on this instrument, we encourage you to get psychotherapy to heal these issues so that you can more effectively help your clients who have Disorganized Attachment. You are welcome to use this self-inventory with your clients to identify the relational behaviors associated with DA.

THE DISORGANIZED ATTACHMENT INVENTORY (ADULT FORM)

Directions: Place the number in front of each item that best represents your experience with that item. Key: 1 = Not at all; 2 = Occasionally true; 3 = Usually true; 4 = True most of the time.

_____ 1. I forget what I am saying in the middle of a sentence.

_____ 2. I get confused when I try to recall negative childhood experiences.

_____ 3. I have momentary lapses in memory while I am talking to others.

_____ 4. I remember being frightened by things my parents said or did.

_____ 5. One or both of my parents were "checked out" when I was growing up.

_____ 6. One or both of my parents were addicted to drugs or alcohol.

_____ 7. I am indirect or manipulate when trying to get others to meet my needs.

_____ 8. My parents said or did things to frighten me into behaving.

_____ 9. I find myself "day dreaming."

_____ 10. I avoided my mother or father's efforts to comfort me.

_____ 11. My parents make scary faces or played monster games with me.

_____ 12. When I was a child, my parents seemed more interested in their career or personal interests than in me.

_____ 13. I assume responsibility for other's feeling and/or behavior.

_____ 14. I seek relationships where I can feel needed and superior in some way.

_____ 15. I am very loyal to others, even when it is not justified.

_____ 16. I have a high tolerance for inconsistent and mixed messages.

_____ 17. I put the needs of others ahead of mine.

_____ 18. I have trouble organizing things to make my life work.

_____ 19. Inside I feel like a coiled spring.

_____ 20. I enjoy taking charge of things when there is a crisis.

_____ 21. Important people in my life have emotionally or physically abandoned me

_____ 22. When I think about my childhood, I draw a big blank.

_____ 23. I feel empty and alone.

_____ 24. I have a hard time defining what I need or want.

_____ 25. I distrust people and their motives for helping me.

_____ 26. I have a short fuse when I feel frustrated with myself or others.

_____ 27. I am at my best when I am helping others and taking care of them.

_____ 28. I enjoy helping other people get their lives together.

_____ 29. It's easy to read other people's moods and know what they want.

_____ 30. I have difficulties in calming myself after an upsetting event.

_____ **Total Score**

Interpretation:

If your score was between:

40-60 - Some evidence of Disorganized Attachment

61-90 – Moderate evidence of Disorganized Attachment

91-120 – Strong evidence of Disorganized Attachment

Table 5-1. Organized vs. Disorganized Attachment

	Organized: Child knows what to do to meet his/her needs	Disorganized: The child does not know what to do to meet his/her needs		
	Secure	Insecure / Avoidant	Insecure / Resistant	Disorganized
Parenting style when child is distressed	Sensitive, loving, (pick up & reassure)	Insensitive, rejecting (ignore, ridicule, become annoyed)	Inconsistent, unpredictable self-centered (overwhelmed or wanting their child to meet their needs,	Frightening, frightened, dissociated, sexualized, or otherwise atypical
Child's response exhibited only when child is distressed and needs caregiver support	Seek out and stay close to parent	Avoid interaction with parent, minimize emotion	Cry and seek out parent even before separation, then show anger and struggle when comforted; exaggerated response to get parent's attention	Inconsistent, contradictory response; freezing, self-stimulating behavior --rocking, pacing, head banging

CHARACTERISTICS OF DISORGANIZED ATTACHMENT

Main's research identifies the following historical factors associated with DA.

- A history of being afraid of the people to whom they are attached.
- A childhood history of physical abuse, trauma, emotional abuse, neglect and rejection.
- Under stress, they fragment psychologically and dissociate to cope with conflicting inner signals.
- Had a parent or primary caregiver with a Disorganized Attachment history.
- Coping mechanisms: "The Little General" organizes the physical world around their mothers as a child, and around other people as an adult;

"The Solicitous Caregiver" organizes the emotional world around their mothers as a child, and for other people as an adult. By the age of six, children with both coping mechanisms have given up their own needs, and focus on caring for other people and their needs.

- They become a 'Lost Child' who doesn't know their needs and have poor coping mechanisms for getting their needs met. They often use the Need/Obligate or Drama Triangle games to manipulate others into meeting their needs.
- Have episodes of anger at others when they don't reciprocate to their caregiving efforts.
- Get triggered easily by people close to them or in situations that remind them of their childhood.
- Have difficulty trusting others.
- Suffer from chronic anxiety or depression.

JOHN BOWLBY: THE FATHER OF ATTACHMENT THEORY

Englishman John Bowlby is considered the father of attachment research. A psychoanalyst, Bowlby was interested in extending psychoanalytic theory. In the mid-1950s, he began working with animals in an attempt to enrich the traditional analytic views of Freud and others. Later he turned to studying children and discovered that whatever their attachment experience was, the eventual outcome was the development of an "Internal Working Model of Attachment."

It was research of Bowlby's student, Mary Ainsworth, that revealed infants' Internal Working Model of attachment was in place by the age of twelve months, and stayed relatively permanent throughout their lifetime, unless there was some kind of relational or therapeutic intervention.

Adults attach to other adults in much the same way infants do with their parents, and usually find mates, friends or mentors with whom to form attachment relationships. One important difference is that adults often have a number of people available to whom they can become attached, where children do not. In addition, the attachment of the infant is necessary for its survival, which is not true of adults.

Mary Ainsworth did careful research on infants using a protocol called the Strange Situation Protocol, which involves observing the mother and a twelve-month-old infant in a laboratory setting. During this 20-minute procedure, the infant plays with toys with the mother present. Then the mother leaves while a stranger is present. They particularly observed the "reunion" reaction of the child when the mother returned. After observing thousands of infants, Ainsworth and her colleagues were able to use this protocol to determine a child's attachment strategy. Through this research, Main and her colleagues identified three distinctly different attachment strategies.

The *secure* infant would be briefly upset at the mother's absence, but would return to playing with the toys. When mother returned the secure infant would run to her, get comforted, and then go back to playing with the toys. The insecure infants acted differently. The insecure/avoidant infant failed to cry when the mother left the room, and would actively avoid her upon her return without showing any emotion. The insecure/avoidant infant focused on playing with the toys during the whole procedure.

The insecure/ambivalent infant appeared distressed even before the mother left the room, and would cling to her throughout the experiment. When the mother left the room, the infant typically got very upset and the experiment was quickly terminated. The insecure/ambivalent infant continued to cling to the mother after she returned and had no interest in playing with the toys.

From these observations, Ainsworth determined an infant's attachment strategy. She did follow-up research to see if this attachment style persisted. Her research validated that the children she studied had the same attachment strategy at age six and again at age nineteen.

DESCRIPTION OF THE SECURE ATTACHMENT PATTERN

Dan Siegel states that an infant must be understood and responded to sensitively by the mother and other caregivers in order to develop a secure attachment. This requires a parent to be able to understand the child's needs and moods and then respond to them in a timely and effective way.[69]

THE AVOIDANT ATTACHMENT STRATEGY

When parents are emotionally unavailable, lacking in understanding of the infant's needs, rejecting, or unresponsive, the child will likely develop an avoidant attachment pattern. This causes an infant to actively avoid contact with the parent, even when the parent initiates it.

THE RESISTANT/AMBIVALENT ATTACHMENT STRATEGY

When parents are inconsistent in their physical and emotional availability, and are not present because they are projecting their own states of mind onto their child, the infant develops a resistant/ambivalent attachment strategy.

These infants are often anxious and fussy, and have difficulty in regulating themselves emotionally. They tend to cling but never actually calm down when a caregiver attempts to comfort them.

THE DISORGANIZED/DISORIENTED ATTACHMENT STRATEGY

This is the most recent strategy discovered by Mary Main and her associates. Parents who frighten their infant in some way or are dissociated or disoriented in their communication with the infant likely had infants who develop a disorganized/disoriented attachment history. These infants tend to freeze as a way of avoiding contact with their parent or caregiver. They also do approach/avoidance behaviors like turning in circles. In cases where these infants are also traumatized or maltreated, the disorganized/disoriented attachment pattern shows up in about seventy percent of infants.

THE ADULT ATTACHMENT INTERVIEW

The work of Mary Main, Erik Hesse and their associates extended Ainsworth's research by developing the *Adult Attachment Interview (AAI)*. This semi-structured interview asks adults to describe the relationship with each of their parents. By reviewing transcribed recordings of their responses, a trained interviewer can determine their attachment history.

Main and Hesse discovered that a person's story of his/her parent relationships was predictive of the attachment pattern of their own children. They actually found in 85 percent of the AAI interviews accurately predicted their child's attachment strategy. In other words, the adult's attachment history largely determines the attachment strategy of their children.

You might ask about the role of genetics in determining the child's attachment strategy. The research on this topic indicates that it helps determine the child's temperament, or the child's sensitivity to handle life's situations, but has no statistically significant effect on the actual attachment strategy. Attachment strategy is determined by the attachment history of each parent or caregiver, which means that children can have several different attachment strategies.

MARGARET MAHLER'S RESEARCH ON SEPARATION-INDIVIDUATION

Margaret Mahler used a similar protocol of observing mother-child interactions to identify the separation-individuation process of toddlers' ages

83

8 months to three years. She found that for children to become emotionally separate from the primary attachment object, another bonded caregiver must be both emotionally and physically present. This additional bonded caregiver supported and assisted the child in navigating the internal conflicts related to this important developmental step.

Mahler found that toddlers who had the support of a nurturing, supportive father or another bonded adult caregiver were able to achieve their "psychological birth" by the age of three. She also identified and charted the separation-individuation stage and its four sub-stages that children had to navigate to complete this milestone. Mahler's research complements that of Bowlby, Ainsworth, Main and Hesse in that she believed that secure mother-child attachments were necessary for the child to successfully complete this essential developmental process.

Again, we encourage you to read Mahler's research carefully, because many clients come to therapy seeking help in completing the separation-individuation milestone. We discuss Mahler's separation-individuation process in detail in the chapter on the counter dependent stage of development.[70]

THE ROLE OF DISORGANIZED ATTACHMENT IN CAUSING DEVELOPMENTAL TRAUMA

Our heuristic research indicates that Disorganized Attachment is the primary cause of developmental trauma. The distorted parent-child interactions associated with DA traumatize infants during the first three years of life in ways that cause codependent or avoidant/ambivalent patterns of coping behavior.

We found that these trauma-related coping behaviors develop even when there are no adverse childhood experiences that involve overt abuse or abject neglect. Children of parents with a Disorganized Attachment history often experienced both abuse and neglect, as their parents were unable to help them become emotionally separate and complete the psychological birth. Children who are unable to complete the psychological birth by age three, will not be able to create and sustain a Self that is separate from their parents. These children have even larger challenges in developing self-organizing and self-actualizing lives.

Developmental trauma has long-term effects on children's lives, making them "developmentally delayed." They stay stuck in the bonding and separation stages unless they have help in completing the developmental processes associated with these stages later in life.

CHAPTER SIX

ATTACHMENT TRAUMA

*Secure attachment has been linked to a child's
ability to successfully recover and prove resilient
in the presence of a traumatic event.*

—Asa Don Brown

WHAT WE LEARNED FROM OUR CLINICAL RESEARCH

Our clinical research revealed that children often experience developmental trauma without anyone being aware that it happened. Parents may be dissociated, distracted or simply fail to understand the needs of infants and how to effectively meet them.

Table 6-1 contains a map of the essential developmental processes that ideally happen during the first eight months of life. During this period, children need constant caregiving, and the new parents need support so that they can provide this constancy.

During this period, many mothers suffer from post-partum depression often triggered by their own unresolved developmental traumas. Drugs or alcohol use can also distract parents who are addicted. Economic stresses can also interfere with parents' efforts to care for their child.

Most parents rely own their own experience of being parented to parent their children. If they are not aware of their own developmental trauma and other adverse childhood experiences, however, they are likely to repeat them with their children. In other words, hidden childhood trauma can interfere with parents being able to provide the constant care that infants need.

Table 6-1. The Essential Developmental Processes
of The Codependent or Bonding Stage[71]

Stage of Development & Primary Task	Essential Developmental Processes	Suggested Experiences for Completing the Essential Developmental Processes
Codependent **(conception to 8 months)** *Bonding & Attachment*	• Mother receives good pre-natal care and support • Experience a non-violent birth with immediate interventions to heal any shocks or birth trauma • Experience secure bonding/ attachment with mother and father and other adult caregivers • Build primal trust with both parents through a consistent resonant connection • Learn emotional resiliency skills from both parents • Create a secure internal model of self/other • Build healthy emotional communication and social engagement skills with both parents & others • Achieve secure bonding experiences with siblings and extended family • Promote effective communication and social engagement skills with both parents and others	•Both parents regularly talk to the child in the womb • Mother maintains a high-quality diet and reduces environmental stressors to prevent the risk of shock and excessive cortisol production during pregnancy • Both parents plan for and want the child • Parents build prenatal relationship with the child • Parents use non-violent birthing practices/ with father assisting in the birth • Mothers nurse and room-in with her child at the hospital; prolonged skin-to-skin contact with both parents in first 12-24 hours following birth • Family leave policies allow both parents to stay home without financial stress • Mother receives effective postnatal emotional & physical support. Father shares in early care of child • Mother and father provide nurturing, respectful touch; eye contact & gazing, singing & speaking in loving ways • Child gets timely emotional and tactile comfort to help heal developmental traumas caused by disruptions in resonant connection to both parents • Child receives unconditional love from both parents

Stage of Development & Primary Task	Essential Developmental Processes	Suggested Experiences for Completing the Essential Developmental Processes
Codependent (conception to 8 months) *Bonding & Attachment (cont.)*		• Child is mirrored and validated for his/her essence by both parents • Immediate & extended family members provide consistent, nurturing, and empathic contact with the child • Parents provide comfortable and protective environment to meet child's needs for safety and survival as he/she begins to crawl or walk

BONDING DURING THE CODEPENDENT STAGE OF DEVELOPMENT

Children build their lives on a foundation of secure bonding with their parents. If this happens effectively, the rest is easy. We believe that parent-child bonding can begin as early as pre-conception and the prenatal development period.

Pre-Conception Bonding. Ideally, the parent-child bonding process begins prior to conception. The prospective parents need information about the essential developmental processes related to conception, gestation, birth, and the first eight months of life. Conscious conception is a practice that couples can use to increase their prenatal bonding. In this little-known body of knowledge, the mother pays particular attention to her diet and nutritional state prior to conception. While making love, a couple can tune in to the yet unborn child and invite him/her to join their family.

A mother wanting to conceive should avoid alcohol; drugs of all kinds; and chaotic, conflictual, or stressful environments that activate her Adrenal Stress Response (ASR). The ASR pumps cortisol and other stress-related hormones into her bloodstream and into the bloodstream of the fetus.

Prior to pregnancy, the father supports his partner by taking some of the normal burdens off of her to reduce her stress by sharing the cooking, cleaning or shopping as she prepares her body for conception.

Prenatal Bonding. Thomas Verny's pioneering research in pre-and perinatal psychology indicates that babies remember everything and are deeply impacted by the events around them from the very beginning of life. Unfortunately, babies are only able to communicate this telepathically, a phenomenon not yet widely understood or accepted.[72]

Parents need to talk and sing to their child while in the womb. Even playing music supports the prenatal bonding process. Research from the field of pre- and perinatal psychology indicates that memory and interactive response patterns begin by the third month of gestation. It is important for both parents to consciously tune in and attempt to make contact with the growing embryo.

Once the pregnancy begins, the mother needs to focus as much of her time as possible on her thoughts and attention on uplifting things that keep her body producing a constant state of endorphins, oxytocin and other pleasure-related hormones. Again, the father can support his partner in this effort by providing her with expressions of his love that help produce these endorphins and oxytocin.

This helps both her and the gestating baby experience harmony and wellbeing. The father can also do this after the first trimester begins, as the child can experience his/her parents communicating their loving thoughts and feelings. As the gestating baby grows larger, both parents naturally draw their attention away from the outer world and attune more deeply to their child.

The womb is the "first school" for the child. Gestating babies are very alert, aware, and attentive to social cues that involve voice, touch, and music. Ideally, the parents should sing and talk to their baby, fill their home with beautiful and inspiring music, rub the baby's body through the mother's belly, and observe his or her cycles of waking and sleeping. They should also talk with the baby about the upcoming transition to the outer world and share their excitement and anticipation about his or her arrival to their family.

Pre- and perinatal experiences are significant not only in forming the personality, but also contribute to the development of the child's attachment and creating the Internal Working Model of reality. Prenates, for example, who are exposed to environmental toxins such as nicotine, alcohol, and prescription or illicit drugs through the mother's blood stream via the placenta, can be born with the same addictions as their mothers.

Birth Bonding. Ideally, parents should wait for their baby to signal his or her readiness to be born, understanding that his or her brain will secrete the hormones that trigger the labor process. They empower their child to direct the birth process, and follow his or her lead in each moment of the final stages of gestation into the birthing process.

They may choose to ignore the well-meaning advice from grandparents or medically trained people who may recommend "inducing" birth, using anesthesia, and other invasive birth practices. These should be avoided unless it is absolutely necessary. Instead, both parents can use tools learned in their natural birthing classes to help them relax and surrender deeply to the birth experience.

If the parents have cleared their own birth traumas, they are free to follow their child's natural birth journey without becoming fearful or being emotionally triggered during the birth process. They also strive to trust those who are assisting them through the birthing experience.

To reassure the grandparents and close friends, parents can choose birth facilitators or midwives who have access to medical support for backup, should it be needed. The parents accept the possibility that their child might have karmic needs for an experience of a breech or cesarean birth and make arrangements for those possibilities should they become birthing options.

At each step in the birth process, the parents and birth facilitators stay in energetic attunement with each other and the baby, and quickly refocus if they get out of harmony. We have found that most birth trauma is the result of the mother being triggered by her own or her partner's unhealed birth trauma.

The Father's Role in Bonding. is imperative that fathers not only be present in the delivery room, but also be an active participant in the whole birthing process. Those who do will be deeply bonded to their children.

Once the child emerges from the womb, the child is gently wiped clean of the birthing fluids, immediately placed naked on the mother's belly, and the umbilical cord is allowed to stop pulsing on its own. Only then, does the father cut it. This act helps to transfer the energy that symbiotically bonds the mother and the child to him. This signals his active participation in the perinatal bonding process. This is also his first initiation of the child, and the first experience of what we call "the divine triangle" between father, mother and child.

The Divine Triangle. The divine family triangle ideally is a tightly woven relational structure in which two bonded parents actively create a triangular form. This insures that their child will complete the essential developmental processes at each stage of his/her development. This Divine Triangle crucible, created prenatally, needs to be nurtured and maintained consciously by both parents throughout the child's life.

A much deeper bond can form when the father initiates the child into the divine family triangle by cutting the umbilical cord. When possible, invite friends and family to surround the couple and infant after the birth with a field of unconditional love and support. The extended family and community of friends can give the parents their first experience of being in a village that helps them raise their child.

If anyone in the support circle gets triggered during the birthing process, they can quietly leave and remove their stressful energy from the group while they work on themselves.

Ideally, all in the birthing area should focus on holding the field of unconditional love to support the couple, the child, and those assisting with the birth. This helps the child not "file" any birth trauma that might have occurred as a result of the twists and turns of the birthing process.

Both parents should talk to the child during this process and acknowledge the cutting of the cord as the child's first separation from the mother. There will be a second "cutting of the cord" when the father helps the child complete his/her psychological birth around the age of three.

After the birth, both parents continue to talk to the baby to reassure him or her of their support while adjusting to entering a new and strange environment. They do everything to make sure their child is fully welcomed into the world outside the womb.

The developmental process of secure bonding and attachment is more achievable when parents avoid excess stresses about their jobs, finances, and obligations to other children or family members. Stressors like these can distract them from this critical first parenting experience and can cause fluctuations in the energy connection between them and their child. If possible, both should seek to stay at home full-time, if possible, with the baby for at least the first twelve weeks.

Unfortunately, not nearly enough parents have financial and social resources that allow them to withdraw from the outside world and focus totally on parenting their child during the first few months. This is why national family leave policies are so important. They permit the mother and father to stay at home for an extended period of time while their jobs are being held for them and they receive pay.

Extended family leave time for both parents would, in our estimation, have a huge impact on advancing human evolution. In 2015, both Netflix and Microsoft corporations extended their parental leave policies, with Netflix employees receiving unlimited leave during their child's first year.

Most fathers, unfortunately, must return to work within a few days and mothers often within a few weeks or months. It is very difficult for children to make these rapid transitions in caregiving without it causing some developmental shock, trauma, and stress to the child. Even though newborn babies cannot speak, they are aware of *everything* that is happening around them, including parents' thoughts, feelings and activities.

Perinatal Bonding. During the first days, weeks, and months after birth, newborns go through many cycles of waking and sleeping that are driven primarily by hunger, the need for pleasure and nurturing, and the need for pain relief.

Their extremely sensitive nervous systems respond to even subtle sensations and energy. This is very visible in something known as the "startle reflex" in which the infant suddenly brings its legs and arms together towards its chest.

These cycles of waking and sleeping are regulated by the baby's need to relieve tension in its nervous system. When babies feel the first pangs of hunger, they begin making small noises and movements.

As the internal tension grows, so do their noises and movements. Eventually the escalating internal tension reaches a point where they release a very clear cry indicating their need. This cry tells the parents to provide comfort, protection, nurturing and safety. If parents do not understand their baby's sometimes subtle signals or are distracted by other demands, the child does not get timely or effective care.

Because infants' nervous systems are still developing, a newborn's cry does not provide parents with much information. At this point, caregiving consists of a series of trial-and-error interventions. As they attune with the child more deeply, they learn to recognize nuances in the child's cries. This allows them to meet the baby's needs more quickly and effectively. Therefore, the child is able to relax more quickly and go into a deep state of equilibrium. Then the cycle starts all over again.

Figure 6-1. The Bonding Cycle

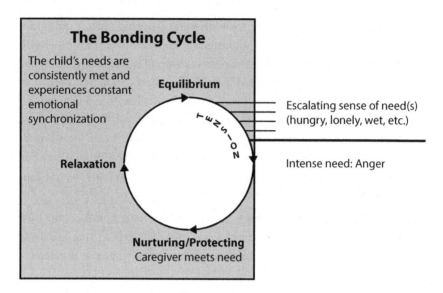

Newborns' sleep and waking cycles can be very short, particularly if they are small—sometimes only two hours long. This short caregiving cycle disrupts parents' regular sleep cycles so that they often do not get the amount of REM sleep they need in order to maintain their energy and sense of wellbeing.

Outside respite support for the parents during this time is very important. It can prevent parents from becoming overly fatigued, cranky, depressed, or emotionally unavailable during this important period of development.

Bonding not only involves the ability of each parent to reestablish emotional synchronization after a disturbing event, it also involves the ability to create positive play states. This stimulates the child's endocrine system to secrete "upper" hormones such as oxytocin and dopamine.

Many newborns cry because they are releasing tension related to birth trauma and may actually be suffering from birth-caused dislocated shoulders, necks, and hips. Dr. G. Gutmann, a German medical researcher who specializes in the treatment of Traumatic Birth Syndrome, discovered that over 80% of the infants he examined shortly after birth were suffering from an injury to the cervical spine and the neck that occurred during the birthing process.[73]

Babies find it more difficult to bond with their mother when they experience a traumatic birth. Parents get frustrated when they are unable to provide comfort and stop the child's pain. This can trigger past memories of feeling helpless. In instances such as this, some parents might even see their child as rejecting them because they are unable to quiet him or her. This disturbs the process of emotional attunement and may cause some developmental shock, trauma, or stress for the child.

After extended periods of unsuccessful comforting and parents trying to cope with their own emotional dysregulation, they may need to take a short "time out" from parenting. This is a time when parents need a support system around them to help them through the rough spots.

Once parents have reregulated their emotions, they can reengage with the child. It is important for parents to stay calm and centered during these episodes and to reregulate any dysregulated emotions generated by the birth process.

SCHORE'S MODEL OF BONDING/ATTACHMENT

Dr. Allan Schore's research provides a comprehensive lens for understanding the complex nature of human bonding and attachment, and how developmental shock, trauma, and stress might affect this process. While Schore and some other developmental psychologists use the term attachment, we often substitute the term "bonding," and use these terms interchangeably.

In his three books on Regulation Theory,[74, 75, 76] Schore uses the language of quantum physics to describe the nuances of parent–child interactions. He identifies the subtle interactions between both parents and the infant that, over time, facilitate children's experiences to move them toward either "growth" or "protection" responses.

His research also helped us validate our two-track model of development: The Optimal Track and the Trauma Track. Children grow when they experience their environment as safe. If a child perceives its environment as unsafe, it automatically goes into a protective, trauma-response mode. According to Schore, this pattern is set in place before the age of two, which also fits our emphasis on the importance of both parents' active engagement in the early bonding process.

Schore's regulation theory defines attachment as a "biological synchronicity between organisms." The term "biological synchrony" can be applied not only to behaviors, but also to the cells in all human beings, as cell biologist, Bruce Lipton, discovered.

Schore's regulation theory describes how the exchange of positive emotions between infants and their caregivers creates a safe emotional environment for the child. According to Schore, this environment stimulates the development of the orbito-frontal portion of the right prefrontal cortex of the brain.[77]

The orbito-frontal regions of the brain are not functional at birth, but develop gradually through a process of relational imprinting. They are also involved in emotional control, and reach a critical period of maturation between the ages of 10 to 12 months. This is also the age by which Ainsworth and Main were able to identify a child's Internal Working Model and attachment history.

This is critical information for parents, as it affirms the importance of their conscious parenting during their child's first year. If orbito-frontal part of children's brains does not develop during this early sensitive period, they grow up with difficulties in regulating their emotions. This loss of brain function is the most acute long-term effect of unhealed early developmental shock, trauma, and stress.[78]

Eckhard Hess's research also indicates that age two months marks a critical developmental milestone in the occipital cortex of infants' brains, one that dramatically increases their social and emotional capacities.[79] For the first time, they can fully see the parents and make direct eye contact.[80]

The mother's and father's emotionally expressive faces become the most potent visual stimulus in an infant's environment, and the intense interest in its mother's and father's faces, especially their eyes, leads the baby to track them and to engage in periods of intense mutual gazing.

The large pupils in infants' eyes serve as a nonverbal communication device that provokes caregiving responses in caregivers. Schore believes that by the age of 2 months, parents and babies are already exchanging high levels of cognitive and social information through their face-to-face interactions. These intense periods of mutual gazing are part of Schore's model of attachment and affect regulation.[81]

The Importance of Right-Brain Synchrony. Schore's research suggests that bonding/attachment involves a right-brain regulation of biological synchronicity between caregivers and children. The right hemisphere, which matures before the left, is specifically impacted by early social experiences with both parents, particularly during experiences of intense excitement. Its development is critical for achieving right-brain synchrony between children and parents. This is how children develop their "Internal Working Model of reality" that directs their interactions with the external world.

The right hemisphere stores the Internal Working Model database based on children's experiences with their parents. It also contains mechanisms that help children maintain positive emotions even when they are experiencing inconsistent care. Schore believes that it is the output from adult caregivers' right brain hemispheres that helps regulate a baby's right brain mechanisms.

This synchrony happens through emotionally synchronized, attuned face-to-face, skin-to-skin, brain-to-brain psychobiological interactions. This energetic system controls babies' regulatory, homeostatic, and bonding functions.

In the first year of a child's life, the right brain begins its hemispheric specialization for processing emotions. Since the brain is use-dependent, children's right brain may not learn how to effectively process emotions unless they receive proper stimulation.[82]

Schore believes that children's brains are shaped by their earliest experiences. He emphasizes that adult interactions with children throughout the first two years of life determine how their brains' sorting system develops: wired for growth and learning or wired for danger and protection.

A child's feelings, cognition, and behavior, he says, only evolve in a growth-facilitating emotional environment.[83] Therefore, the role of parents and early caregivers are crucial in facilitating the development of this very important right-brain function during the first two years of your child's life.

Schore also believes that the right brain is the seat of unconscious emotional regulation. He says it is critical for learning stress-coping skills and effective interpersonal behavior throughout the lifespan.

He cites a growing body of interdisciplinary studies suggesting that these interpersonal emotional experiences are critical to the early organization of the limbic system in children's brains. This part of the brain not only processes emotions but is responsible for organizing new learning and adapting to a rapidly changing environment.

Schore also emphasizes that psychology and neuroscience are currently moving away from a long-standing focus on cognitive processes, and towards a focus on the importance of emotions, the Self, and the overall personality.

Perhaps the most significant part of his research on infant bonding/attachment is his ability to articulate the core psycho-neurobiological processes involved in the emotional synchronization between parents and infants.

This means it is important for them to connect and stay connected to their child during this early period of development.

Schore uses the term "emotional synchronization" to describe the human experience of deep emotional connection, which is based on the developmental principle of reciprocal mutual influence. He recognizes that adults' right brain and Central Nervous System and can naturally shift into a pattern of resonance with children's right brain and Central Nervous System. This experience of resonance is commonly referred to as "being on the same page" or "same wavelength" with someone. Schore says that "the self-organization of the developing brain occurs in the context of a relationship with another self, another brain," that of the mother.[84] Schore's illustrates this relational dynamic in Figure 6.2.

Figure 6-2. Emotional Synchronization

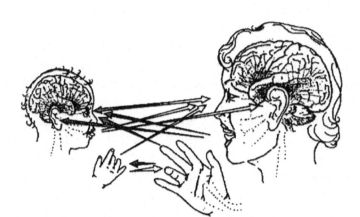

If children have sufficient experiences of nervous-system-to-nervous system and brain-to-brain resonance by two to three months of age with both parents, they will become sensitive and responsive to this reciprocal attunement. Children who do not have enough of these experiences will struggle with relational reciprocity and social engagement as they grow older.

Hofer describes how infants' immature internal homeostatic systems are regulated by the caregiver's more mature and differentiated nervous system.

In this symbiotic pleasurable state, parents' and children's individual homeo-static systems become linked together and provide "mutual regulation of vital endocrine, autonomic, and central nervous systems of both parents and their child by elements of their interaction with each other."[85]

The critical aspect of bonding is parents' conscious use their nervous system as an instrument for attuning to their baby in order to create a state of bio-psychological synchronization. This process requires learning to follow very subtle cues coming from their child.

Creating a solid infant–mother and infant-father bond also requires reciprocal interaction. Babies mirror back parents' loving gaze, causing their endorphin levels to rise. This completes a closed loop emotional circuit, a sort of "love loop."

This loop creates a dynamic, interactive system that is less about what you are "doing" to your baby and more about how you are "being" with your baby and how your baby is learning to be with you, according to Schore.[86]

This attunement between adults and children helps them learn to regulate their emotions and their bioenergetic systems, including hormone production. It is especially important in helping children modulate their production of cortisol and other adrenal hormones, so that they can quiet themselves after an upsetting experience.

Many new studies link early attachment disturbances with chronic and degenerative adult health issues, such as cardiovascular disease and cortisol function.[87] When in sync, says Schore,[88] adults and babies both experience positive emotions. When they are out of sync, both experience negative emotions. When adult reactions involve negative emotions, they are likely being triggered by their own unhealed developmental shocks, traumas, and stresses.

These human love dialogues involve many cycles of appetite, anticipation, and consummation, also contain the first experiences of rationing, frustration, disappointment, disruption, separation, and limitation. Having experiences of being out of sync with a baby isn't such a bad thing. It can actually be quite valuable.

Short-term misattunement is not a bio-neurological disaster, if the adult and child can quickly re-attune. The process of falling out of sync and then repairing the disruption actually teaches a child resilience and builds a sense of confidence that the world will respond to his/her needs for comfort.

Misattunement becomes a biological crisis only when caregivers do not help a child re-attune. Unfortunately, they may not have a good understanding of the subtleties of parent/baby interactions and are unable to recognize when they are not attuned.

This misattunement is not out of malice, but out of ignorance—it is simply where humans are in their evolution as a species. The lack of understanding about how we bond with each other is, from our perspective, still the biggest problem facing humanity. It certainly is the primary cause of many unintentional developmental shocks, traumas, and stresses that occur during the critical first three years of children's development.

THE CHEMISTRY OF BONDING

Unconditional Love and LOVEvolution. Allen Schore's model of attachment also includes research findings describing the chemistry of bonding and attachment. It indicates that the intimate contact between adults and children activates both of their hormonal systems.

During mutual gazing interactions, for example, the adult's face activates the production of "upper" hormones such as dopamine in the child's brain. It also helps children to regulate their levels of dopamine and other neurotransmitters. This mutual gazing generates high levels of arousal and elation in a child's behavior that are quieted by the adult caregiver's soothing and calming behaviors. This interaction also helps children learn to regulate their oxytocin levels.[89]

Oxytocin is known as the "anti-stress hormone" because it counteracts the impact of too much dopamine and high levels of cortisol associated with stress.[90] This factor is critical in understanding how to help children re-regulate themselves during any times of mis-synchronization. Restoring the mutual gazing process helps the child to calm.

Oxytocin creates feelings of optimism, calmness and connectedness. It also increases curiosity and reduces cravings associated with addictions. It increases sexual receptivity, facilitates learning; repairs, heals and restores wellbeing; encourages wound healing, diminishes pain, lowers blood pressure and protects against heart disease. It is also plays a key role in pair bonding.[91]

Oxytocin is also released in the brain during social contact, but it is especially pronounced with skin-to-skin contact. This contact promotes bonding between caregivers and children. When the birth and earliest bonding processes are not disturbed by excessive medical interventions, oxytocin acts as one of nature's chief tools for activating the birth process and bonding instincts of both caregivers and children.

Roused by the high levels of estrogen ("female hormone") during pregnancy, the number of oxytocin receptors in the expecting mother's brain multiplies dramatically near the end of her pregnancy.[92] This makes the new mother highly responsive to the presence of oxytocin. These receptors increase in the part of her brain that promotes maternal behaviors.

Oxytocin's first important surge is during labor, which helps ensure a final burst of antibodies for the baby through the placenta. Passage through the birth canal further heightens oxytocin levels in both mother and her baby. Oxytocin not only influences maternal behavior, it also stimulates the milk "let down" during nursing. Nursing during the initial hour after birth causes oxytocin levels to surge in both mother and her baby.

Mothers who postpone nursing lose part of the ultimate hormone high that is available immediately after birth. Nature designed this powerful initial imprinting as a fail-safe system that helps mothers and babies find and recognize each other in the hours and days after birth.

Mothers continue to produce elevated levels of oxytocin through nursing and holding their infants, which provides both with a sense of calm and wellbeing. Oxytocin levels are higher in mothers whom exclusively breastfeed than in those who use supplementary bottles.

Under the early influence of oxytocin, nerve junctions in certain areas of mother's brain actually undergo reorganization, thereby "hard-wiring" her maternal behaviors. In addition, chemicals such as vasopressin have a huge effect on the brain and behavior of fathers of newborns.

ATTACHMENT TRAUMA DURING THE CODEPENDENT STAGE OF INDIVIDUAL DEVELOPMENT

It is quite common now for infants and young children to be cared for by strangers to whom they are neither related nor securely bonded. These caregivers may not be interested in or even capable of attaching to them. When young children are left with emotionally indifferent caregivers for periods that are too frequent, too long, or both, their young nervous systems are unable to cope and they suffer bonding breaks with their parents or caregivers.

When infants and caregivers completely lose their mutual bioresonant attunement, their autonomic nervous systems become dysregulated and the infants go into shock. They collapse into a dissociated emotional state that, from the outside, looks as though they are falling asleep.

This dissociative experience is often referred to as the "Black Hole," an intrapsychic abyss where infants lose contact with what is going on around them and fear they will not survive. Black Hole memories, when triggered later in life, evoke primordial emotions, and highly disturbing feelings driven by unconscious fears about the possibility of annihilation—the archaic "fears without solution" associated with Disorganized Attachment.[93] Figure 6-3 illustrates this collapse into dissociation and the Black Hole.

Figure 6-3. Breaks in the Bonding Cycle

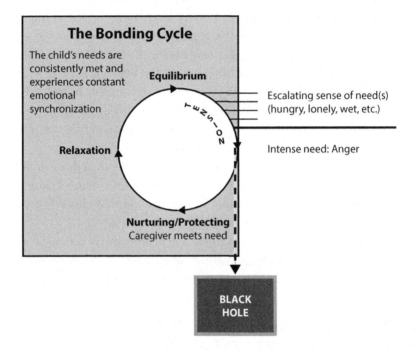

The Black Hole is a dissociative state of consciousness that stores memories of overwhelming experiences related to the loss of caregiver attunement. Infants' first shock-related memories create the beginning of compartmentalized intrapsychic structures, and may develop into a complex and compact system of dissociated memories, if they are exposed to subsequent experiences involving caregiver abandonment or neglect.

After several episodes of falling into the Black Hole, infants learn a variety of coping mechanisms to avoid it. Figure 6-4 below shows how babies learn to use oral substitutes such as thumbs, fists, soft blanket, or pacifier as oral substitutes for the missing nurturing, love, and emotional attunement. This helps them cushion or avoid falling into the Black Hole in an effort to self-regulate their emotions.

Figure 6-4. Attachment Trauma Coping Strategies

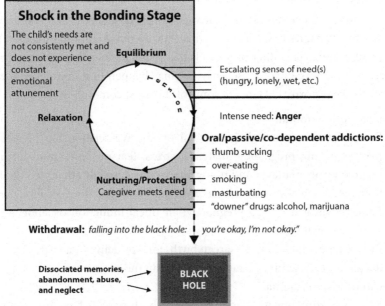

Oral mother substitutes during the bonding stage of development serve an important function for children who are shocked or traumatized. They provide the physical and emotional support that children need from their mothers and other bonded caregivers. Because the unconditional love energy is missing, however, the substitute never completely satisfies children's deep yearning need for physical touch, attunement and resonance with loving caregivers. In a desperate attempt to relax and emotionally self-regulate, the child often uses more and more of the mother substitute substance or activity in search of the missing connection to and energy from the mother.

These early coping behaviors lay the foundation for adult "downer" addictions such as smoking, eating, masturbating, using drugs such as alcohol and marijuana, and attaching to others in a codependent way. If children are not able to slow or prevent their fall into the Black Hole because of a lack of emotional care giving from their mothers, they may go into a long-term shock state of weight loss and unresponsiveness that characterizes a "failure to thrive" baby.

"NORMAL" EVENTS THAT CAUSE ATTACHMENT TRAUMA DURING THE CODEPENDENT STAGE

We believe that most parents and early caregivers do the best they can to be present during babies first their year, that they do not intentionally cause attachment trauma. The other problem is that many parents don't understand or recognize that many of these early traumas happen to everyone, so they are considered "normal." Here are some of the most common ones:

- Conception trauma.
- Prenatal trauma, including stressful or abusive relationship between parents during pregnancy; maternal stress, fear or depression during pregnancy or infancy; child not wanted; considered or attempted abortion; biochemical stresses during pregnancy from nicotine, alcohol, pesticides; twin lost during pregnancy; chemical induction of labor; and intrustive fetal monitors.
- Birth trauma, including Cesarean birth, forceps delivery, anesthesia, induced labors, vacuum extractions and scalp monitors.
- Circumcision trauma.
- Relational disconnects caused by one or both parents having Disorganized Attachment.
- Prolonged illness of a parent or a child causing prolonged breaks in the bonding cycle.
- Undue stress in the family due to economic conditions, spousal abuse or parents fighting, an absent father or young siblings competing for attention.
- Addictions that keep the parents from being present to attend to the daily needs of the child.
- Post-partum depression or emotional overwhelm of the mother.
- Parents' lack of understanding of infant's needs, causing unintentional neglect.
- Not comforting an infant who is emotionally dysregulated.

DISORGANIZED ATTACHMENT AND ATTACHMENT TRAUMA

The most common cause of attachment trauma is the result of disorganized caregiving by adults with Disorganized Attachment. It creates an intergenerational parenting dynamic known as *the reversal process*. Also known as *parentizing* and *parentification*, it involves parents and other care-giving adults unconsciously reversing roles with the children they care for. The children decide to give up their own needs and become physical and/or emotional caregivers for narcissistically deprived adults.

Disorganized Attachment (DA) creates a form of attachment trauma that happens under threatening relational circumstances and conditions. Mothers can be hostile, domineering, tense, angry and aggressive, or withdrawn, helpless and dissociative. By age six, children have learned how to adapt to mothers who are hostile, domineering, tense, angry and aggressive, or withdrawn, helpless and dissociative. Children respond to their parents' disorganized care giving by developing a Disorganized Attachment.

By this age, children display controlling behavior towards one or both parents. This behavior falls into three categories: 1) behaviorally disorganized, 2) controlling-care giving and 3) controlling-punitive. The first and second categories appear during the codependent stage of development, and the third during the counterdependent stage of development.

I have given names to these behavior categories (they aren't Main's) to help distinguish more clearly between them. I think my names also capture the heart of children's valiant effort to support their mothers so that they can take care of them.

Categories #1 and #2 involve role-reversals or parentizing behaviors in which the child cares for the adult and are more related to attachment trauma and create codependent behaviors. The third category is related to separation trauma and creates counterdependent behaviors. More about it in the next chapter.

1) I call the behaviorally disorganized strategy, the Lost Child. This category is the most dysfunctional, as these children have the fewest internal resources to influence or control their parents' anxiety and fearfulness. It is also often related to caregiver abuse, and characterized by verbal and non-verbal disorganization that cause abrupt changes of emotional states. These children also appear apprehensive, and confused when caregivers approach them. Parents of these children are typically deficient in their care giving, struggle with ongoing stress such as marital problems, hospitalizations and ongoing health problems, accidents and shifting alliances in care giving.

Figure 6-5. Disorganized Attachment Coping Category #1: The Lost Child

As a group, they show the highest impact of multiple family and environmental risks. They also are the most likely to struggle with internal conflicts related to external vs. internal locus of control issues as they grow older.[94]

2) I call the controlling-care giving strategy, The Solicitous Caregiver. Children using this coping strategy look behaviorally organized but lack cognitive organization. They often display inhibition and anxiety while appearing cheery and polite, showing few signs of distress when with the mother.

Figure 6-6. Disorganized Attachment Coping
Category #2: The Solicitous Caregiver

The Solicitous Caregiver provides emotional support for the mother, often being the peacemaker and smoothing out any upsets or conflicts in the family environment. These children are often empathic and overly sensitive, and become emotionally hypervigilant to the mother's needs. They become highly skilled in identifying other people's emotional needs, but develop virtually no skills in understanding their own. These children become the ultimate caretakers and rescuers. From a gender perspective, girls tend to adopt the Solicitious Caregiver strategy more frequently than do boys.

The mother appears to respond positively to this role-reversing behavior, often praising the child for being precocious. She is often passive, disengaged and not able to meet the child's needs for protection, safety and reassurance. Mothers' dazed, absent and dissociated behaviors often indicate that she has unresolved, complicated trauma. This history interferes with her ability to respond to her child's distress signals.[95]

The first two coping patterns for Disorganized Attachment both involve codependent behaviors that keep the child attached to the mother's world and revolving around her emotional needs.

The research of Mary Main and Erik Hesse indicated that between 80 and 90 percent of the clients who seek therapy have Disorganized Attachment.[96] Their research findings suggest that this statistic might also apply to mental health professionals, making it likely for many of them to also have DA. For this reason, I strongly encourage mental health professionals to know their own attachment histories. Because of the importance of the client-therapist relationship in the healing process, disturbed relationship dynamics associated with Disorganized Attachment, and the high probability of mental health practitioners also having a Disorganized Attachment history create considerable risk of therapists encountering their own countertransference issues. From an attachment perspective, this mirroring phenomenon makes it virtually impossible for practitioners to uphold the "no harm" ethic in their professional work with clients.

THE LASTING IMPACT OF ATTACHMENT TRAUMA DURING THE BONDING STAGE

In our book, *Breaking Free of the Codependency Trap*, we discuss extensively the impact of developmental trauma during the codependent stage of development.[97] Here are some of the most common adult behaviors that associated with attachment trauma:

- Being "addicted" to people.
- Feeling trapped in abusive, controlling relationships.
- Having low self-esteem.
- Needing constant approval and support from others in order to feel good about yourself.
- Feeling powerless to change destructive relationships.
- Needing alcohol, food, work, sex, or some other outside stimulation to distract you from your feelings.

- Having undefined psychological boundaries.
- Feeling like a martyr.
- Being a people-pleaser.
- Being unable to experience true intimacy and love.

The following is a list of common behaviors that children and adults display after early experiences that involve developmental shock, trauma, or stress.[98]

1. Attachment problems: Uncertainty about the reliability and predictability of the world, distrust and suspiciousness, social isolation, interpersonal difficulties, difficulty attuning to other people's emotional states and points of view.

2. Biochemical disturbances: hypersensitivity to physical contact, analgesia, somatizing the trauma in the physical body, increased health and medical problems.

3. Affect or emotional dysregulation: easily aroused high-intensity emotions, difficulty deescalating, difficulty describing feelings and internal experience, chronic and pervasive depressed mood or sense of emptiness or deadness, chronic suicidal preoccupation, over-inhibition or excessive expression of anger.

4. Dissociation: distinct alterations in states of consciousness, amnesia, depersonalization, and de-realization.

5. Impulse control problems: poor modulation of impulses, self-destructive behavior, aggressive behavior, sleep disturbances, eating disorders, substance abuse, oppositional behavior, excessive compliance.

6. Cognitive disturbances: difficulties in regulating attention, problems managing life situations, problems focusing on and completing tasks, difficulty planning and anticipating, learning difficulties, problems with language development.

7. Poor self-concept: a lack of a continuous and predictable sense of self, low self-esteem, feelings of shame and guilt, generalized sense of being ineffective in dealing with one's environment, belief in being permanently damaged by a trauma.

8. Narcissistic disturbances: unwillingness to admit mistakes; needing to be the center of attention, grandiose and inflated self-image; drug, alcohol or food addictions; cut off from feelings, lack of empathy, feelings of entitlement.

Again, these problems fall along a continuum from mild to severe. The critical point in this discussion is that "subtle and ordinary" early trauma creates the same symptoms and problems as acute trauma that is "extreme and dramatic." All contribute to the foundational experiences that ultimately determine a person's ability to form and sustain healthy relationships, to succeed in the world, and to experience positive mental health.

(This page intentionally left blank)

CHAPTER SEVEN

SEPARATION TRAUMA

Counterdependency involves avoiding any dependence on others, being uncomfortable opening up to or trusting others, pushing others away, appearing overly independent, acting strong, and keeping overly busy. It is common in people with early childhood trauma or abuse. Counterdependency is a pattern of behavior, not an illness, and it can be changed.

—Barry & Janae Weinhold, *The Flight From Intimacy*

THE COUNTERDEPENDENT STAGE OF INDIVIDUAL DEVELOPMENT

This stage of individual development begins around eight or nine months of age. By this time children are becoming physically mobile, and shifting their attention away from the oneness of bonding and towards exploration and separation. The most important developmental process in this stage involves creating a separate identity and sense of self.

Jungian psychologists refer to this as the *individuation process*, and developmental researcher Margaret Mahler calls it the *psychological birth*. During this process, children learn to experience themselves as emotionally and psychologically separate from their parents. They create a foundation for the development of a fully individuated self.

During the counterdependent stage of development, children venture further and further from the bonded safety of the codependent stage. The exploring child who falls or gets frightened quickly returns to a parent for comfort, so this stage is characterized by "coming and going" behaviors.

Also known as the "terrible twos," it consists of several sub-phases that are characteristically punctuated by emotional outbreaks and tantrums related to a child's internal conflict about separating. The latter part of the stage is characterized by a lot of "no" responses and oppositional behaviors that help children build boundaries between themselves and others. This opposition is directed not just towards the parents, but also siblings, grandparents and other caregivers.

Table 7-1 below describes the essential developmental processes of the counterdependent stage of individual development. Our research indicates it takes the cooperative and conscious effort of two bonded caregivers to help children complete these developmental processes successfully and on schedule.

Most parents rely own their own experience of being parented to parent their children. If they are not aware of their own developmental trauma and other adverse childhood experiences, however, they are likely to repeat them with their children. In other words, hidden childhood trauma can interfere with parents being able to provide the constant care that infants need.

Table 7-1. The Essential Developmental Processes of the Counterdependent Stage of Individual Development[99]

Stage of Development & Primary Task	Essential Developmental Processes in Counter Dependent Stage	Experiences for Completing the Essential Developmental Processes of the Counter Dependent Stage
Counter-dependent **(8–36 months)** *Separation & Individuation*	• Develops a "love affair" with the world beyond the immediate bonding/connection with parents • Learn to explore one's environment in safe ways • Learn to trust and regulate one's own thoughts, feelings, behaviors in socially-appropriate ways • Internalize appropriate physical & social limits • Develop healthy narcissism	• Parents offer timely help to heal any narcissistic wounds or developmental traumas in both themselves and the child that disturb resonance • Parents give permission and support to safely explore your environment; • Parents give the child twice as many "yes's" as "no's" as he/she explores the world • Parents arrange environment to provide safety • Parents help the child internally regulate his/her emotions, especially shame • Parents help the child to identify self-vs.-other needs

Stage of Development & Primary Task	Essential Developmental Processes in Counter Dependent Stage	Experiences for Completing the Essential Developmental Processes of the Counter Dependent Stage
Counter-dependent **(8–36 months)** *Separation & Individuation (cont.)*	• Resolve internal conflicts between oneness & separateness • Bond with self • Continue building secure Internal Working Model of reality •Completing the psychological birth process by age 3.	• Parents model for the child how to effectively meet his/her needs • Adults help the child learn to quickly reestablish the resonance with his/her parents when it is disrupted • Parents use non-shaming responses with the child in setting limits & giving consequences • Caregivers offer empathy & compassion as the child learns to regulate his/her conflicting emotions, thoughts and behaviors • Caregivers authentically mirror the child's essence • Caregivers support the child in becoming a separate individual and trusting his/her internal impulses and needs • Parents give positive support for the child's efforts to develop an autonomous Self

COMPLETING THE COUNTERDEPENDENT STAGE OF DEVELOPMENT

Only children with secure bonding have a solid enough psychological foundation for them to successfully complete the counterdependent stage of individual development. This secure foundation helps them gradually move away from the safety of being with mother and father, and venture into an unknown and sometimes scary world.

The more secure children's bonding, the more easily they complete the separation process. Their natural drive to separate and explore the world, however, requires a different kind of support than they needed during the bonding stage.

Separation requires supervision, limits, consequences and experiences that help children learn cause-and-effect thinking, but without the possibility of encountering life-and-death situations. For example, a child only learns what "hot" means by touching something hot enough to make the appropriate connections in the brain, but without burning them.

Once children have completed their psychological separation, they have sufficient self-confidence to rely on their own internal guidance, their own knowing and life experiences, to help them make age-appropriate day-to-day decisions. They no longer need to rely on others to direct their lives. This is at the heart of the psychological birth.[100]

Children with a healthy sense of self are able to accept responsibility for their actions, share and cooperate, cope with frustration and stress in appropriate ways, respond effectively to the authority of others, and express their feelings in healthy ways.

As we stated earlier, children need secure bonding with their mother and father or other adult caregivers during the first six to nine months of life in order to complete the psychological birth. Margaret Mahler,[101] a researcher and child psychologist, did extensive observational research with mothers and their babies to better understand the components of the essential developmental processes that need to be completed during the first three years.

She found that holding, singing and talking to the child, mirroring back the child's essence, patient attention to the child's needs and nurturing touch were essential for strong parent-infant bonding. She described this experience as "symbiosis."

The innate drive for both mother/father and child to enter a deep state of psychological and biological attunement with the child is at the core of symbiosis. Mahler and others found that there are degrees of symbiosis, depending on the quality of the connection between parents and children.

Mahler found that the stronger the parent-child emotional attunement, the stronger the children's foundation for completing the psychological birth and becoming emotionally separate from their parents. She also believed that the separation stage is motivated by children's innate drive to explore the world and to become autonomous. This drive, however, creates an internal conflict for them.

When children begin to separate emotionally, the quality of the bonding relationship with both parents is crucial. If, for example, the mother is depressed, tired, or not available emotionally because she is unable to cope with the demands of parenting, or is anxious because the father is unavailable, this affects the pace of the separation process.

Incomplete bonding makes it more difficult for children to begin their separation. They need more bonding before they feel safe enough to explore.

If the need for more bonding is not completely met, children will continue to grow physically, but without developing the internal security and confidence they need to venture out to encounter an unknown world

According to the principles of human development, physical development continues forward to the next stage, even if children's social and emotional development lags behind. They learn to fake their independence with an "I'm strong and can take care of myself, I'll show you I don't need you" attitude. This is the first step in constructing a narcissistic or False Self. In such cases, children learn to focus on performing and pretending "as if" in their interactions with the outer world.

Some children separate prematurely because of early experiences involving developmental shock or trauma. Perhaps there was intense birth trauma, a milk allergy, or "helicopter" parents who clung too tightly and were overly intrusive, trying to control every facet of their lives.

Shock or trauma can occur if a parent dissociates or does scary things that cause a child's brain to short-circuit. This prevents children from building trust and bonding. They may prefer strangers as early as three months, and stiffen against their parents' efforts to hold and comfort them.

Naturally this reactive behavior causes anxiety in the parents. A mother or father may wonder, for example, "Why doesn't my child like me?" Depending on their self-esteem, they may see the child's attempts to separate prematurely as rejection, or even a threat to their identity as a mother or father.

In either case, the movement from bonding into separation is a delicate process, requiring that parents not only have good information about child development, but also have healed their own developmental shocks or traumas related to bonding and separation experiences.

THE LIMITS OF PARENTAL SEPARATION

Children's inner struggle between the desire for oneness and the desire for separateness creates the framework for their journey towards individual selfhood. Parents, however, also desire to separate from their children. This makes the separation process a "dance" between the parents' desire for separation, particularly the mother's desire to return to some of the life she had previous to her child's birth, and the child's struggle between staying close and exploring.

cInfants and toddlers can only tolerate a certain length of separation time from their parents. If these limits are exceeded this can cause a trauma in the child. Below Table 7-2 shows the safe limits of separation.

Table 7-2. The Limits of Parental Separation

Age of child	Preferable limit	Acceptable limit	Harmful limit
Under one year	Two days	Seven days	More than seven days
1 – 2 years	Three days	Ten days	More than ten days
3 – 5 years	One week	Three weeks	More than three weeks
6 – 9 years	Two weeks	Four weeks	More than four weeks
10 – 13 years	Four weeks	Six weeks	More than six weeks

THE FATHER'S ROLE IN SUPPORTING THE SEPARATION PROCESS[102]

During the Early Exploration Phase, you moved away and back many times during a day to confirm that the bond with your mother or father was still intact. You may also have gotten touched, given a loving smile, a brief cuddle, a bottle by your father, or an opportunity to nurse on your mother's lap. Each time, however, you were lured back to exploring the world because your drive to explore the world around you grew stronger by the day.

Your father knew that his role was to play with you, hold you, and help you move away from your mother. Soon you learned that your father wasn't just a part of your mother, but a separate person. You saw these differences and similarities between your father and your mother. She let you know in many ways that she trusts your father, which also helps you trust him.

If your mother was afraid of your father and tried to keep you from him, then you likely picked up this fear. You also needed other relatives and friends with whom you could bond, and trusted your parents' judgment about who was trustworthy.

One of the essential developmental processes of this phase involved developing a specific smile of recognition for your mother, father or other caregivers. Games of peek-a-boo are common ways to interact with a child during this stage. It's also how you learned to discriminate between your parents and strangers.

If the bonding with your mother and father was secure, you showed more curiosity and wonderment toward strangers. If it was insecure, you might have pulled back from strangers out of fear and uncertainty, especially when you were around the age of eight months.

THE FATHER'S ROLE IN ACHIEVING OBJECT CONSTANCY

Parents and bonded caregivers play a critical role in helping children move through the oppositional sub-stage of development and achieve object constancy. Object constancy is a child's ability to maintain a sense of an "okay" Self when they don't get their way.

Parents' most difficult task is to avoid participating in children's oppositional behavior. Splits typically manifest in the two-against-one game where a child allies with one parent against the other. This kind of polarized thinking often involves keeping secrets, or parents using the child in a Drama Triangle conflict. In this situation, the child tests the strength of the bond between the parents or a parent and another caregiver, not the adults' psychological maturity.

Adults who haven't completed their own psychological birth will inadvertently play into children's splitting behaviors during conflicts with them, getting into useless power struggles. This follows the old saying, "never get into a power struggle with a skunk."

When this happens, adults often find it difficult to validate a child's reality and support their feelings. This makes the child's separation process even more difficult to facilitate. A father with unhealed abandonment trauma, for example, may reveal his polarized thinking by criticizing his wife and making her bad in front of the child when she pays more attention to the child's needs than she does to his needs.

Most men without "male mothering" skills feel trapped in the middle of a "no-win" struggle between their partner and their child, and don't know how to handle the situation. It is no surprise, therefore, that the most common time for fathers to leave a marriage or file for divorce is when the first child is about two years old. This is when the need for a father with male mothering skills is also most critical.

THE FATHER'S ROLE IN COMPLETING THE COUNTERDEPENDENT STAGE

In order to support the completion of the essential developmental processes of the counter dependent stage, fathers need to:

- Identify and heal any remaining developmental traumas from his own separation stage of development.
- Avoid getting personally triggered by his child's good-bad splits in perception.
- Give his child twice as many "yes" as "no" responses while they are exploring their world.
- Childproof his home to allow safe exploration thus reducing the number of limits that need to be set.
- Set appropriate and safe limits without use of shame or physical punishment.
- Show respect and compassion for the feelings of his child.
- Take his child's needs seriously.
- Meet his child's needs in appropriate and timely ways.
- Use "time-in" activities rather than "time-out" to help his child regulate emotions.

'TIME-IN' VERSUS 'TIME-OUT' IN

"Time-out" has become a very common way of disciplining dysregulated children. While it is a big improvement over corporal punishment, we personally believe that it is also a primary cause of developmental trauma during the counterdependent stage of development.

So, we want to say very clearly: Time-outs serve the needs of adult caregivers, not the needs of children. They provide adults with time to re-regulate their own emotions when they get upset.

This approach gives adult caregivers a justifiable reason for separating from a child so they can calm themselves down. They may frame it as time for their child to think about and correct their behavior and to re-regulate themselves emotionally, when the opposite is actually true.

While time-outs are helpful for adults, they are absolutely one of the worst things for a toddler. Why? Time-outs violate the most basic principles of adult-child relationships and the research of Allen Schore and others whom we have cited earlier in this book.

Schore is very clear in his position that the attuned parent-child dyad is the mechanism that controls children's ability to regulate both their biological and emotional states. The closer in proximity the child is to an adult, the easier it is for children to re-regulate themselves during or after an emotional meltdown.

Separating a child from their adult regulator when the child is emotionally dysregulated just reinforces the developmental trauma, and helps hardwire insecure behavior patterns even more deeply into his or her developing nervous system. When adults correctly understand the cause of toddlers' emotional outbursts, they recognize that "meltdowns" are an extreme case of emotional dysregulation.

Emotional outbursts are usually the result of an inner conflict between the desire to be separate and the drive to explore, while also wanting parents' love and approval. Toddlers need adults' understanding about their feelings of frustration and anger when someone limits their exploration and their efforts to be independent.

When dysregulated children get a "time-out," they become even more disconnected from caregivers. This not only increases their emotional dysregulation, it can cause experiences of feeling abandoned.

Many adults, unfortunately, make the situation worse for a two to three-year old child by saying, "I don't want to be close to you when you are behaving this way. Go to your room until you can get yourself quieted down."

This message often comes with a facial expression showing scorn, which the child internalizes as, "There is something wrong with me. I feel ashamed of myself and I don't know how to stop my feelings. I need help." This dynamic creates even more internal conflict. The child believes that "There actually is something wrong with me because I don't know how to get myself to feel better," and he/she experiences toxic shame.

If this happens repeatedly, the self-judging belief and the shame get reinforced. This is the core of shame-based behavior in adults. What children really need is a "time-in" where they sit on or by you, be touched, and talked to in a calm, soothing way. This not only helps them re-regulate their feelings, it stops the feelings of shame from developing.

When this happens, children realize there is nothing wrong with having these feelings and they can calm down. Adults are much more empathetic when they understand correctly that the emotional outburst is a symptom of children needing help to re-regulate their emotions.

Rather than feeling angry and frustrated at the child, adults can intervene empathetically in ways that truly help them. This normalizes the negative feelings and communicates an acceptance of children's struggle to become independent and learn how to regulate their emotions.

The developmental trauma caused by "time outs" and the resulting prolonged shaming is not only too much for toddlers to endure emotionally, it has damaging long-term consequences. Toddlers not only fail to learn how to discharge or regulate their feelings of shame in a healthy way, they learn to cope by blaming themselves or others. They also learn to project the energy of their shameful emotions away from themselves and onto others to relieve their inner stress.

If you are a conscious parent or caregiver, it's important to heal your own developmental traumas. This makes you more able to help children successfully complete their psychological birth and the essential developmental processes of the counter dependent stage of development on time between ages two and three. This allows children to develop object constancy, go on "internal power" and experience both/and, "I'm okay, you're okay" thinking.

Janae has presented this information to many childcare professionals and early childhood educators at conferences and trainings and found them very receptive. There were a few, however, who insisted that children are able to re-regulate their emotions through time-out. What she eventually saw was that these people preferred to blame, shame, punish and traumatize emotionally dysregulated children than look at how some children were triggering their own unhealed developmental traumas.

She remarked, "I can't tell you how much it upsets me to see some of these individuals in positions as behavioral experts in the childcare profession using their work as an avenue for transmitting intergenerational cycles of trauma... and doing so in spite of my very direct efforts to help them see what they were doing and why."

THE FATHER'S ROLE IN COMPLETING THE PSYCHOLOGICAL BIRTH

If you did not have a father or other bonded caregiver who could be present and show empathy toward you for your struggles and support your feelings, you likely have yet to complete the individuation process. It's likely that you developed a False Self to help you cope by making you look strong and independent ("fake it till you make it").

Perhaps you hoped this False Self would be more acceptable than your True Self. As an adult, you've retained aspects of your False Self while working to complete the vital process of individuation.

People with developmental traumas from the bonding process generally develop a deflated False Self. Inside they feel weak and helpless. If you suffered from developmental traumas related to the separation process, you may have an inflated False Self.

If you had very early developmental shocks or traumas, you may be more prone to depression. If you suffered with developmental traumas during the separation process, you are more likely to be grandiose and adrenalized into hyperactivity to help you avoid feeling depressed. To complete your psychological birth as an adult, it is necessary to master the internal struggle between two seemingly opposite forces: the natural drive toward oneness and closeness and the equally powerful drive to be an emotionally separate, self-determining individual.

Understanding what happened to you in your childhood, healing your developmental traumas, and developing new relationship skills are important steps in completing your psychological birth. Many people ask, "How will I know when this is complete?"

You will have a keen sense of who you really are and handle life's challenges and conflicts with a minimum of stress, while feeling good about yourself and good about others. You will be able to maintain your object constancy in the midst of most of life challenges.

You will be able to be both close and intimate and be separate and alone when you want. Only adults who have worked on themselves both psychologically and spiritually, can expect to complete this essential developmental process successfully.

So, what about single-parent families? No research has been done about how bonded caregivers such as a babysitter or grandparents can fill the missing parent's role. However, if a male child's primary parent is a woman and the father is either absent or very emotionally unavailable, he will have more difficulty in separating from her. This area certainly needs much more research and study.

When functional family dynamics are not present in the parent-child structure, a dysfunctional family triangle known as the Drama Triangle develops instead. The dynamics of the Drama Triangle are the result of developmental traumas originally from the counter dependent stage of development. You can read more about the nuances of the Drama Triangle in our book, *Breaking Free of The Drama Triangle and Victim Consciousness*,[103] available at Amazon.

DISORGANIZED ATTACHMENT AND SEPARATION TRAUMA

Many children experience separation trauma during the counterdependent stage. These unhealed separation traumas prevent the psychological birth of the individual from occurring on schedule. This inhibits the full development of an individuated self. Because of this, we believe that very few people have fully completed the essential developmental processes of this stage that would provide a solid foundation for their efforts as an adult to become fully individuated.

The most common cause of separation trauma is disorganized caregiving by adults with Disorganized Attachment and a related intergenerational parenting dynamic known as *the reversal process*. Also known as *parentizing* and *parentification*, it involves parents and other care-giving adults unconsciously reversing roles with the children they care for. This happens during the counterdependent stage of development when children decide to give up their own needs and become physical caregivers for their disorganized adult caregivers.

This caregiving reversal is particularly visible during the separation stage of development when children have just begun to develop a Self, and learning to use their will to direct what happens in their physical environment. Children learn to survive in reversal situations by giving up their need to be cared for. Instead, they organize things in their physical environment around their mother with the hope that she will become more available to care for them. This reversal pattern is quite common in the eldest child.

Reversals allow adult caretakers to unconsciously avoid encountering their own developmental traumas. Perceptive children are aware of times when their parents are triggered and regressed, and unable to attend to their needs. In order to survive, these children step in and take charge of things. The sad dynamic in all of this is that toddlers also give up their needs for affection, nurturing and safety and begin behaving as little adults. This premature separation causes them to "split" against their mother and other caregivers, which requires closing their hearts. Figure 7-1 below shows how this split into counterdependent behavior happens.

Figure 7-1. Separation Trauma & Splitting

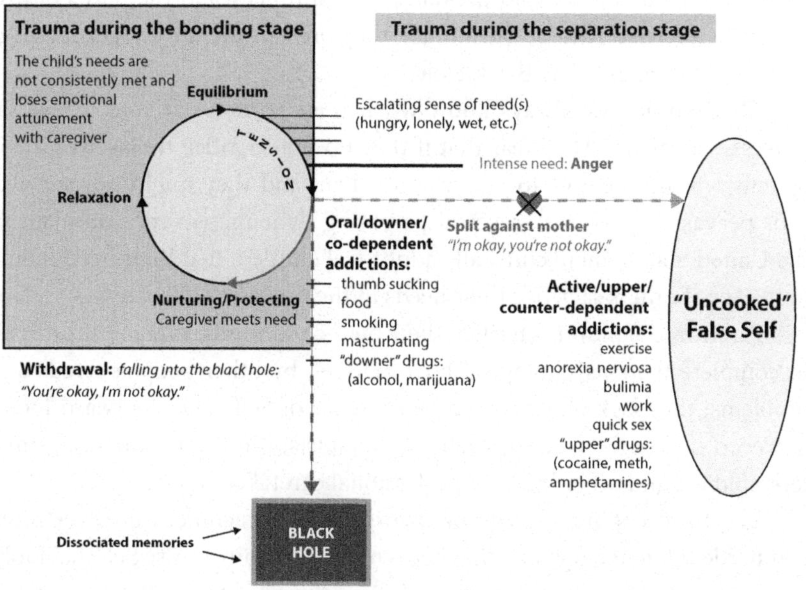

Trauma during the bonding stage

The child's needs are not consistently met and loses emotional attunement with caregiver

Equilibrium

TENSION

Escalating sense of need(s) (hungry, lonely, wet, etc.)

Intense need: **Anger**

Relaxation

Trauma during the separation stage

Split against mother "I'm okay, you're not okay."

Oral/downer/ co-dependent addictions:
- thumb sucking
- food
- smoking
- masturbating
- "downer" drugs: (alcohol, marijuana)

Nurturing/Protecting
Caregiver meets need

Withdrawal: *falling into the black hole:* "You're okay, I'm not okay."

Active/upper/ counter-dependent addictions:
exercise
anorexia nerviosa
bulimia
work
quick sex
"upper" drugs:
(cocaine, meth, amphetamines)

"Uncooked" False Self

Dissociated memories → **BLACK HOLE**

This image also shows how toddlers create a False Self as a defense against their needs and being vulnerable. They learn to project an image of strength and competency to the outer world. Internally, however, their hearts are closed, and unable to give and receive unconditional love. The Self does not develop because it is cut off from normal internal yearnings and impulses that are at the heart of intimacy.

The False Self requires a lot of energy to build and sustain. Children learn very early to use "upper" activities and substances that keep them adrenalized. This hyperactivity helps them cope with their isolation and pseudo-maturity by moving fast and "looking good." Two-year old defenses such as addiction to sugared and processed foods, yelling, screaming, running, hitting, breaking things and refusing to eat or sleep become more sophisticated as the child matures.

They morph into adult defenses such as excessive exercising, working, shopping, traveling, and managing other people's lives. When this hyperactivity becomes difficult to sustain, they move to more sophisticated upper substances such as meth, cocaine and amphetamines to help maintain their pace.

Figure 7-1 also lists some of the most common adult addictions that the False Self uses to maintain an appearance of strength. These activities and substances help adults avoid the dangers of intimacy and the perils of loss that are associated with it. Most of all, they prevent them from getting triggered and falling into the Black Hole.

Children almost always know when their parents are into a reversal process with them. They fear that if they do not sacrifice themselves, their parents will not be able to take care of them and they might not survive. This pervasive, powerful, reversal parenting dynamic is very dominant in the United States where culturally adults feel entitled, that their needs come first, even if others sacrifice their needs in the process.

Parentized children sacrifice their own childhoods, making it difficult to complete their psychological birth. Driven by other people's needs and problems, they lack of a strong enough sense of Self. Their outward focus, however, makes them ideal teachers, therapists, physicians, nurses, ministers, soldiers and other kinds of professional caretakers.

The third coping strategy of Disorganized Attachment involves more counterdependent behaviors that help children sustain a False Self that looks much more independent and self-sufficient than it actually is. It also allows people to feel more in control and to make their environment physically safer.

This aggressive, confrontational False Self feeds the "Little General" category of coping with Disorganized Attachment. This counterdependent False Self creates a strong wall of defense mechanisms against the dangers of intimacy.

DISORGANIZED ATTACHMENT COPING CATEGORY #3: THE LITTLE GENERAL

We call the controlling-punitive disorganized category for coping with Disorganized Attachment the *Little General*. Children using this coping behavioral pattern often control the mother through harsh commands and verbal threats and by using physical aggression towards her. She appears intimidated, helpless, withdrawn and stressed by her child, who becomes increasingly moody, hyperactive and out of control, resenting the role-reversing situation. The child experiences the mother's chaotic communication, her unresolved fears and her intermittent dissociation very disturbing.[104]

The Little General is directive, telling the mother what to do, when to do it, and how to do it. Little General types care for their overwhelmed parents by assuming some of their daily responsibilities in the physical environment hopes that parents will be able to care for them. They often take charge of shopping for food, cooking for the family, and providing essential care for younger children. This is particularly true in families where parents have serious addictions and are nonfunctional in important ways.

Figure 7-2. The Little General

As adults, Little Generals make great managers, directors and administrative workers. They are highly effective in human and social services professions where they can use their well-developed strategic thinking skills to organize other people's lives. While all three of the strategies for coping with disorganized caregiving are adaptive and look very different in children's interactions with their mothers, their purpose is exactly the same: controlling parental chronic unpredictability or malevolence, or both.[105] From a gender perspective, boys tend to adopt the Little General coping strategy more frequently than girls.

The outcome of all three strategies is also the same: neither the disorganized mother or her children ever focus on identifying or meeting the child's needs. These emotionally neglected children may become quite effective and efficient in organizing the lives of others, but have virtually no skills or understanding about how to organize their own lives.

Defense mechanisms learned during the separation stage of development form the foundation for attachment disorders in early childhood. As children grow older, they can turn into developmental trauma-based personality disorders. Defiant and oppositional behavior that persists beyond the age of 3 are an indication that the unrecognized and unhealed effects of developmental shock, trauma, and stress are being hard-wired into children's brains and personality structures.

One of the rules in developmental psychology is that a person can only become psychologically and emotionally separate to the degree that they have secure attachment. Those with insecure attachment, particularly Disorganized Attachment, encounter more difficulty during the separation process because of their higher exposure to unhealed experiences of developmental shock, trauma and stress. Their developmental delays, caused primarily by narcissistic or other controlling parenting behaviors, make the individuation process much more difficult to complete on schedule.

"Normal" Events That Cause Separation Trauma

- Too many "no's" during the exploratory process.
- Limits are set in angry, rigid or abusive ways.
- Use of physical punishment, shaming or name-calling to set limits.
- The birth of a younger sibling before the older child is three years old.
- No limit-setting to create safety.
- An emotionally or physically absent father.
- Separations of two weeks or more, without any contact with the child.
- Sibling rivalry promoted or supported by parents.
- Not enough "kid proofing" of the environment
- Physical injuries that lead to a belief that the world is not safe.
- Parental expectations are too high causing performance anxiety.
- Little support for the child to become a separate person.
- Holding on and keeping your child dependent to meet your needs.

The Long-term Impact of Separation

- Addictions to "upper" substances or activities.
- A belief that the world is a scary place.
- OCD behaviors.
- Social disengagement/dissociation.
- Low self-esteem.
- Frequent experiences of severe emotional dysregulation.
- Difficulty in reregulating yourself, without assistance.
- A stressful disorganized lifestyle.
- Becoming overly involved in the lives of your children or spouse.
- Not feeling lovable, leading to compulsive "doing."
- Difficulties with intimacy.
- Erect walls to keep people from getting too close.
- Defensive behaviors.
- Problems with intimacy, narcissism

CHAPTER EIGHT

DEVELOPMENTAL SYSTEMS THEORY

Today the network of relationships linking the human race to itself and to the rest of the biosphere is so complex that all aspects affect all others to an extraordinary degree. Someone should be studying the whole system, however crudely that has to be done, because no gluing together of partial studies of a complex nonlinear system can give a good idea of the behavior of the whole.

—Murray Gell-Mann

DEVELOPMENTAL SYSTEMS THEORY

Drawing from what we learned in our relationship laboratory, we began using a heuristic research approach to study human development. We used optimal individual development as the baseline for tracking evolution in both micro and macro human systems.

Over a period of about 15 years, we applied the principles of optimal individual development to larger, more complex human systems—first in micro systems (individuals, couples and families) then in macro systems (groups/organizations, cultures/nation–states, and the whole human race). Our book, *Conflict Resolution: The Partnership Way*[106] describes how seven levels of human systems evolve through the same four stages of development: codependent, counterdependent, independent, and interdependent.

Our systemic research revealed that fractal patterns of both optimal development and shock, trauma, stress are present in all seven levels of human systems. We could see how precisely these fractal patterns operate as templates that organize all biological, psychological, and social development in systems.

We eventually consolidated our research into a systemic meta-theory, *Developmental Systems Theory* (DST). It is based on principles of fractal evolution in which a series-reiterated pattern of "structures" nests within one another, like Russian Matryoshka dolls. More specifically, the pattern of the whole is reflected in the parts of the whole.[107] When we applied these fractal principles to the history of the human race, we could see an evolutionary fractal pattern of the human race that is also reflected in each individual human.

We saw how this fractal perspective of both optimal and trauma-based evolution revealed the interconnectedness of all life. In a fractal, any small part of a larger image contains the pattern of the whole. If you look at a nation–state as a human system and then focus on one citizen of that nation–state, it is possible to understand something about that individual's behavior. Likewise, looking at one citizen of a nation–state will help you understand how the larger system behaves. Behaviorally and structurally, they mirror each other.

Bruce Lipton's work helped us understand the functional structure and behavior of a cell.[108] While Lipton used a single cell as his theoretical model, we used an individual as our theoretical model. Once we understood how an individual develops, it helped us understand and map the development and organization of larger and more complex human systems, including couples, families, groups/organizations, cultures/nation–states, and the human species. Using this fractal framework, we mapped evolution showing how each larger system contains the same patterns of organization and behavior that are found in the subsystems contained within it.

Based on our new research findings, we decided that the earlier models of evolution are outdated and that Lipton's model of fractal evolution is more useful. His model offers an alternative theory to Neo-Darwinism. It is based on the primacy of all development on the individual cell receptors' perception of its environment rather than on nature or genetics.

Lipton bases his biological premise on extensive research. He draws from unified field theory and asserts that receptors on the membranes of individual cells read the "field" surrounding them. The cells' perception of the field determines how they respond. When the cells perceive danger, their receptors close and direct the organism to go into a protective mode. When the cells perceive safety in their environment, the receptors open, and they direct the organism to go into a growth mode.

Lipton's operational model has no middle ground: cells and organisms can only be in one mode at a time. Cells are either in a growth mode and able to give and receive information, sustenance and unconditional love; or they are in a protection mode and closed to receiving supportive information and energy. We find Lipton's model of fractal evolution, along with principles from quantum sciences, particularly quantum biology and neuroscience, supportive of our DST framework.

Lipton's pioneering work in the field of epigenetics[109] also provided us with a scientific foundation for *Heart Field Therapy*, our clinical approach.[110] Epigenetics, a revolutionary field in biology, says that our DNA is mutable rather than fixed. Rather than being "destiny" in a Darwinian sense, DNA can be modified without changing the basic blueprint. The DNA blueprint cannot only be damaged by trauma, shock, stress and environmental toxins, but it can also by healed using modalities such as meditation that help heal damage to the DNA strands.[111]

THE CONTRIBUTIONS OF ALLAN SCHORE

Schore[112] applies three interacting principles of dynamic systems theory to the study of normal and abnormal human development. His first key principle is *state changes*. This principle involves looking for the underlying complex psychobiological states that evoke change in humans. In individuals, the brain and nervous system determine and regulate these state changes.

Advances in brain imaging technology have made it easier to identify the internal states that cause changes in the brain and nervous system and ultimately cause a biological system to shift. For example, the study of infant bonding and attachment now involves studying the developing brain and nervous system as a child evolves into a self-organizing being.

Schore's second key principle is the *psychobiological state* that marks the common boundary between the psychological and biological sciences and helps reunite mind and body. His third key principle of *self-organization* is essential for identifying the impact of early childhood experiences on brain development, particularly the development of the right hemisphere.

Bruce Perry[113] and others recognize the developing brain as use-dependent: The quality of the bonding interactions between infants and their mothers determines which parts of the brain fully develop and which do not.

Schore's review of recent brain research suggests that "the self-organization" of the brain occurs in the context of another self, another brain."[114] He contends that an infant's early bonding experiences with his or her mother involve the energetic attunement of their two right brains. If the mother has a well-functioning right brain and is able to attune to her child's right brain through mutual gazing, kind words, soft singing, and gentle touch, this allows the infant's cell receptors to open and causes the brain and nervous system to grow and develop.

Schore focuses much of his attention on the experience-dependent maturation of the fronto-limbic system in the human brain. This part of the brain directs traffic and regulates psychobiological states and organismic energy flow and balance.[115] He contends that less than optimal gene–environment interactions (developmental shocks, traumas, or stresses) during the crucial attachment and separation developmental processes during the first three years of life can cause this condition. This is where these adverse childhood experiences can produce a fronto-limbic brain organization that is vulnerable to a later spectrum of psychopathologies.[116]

Both Lipton and Schore use language from the field of quantum mechanics, particularly quantum biology. Their paradigms recognize a psychobiological transfer of energy generated during shared emotional states that is transmitted between living systems, both at micro- and macroscopic levels.

Schore sprinkles his description of the mother-child relationship with quantum language such as attunement, energetic resonance and synchronization. In the introduction of Janae's *LOVEvolution* book, she presents research showing that the beating human heart generates some 2.5 watts of electrical activity with each heartbeat that creates a pulsing electromagnetic field of energy around the body.[117]

We know that the developing brain demands massive amounts of energy and nutrients to fuel its growth, making a young child's brain operate at a much faster metabolic rate than an adult brain. This is why it can shift more rapidly to organize and reorganize. We also know that self-organization increases the rate of energy/matter transfer, so the more open a complex system is to receiving energy, the faster and easier the energy/matter flows in that system.[118]

This concept supports Lipton's notion that when the cell perceives that it is safe to open and receive new energy/matter, it relays this information on to the fronto-limbic brain, which increases the rate of self-organization.

Based on his review of the new research on neurobiology and neurochemistry, Schore lists a number of useful and important systems principles for studying self-organizing systems.[119] The following principles describe how humans get their needs met and evolve:

- They are open to interact with their particular environment. For human infants, it is important to monitor their interactions with the social environment, particularly their attachment pattern with their primary caregivers.
- Infants' ongoing development requires an open system in which both matter and energy can be openly exchanged with the environment. This is the same principle that Lipton observed at a cellular level. If the receptors on the lining of the cell wall perceive the environment as safe, they open and receive both matter and energy that supports further development.

At certain key moments in the development of a system, a flow of new energy/matter from the environment allows the components of infants' self-organizing systems to become increasingly more integrated. We describe these as *essential developmental processes*. An example is the secure attachment that occurs during the first year of life as the result of an infant's consistently repeated experiences of connecting, disconnecting and reconnecting with its mother and other adult caregivers. Completing this essential developmental process during the Codependent Stage allows children to build basic trust and move on to the Counterdependent stage of development. This process is integral in not only individual human development, but in all self-organizing biological systems.

PRINCIPLES OF SELF-ORGANIZING SYSTEMS

- All human systems, including infants, function hierarchically. One can track the path of their development to see where environmental inputs (developmental shocks, traumas, stresses, or exceptional developmental support) may have caused the system to modify its trajectory.
- The different organizational levels of both human individuals and larger and more complex human systems unfold through a hierarchical process of development and maturation. This unfoldment is characterized by an alternation between rapid and slower rates of development that finally plateaus and sets the limits on the stages of development. Thus, a plateau in development marks the end of one stage of development before an acceleration of development marks the beginning of the next stage.
- Developmental change is the result of a series of alternating states of stability and instability. These changes are marked by transitions that irreversibly alter the trajectory of the system and help it reach new and higher levels of self-organization.

- Complex systems are sensitive to bifurcation points where the system can choose to divide. At these sensitive points, small differences in inputs can become amplified and are able to activate large system-effects over many cycles of change. In chaos theory, these inputs are called *strange attractors*. When these inputs are integrated into the system, they have the potential to produce system-altering changes.
- Strange attractors can be introduced deliberately to both stabilize a system or to rapidly change the path of a system trajectory to a desired state. They also cause systems to become more flexible in their performance and more open to adapting to changes in their environment. Those who perform this function for individuals, couples and families are called therapists. in organizations, they are known as *change agents*, or in our terminology, *developmental process consultants (DPCs)*.
- Information is a special kind of energy that is required to establish biological order. Emotion (e-motion or energy in motion) acts as a strange attractor to direct the system's attention to relevant information coming in from its environment. It helps the system monitor and interpret environmental events according to their significance to the system.
- Interpersonal strange attractors, such as therapists, also help determine the stability of a system. They help maintain the system's equilibrium and help the individual to effectively regulate any disequilibrium caused by emotions.

THE ESSENTIAL DEVELOPMENTAL PROCESSES OF ALL HUMAN SYSTEMS

While we know the map is not the territory, we mapped the essential developmental processes for each of six human systems, from the individual through the whole human species. Our Developmental Systems map below shows what each system needs in an optimal model through four stages of human development in order to truly evolve.

As you look at the map shown in Tables 8.1 and 8.2 below, you can see how these four stages of development operate in all human systems. We could have divided the pie even smaller, but felt outlining the essential developmental process in each of these human systems is sufficient to grasp the concept. Mostly, therapists work with the three Microsystems: the individual, the couple and the family.

Table 8-1. The Developmental Evolution of Human Microsystems

Stage of Development & Primary Task	Essential Developmental Processes of an Individual	Essential Developmental Processes of a Couple	Essential Developmental Processes of a Family
Codependent Stage: *Bonding & Attachment*	• Mother receives good pre-natal care and support • Experience a nonviolent birth with immediate interventions to heal any shocks or birth trauma • Experience secure bonding/attachment with mother and or other adult caregivers • Build primal trust with both parents through a consistent resonant connection • Learn emotional resiliency skills • Create a secure internal model of self/other • Build healthy emotional communication and social engagement skills with both parents & others • Achieve secure bonding experiences with siblings and extended family • Promote effective communication and social engagement skills with parents and others	• Create secure and consistent bonding experiences with each other • Establish deep primal trust in each other • Develop ways to quickly repair any disruptions to couple resonance • Establish good communication and social engagement skills with each other • Establish an identity as a couple • Create secure bonding experiences in the family between parents and children • Establish primal trust among family members • Establish healthy emotional communication and social engagement skills among family members • Establish an identity as a family.	• Create secure bonding experiences in the family between parents and children • Establish primal trust of family members with one another • Establish healthy emotional communication and social engagement skills among family members • Initiate a healthy family vision and induct family members into it •Establish a healthy identity as a family

Stage of Development & Primary Task	Essential Developmental Processes of an Individual	Essential Developmental Processes of a Couple	Essential Developmental Processes of a Family
Counter-dependent Stage: *Separation*	• Achieve complete psychological separation from both parents • Learn to explore one's environment in safe ways • Learn to trust and regulate one's own thoughts, feelings, behaviors in socially appropriate ways • Internalize appropriate physical & social limits • Develop healthy narcissism • Resolve internal conflicts between oneness & separateness • Bond with self • Continue to build secure Internal Working Model of reality • Successfully complete the psychological birth process	• Become functionally separate individuals in the relationship • Identify and accept individual differences in thoughts, feelings, and behaviors in each other • Resolve internal conflicts between needs of self-other • Develop effective partnership ways to resolve conflicts of wants and needs, and conflicts of values and beliefs	• Parents and children learn to assert their individual needs and have them supported by other family members • Use fair, equitable, and non-shaming methods of limit setting and discipline • Parents are able to set effective limits for themselves and their children • Resolve conflicts effectively between needs of parents and needs of children
Independent Stage: *Mastery*	• Master basic self-care • Master the process of becoming a functionally autonomous individual separate from parents • Develop object constancy	• Listen empathically and non-defensively to each other • Communicate feelings directly and responsibly	• Support development of individual initiative in family members • Develop individual and couple autonomy within the family structure

Stage of Development & Primary Task	Essential Developmental Processes of an Individual	Essential Developmental Processes of a Couple	Essential Developmental Processes of a Family
Independent Stage: *Mastery (cont.)*	• Develop trust in core values and beliefs •Achieve secure bonding experiences with nature • Learn effective social engagement skills • Develop secure self/other Internal Working Model • Develop secure Internal Working Model of self/other •Achieve secure bonding with peers	• Take responsibility for the influence of past shocks, traumas, or stresses on behavior • Master financial, psychological, and professional self-sufficiency within the relationship • Move beyond an idealized, romanticized approach to love and intimacy • Develop core values and beliefs as a couple • Achieve object constancy as a couple • Bond with nature as a couple	• Set limits on children, selves, extra-family involvement to preserve couple relationship/couple autonomy within the family structure • Develop core values and beliefs as a family • Achieve object constancy as a family • Bond with nature as a family
Inter-dependent Stage: *Cooperation*	• Learn how to cooperate with others • Learn how to negotiate with others to get needs met • Learn to accept responsibility for personal behaviors and life experiences • Experience secure bonding with peers & other adults • Develop a social conscience	• Create a well-differentiated and clearly defined sense of self • Support partner's development • Learn to cooperate with each other in getting important needs met in the relationship	• Build consensus in decision-making skills among family members • Teach family members to cooperate with each other so all get important needs met.

Stage of Development & Primary Task	Essential Developmental Processes of an Individual	Essential Developmental Processes of a Couple	Essential Developmental Processes of a Family
Inter-dependent Stage: *Cooperation (cont.)*	• Achieve a secure bonding with the main culture • Develop a secure bonding with the planet • Live out of an authentic adult self • Achieve secure bonding with own children • Understand the influence of incomplete developmental processes on own life and the how to heal own developmental shocks, traumas, or stresses successfully	• Experience the deepest human connection possible with each other • Develop equality in the relationship • Cooperate to help each other heal developmental shocks, traumas, or stresses • Cooperate to develop each person's fullest human potential	• Create rituals that sustain the spiritual dimension of the family • Create divisions of labor based on individual interests and abilities • Help family members cooperate to help each other to heal their developmental shocks, traumas, or stresses • Teach family members how to cooperate to develop each member's fullest potential as human being.

Table 8-2. The Developmental Evolution of Human Macrosystems

Stage of Development & Primary Task	Essential Developmental Processes of an Organization	Essential Developmental Processes of Cultures & Nation–states	Essential Developmental Processes of the Human Race
Codependent Stage: *Bonding & Attachment*	• Create bonding experiences for employees	• Create bonding experiences that unify all subcultures around common values and practices	• Establish secure bonding with the world of Nature

Stage of Development & Primary Task	Essential Developmental Processes of an Organization	Essential Developmental Processes of Cultures & Nation–states	Essential Developmental Processes of the Human Race
Codependent Stage: *Bonding & Attachment (cont.)*	• Build trust between employers and employees • Create an organizational identity • Provide for basic needs of employees and managers • Foster healthy emotional communication and social engagement skills with employees and employers • Build organizational esprit de corps	• Build trust between leaders and citizens • Create healthy national identity • Establish healthy emotional communication and social engagement skills for all citizens • Provide opportunities for all citizens to get their basic needs met • Understand the true history of the nation • Build national esprit de corps	• Create a respect for the supernatural and spiritual elements of human life • Establish a unique identify as a species • Promote the development of right-brain functions within the individual • Understand the true history of the human race
Counter-dependent Stage: *Separation*	• Support employees to assert their needs and have them taken seriously by employers • Identify and promote unique contributions of each employee to the organization • Use fair, equitable, and non-shaming methods of limit-setting with employees • Establishing rules and policies in equitable ways.	• Encourage all citizens to assert their needs and insist they are taken seriously by leaders • Guarantee freedom of expression and protect minority and cultural rights • Identify and promote unique contributions of every citizen to the nation	• Explore ways to become functionally separate from Nature • Establish and respect diversity in the species • Develop left-brain functions within the individual • Create separate nation–states

Stage of Development & Primary Task	Essential Developmental Processes of an Organization	Essential Developmental Processes of Cultures & Nation-states	Essential Developmental Processes of the Human Race
Counter-dependent Stage: *Separation (cont.)*	•Resolving internal conflicts between the needs of employees and the needs of employers in partnership ways • Understand the influence of incomplete developmental processes on work performance and provide ways to heal developmental shocks, traumas, or stresses that show up at work	• Establish fair, equitable, and non-discriminating laws and national policies • Use rule of law to provide equal justice for all citizens. • Identify unique strengths of cultures and nations • Develop effective ways to resolve conflicts of needs between cultural groups and between nations • Understand how incomplete developmental processes influence national health and provide ways to heal developmental shocks, traumas, or stresses of all citizen	• Create religions based on beliefs in the supernatural and separate from Nature • Resolve conflicts between nations and religions in partnership ways • Understand how incomplete developmental processes influence human development and provide ways to heal developmental shocks, traumas, or stresses of all humans
Independent Stage: *Mastery*	•Create an organizational culture with mutually determined values and beliefs • Support individual autonomy within the organizational structure	• Create a national culture that honors and protects diversity of all cultures. • Create economic/social safety net for those in need • Insure that voting rights of all citizens are guaranteed	• Reunite with the world of Nature as partners • Develop whole-brain thinking functions including both/and thinking • Create & support individual cultures

Stage of Development & Primary Task	Essential Developmental Processes of an Organization	Essential Developmental Processes of Cultures & Nation–states	Essential Developmental Processes of the Human Race
Independent Stage: *Mastery (cont.)*	• Give employees responsibility for self-regulation of emotion and self-care. • Support employees' achievement of true pride in their work • Providing specialized training and development for each employee to enhance individual contributions to the organization	• Teach citizens how to take responsibility for self-regulation of emotion and self-care • Help citizens develop true cultural and national pride	• Celebrate diversity among all cultures • Resolve conflicts of needs between cultures in partnership ways • Provide for the basic needs of all citizens • Utilize systemic thinking in making major decisions
Inter-dependent Stage: *Cooperation*	• Create organizations that run cooperatively by employees and employers • Utilize cooperative team-building activities • Promote cooperation- building among teams • Create rituals that build and sustain employee morale • Creating divisions of labor based on individual interests and abilities	• Citizens and their representatives cooperate to create three interdependent and balancing branches of government with equal power to govern • Leaders cooperate to build consensus policies to handle relations between cultural groups and between nations • Leaders cooperate to create meaningful national rituals that build and sustain citizen morale	• Establish a planetary partnership culture based on cooperation and respect for differences • Develop the global brain and utilize global thinking in major decision-making bodies • Develop trans-systemic thinking

Stage of Development & Primary Task	Essential Developmental Processes of an Organization	Essential Developmental Processes of Cultures & Nation–states	Essential Developmental Processes of the Human Race
Inter-dependent Stage: *Cooperation (cont.)*	• Foster coop-eration that helps each employee develop his or her fullest potential as a human being	• Create equal op-portunities for all citizens to develop their fullest poten-tial	

A LIST OF DST'S TESTABLE HYPOTHESES

Here are some of the testable hypotheses that we used to validate our *Developmental Systems Theory*. We also include here some instruments that we used to test these hypotheses.

1. The more that therapists help their clients connect the dots between their unhealed developmental shocks, traumas and stresses and the problems they are currently having in their adult lives, the more likely they will be able to transform their lives. (*Developmental Trauma Inventory, Two Lists Self-Inventory, Family Patterns Inventory*)
2. The more therapists are able to help couples identify their hidden core unhealed developmental shocks, traumas or stresses causing their current intractable conflicts, quicker these couples can heal the effects of their shocks, traumas or stresses.
3. The more therapists can help couples identify their core unhealed developmental shocks, traumas or stresses that they each brought to the relationship and are triggering reenactments, the quicker they will develop the compassion and empathy for their partner. These qualities are needed to be able to help each other heal these shocks, traumas or stresses.
4. The more therapists are able to help their emotionally dysregulated clients' clear unhealed developmental shocks, traumas or stresses and how to re-regulate themselves, the better their outcomes will be with these clients. (*Trauma Elimination Technique*)
5. The more effective therapists are in attuning to and following the clients' process (and does not direct it), the more likely clients will discover how their own incomplete developmental processes are related to unhealed developmental shocks, traumas and stresses in their childhood.

6. The more effective therapists are in getting clients to understand the connections between their innate physical and emotional healing process and their reported presenting physical or emotional symptoms, the more likely they can heal these conditions.
7. The more effective the therapist is in helping clients to resolve their intractable conflicts, the more they will free themselves from degenerative physical and psychological conditions.
8. The more therapists help clients heal their developmental shocks, traumas and stresses, the more they will also be able to heal any degenerative physical conditions related to these shocks, traumas or stresses.
9. The better that therapists understand how to use a developmental, constructivistic approach to therapy, the more effective they will be in helping their clients.
10. The more intervention tools that therapists effectively integrate into their therapeutic approach designed to heal the seven major elements of developmental shocks, traumas or stresses on the Mind Body, the more timely and effective their interventions will be.
11. The more of the basic skills that therapists have integrated into their therapy approach, the more effective their work with clients.
12. The better therapists can create an effective therapeutic relationship with their clients, the more likely they will achieve a positive outcome in therapy.
13. The more that teachers and therapists can allow clients or students to explore their own developmental issues in depth and provide appropriate modeling, the more they will be able to make a significant shift in their consciousness.

RESEARCH RESULTS: OUR MOST EFFECTIVE INTERVENTIONS

Code: (S=Shock, T=Trauma & St=Stress) (See Chapter Two for detailed explanation of the Trauma Continuum)

SUCCESSFUL INDIVIDUAL INTERVENTIONS – THERAPY, COACHING AND PSYCHOEDUCATION.

Goal: To help individuals complete their incomplete developmental processes from the first three years of life and complete their individuation process.

- Use of self-study (books, online courses, articles & self-inventories) to discover hidden & unhealed developmental shock/trauma/stress from early childhood. (S, T & St)
- Use of Two Lists exercise to identify core causes of current problems. (S, T & St)
- The therapist attunes with clients & effectively follows their process. (S, T & St)
- The therapist creates an attuned relationship with the client. (S, T & St)
- The therapist does appropriate personal sharing and modeling. (S, T & St)
- Clients learn to use the Trauma Elimination Technique when they are triggered. (T)
- Clients learn about Drama Triangle dynamics and how to get off the Triangle. (T & St)
- The therapist facilitates the Parental Completion Process with both parents. (T & St)
- Clients learn emotional regulation skills (breath work, centering, Presence. S & T)
- The therapist reframes client's presenting problems to facilitate the healing-in-process. (S, T & St)

Results: Most clients report making significant progress in 3-6 sessions, and some chose to do work that is more extensive.

SUCCESSFUL COUPLE INTERVENTIONS – CO-THERAPY, COACHING AND PSYCHOEDUCATION.

Goal: To shift relationship dynamics from a competitive to a cooperative structure.

- The therapist uses the *Couple Sculpting Diagnostic Tool.* (S, T & St)
- The therapist teaches the couple conflict resolution skills using worksheets for each type of conflict from CR book. (T & St)
- The therapist reframes the presenting issues into a healing paradigm. ((S, T & St)
- Couples learn about Drama Triangle dynamics and how to get off the Triangle. (T & St)
- The therapist helps couples shift from a competitive to a cooperative approach in resolving conflicts. (T & St)

- Couples use structured role-playing to help heal early incidents of shock, trauma or stress & to help complete the developmental processes from that time. (S, T & St)
- Couple completes *Betrayal Clearing Exercise.* (S, T, & St)
- Couple learns ways to recognize and reclaim projections. (T & St)

Results: More sophisticated couples learn skills to work on the unhealed shock, traumas or stress that appear in their relationship in 3-6 sessions. They report success in helping each other heal their developmental shocks, traumas or stresses.

SUCCESSFUL FAMILY INTERVENTIONS – CO-THERAPY, PROCESS CONSULTATION AND COACHING.

Goal: To shift family dynamics from a competitive to a cooperative structure.

- Home visits – Conduct therapy in clients' home when possible. (S, T & St)
- Provide process consultation at Family Meetings. (St)
- Teach couple new parenting skills especially limit-setting and discipline skills. (St)
- Provide family members with experiences of a supportive family climate. (St)
- Coach members in restoring emotional balance during family interactions. (S, T, & St)
- Teaching family members how to recognize and reclaim their projections. (T & St)

Results: Family climate became more positive and supportive, with more direct expression of positive feelings, and more effective limit setting by parents. Family meetings implemented to provide family structure.

SUCCESSFUL COMMUNITY INTERVENTIONS – THE KINDNESS CAMPAIGN (A VIOLENCE PREVENTION PROGRAM).

Goal: To shift the community climate from fear-based to one based on love and kindness by providing residents with public recognition of their kind behaviors.

- Distributed over 80,000 Kindness Buttons in Colorado Springs, CO (Spread Kindness…its Contagious). Buttons were to be worn and passed on when witnessing an act of kindness. This person was then told to do the same. (T & St)

- Media (TV, radio, print, electronic) emphasize reporting acts of kindness. (T & St)
- PSA's by community leaders on the importance of kindness. (T & St)
- Kindness Line to report acts of kindness (over 22,000 calls). End evening TV news show with one of the calls. (T & St)
- News features about acts of kindness of residents. (T & St)
- Neighborhood and community-wide awards ceremonies honoring the kindest citizens. (T & St)

Results: TV viewers' survey after 6 months showed that 75% of those polled believed the Kindness Campaign had significantly reduced violence in the community.

SUCCESSFUL SCHOOL INTERVENTIONS – THE KIND & SAFE SCHOOLS INITIATIVE (A SUCCESSFUL BULLYING & PUT-DOWN PREVENTION & CHARACTER EDUCATION PROGRAM).

Goal: To change the school climate from negative to positive by emphasizing recognition of kind acts.

- Conducted staff in-service training. (S, T & St)
- Trained teachers to distribute Kindness Buttons to students displaying kind acts. (T & St)
- Held school-wide recognition assemblies to honor the kindest kids. (T & St)
- Created a character education curriculum embedded in all subject matter classes. (T & St)
- Taught conflict resolution to all students. (T & St)
- Establish a peer mediation program. (S, T & St)
- Developed a bullying & put-down prevention program. (S, T & St)
- Initiated a restorative justice approach to the school discipline program. (S, T, & St)
- Educated with parents on kind discipline methods through the PTO organizations. (S, T & St)

Results: Reports show that bullying & put-down behavior was reduced by over 90%, and discipline referrals dropped by 35%.

**SUCCESSFUL BUSINESS/ORGANIZATIONAL INTERVENTIONS
– DEVELOPMENTAL PROCESS CONSULTATION.**

Goal: To shift the organizational climate from a competitive to a cooperative climate.

- Do collaborative data-collection with key managers and employees to determine where incomplete developmental processes are interfering with the evolution of the organization. (S, T, & St)
- Provide process consultation at key organizational meetings. (S, T, & St)
- Conduct coaching session with key executives (S, T & St)
- Train employees & managers in systemic ways to recognize kind acts. (T & St)
- Give employees skills to help them address any unhealed developmental shock, trauma and stress on their job performance including conflict resolution skills. (S, T & St)

Results: Employees are empowered to change the work place climate from competitive to supportive & cooperative, with higher employee morale and fewer turnovers.

TECHNICIAN OR A PROFESSIONAL COUNSELOR: WHAT'S THE DIFFERENCE?[120]

Technicians use specific techniques in a counseling session for treating symptoms of clients' identified diagnoses. The goal is to reduce the severity of clients' symptoms, which create the outcome criteria used to determine their success.

Professional counselors have their own personal theory of counseling, which they use to evaluate the effectiveness of their practice. If you have not created your own personal theory of counseling, here's an outline for creating one. Write your answers to the questions in the outline and identify testable hypotheses to help you determine your effectiveness.

AN OUTLINE FOR CREATING YOUR PERSONAL THEORY OF COUNSELING

What are my personal values, beliefs, and assumptions?
- What is my view of the "good life?"
- What is my view of an effective, well-functioning, mature person?
- What is my purpose in this life?

- What is my responsibility to others?

Biographical information
- What life experiences have contributed the most to my uniqueness?
- What events and family patterns have influenced my theory?
- What client population am I most effective and least effective in working with?

My beliefs about human nature
- What motivates people to behave the way they do?
- What influences the thinking of people?
- What are the relationships among thinking, feeling, and valuing?
- How do people make choices?

My beliefs about behavior change
- How do people learn?
- Which behaviors are innate or learned?
- What counselor and client behaviors promote change?
- What are the basic principles of behavior change?
- What is the normal sequence of behavior change?

The theories that impacted me the most and why
- Which theories am I most attracted to and why? Be specific.
- Which theories am I least attracted to and why? Be specific.

My main strategies and methods
- What is the role of a counselor?
- What techniques and skills do you use to facilitate change?
- How do you believe changes made in counseling transfer to other situations?

The outcomes I expect
- How do I establish goals for my counseling or conflict resolution work?
- What criteria do I use to evaluate the effectiveness of my interventions?

The evaluation procedures I use
- What ways do I use to evaluate my effectiveness?
- What ways do I use to determine my personal and professional accountability?
- How will I test my personal theory of counseling and conflict resolution?
- What hypotheses can I develop to test the effectiveness of my theory? Be specific. (See above hypotheses we used to test the effectiveness of DST.)

PART THREE

HEALING DEVELOPMENTAL TRAUMA

(This page intentionally left blank)

CHAPTER NINE

OUR SYSTEMIC APPROACH
TO HEALING

Therapists will have much more impact when they are
able to conceptualize or discern more precisely what
this client's core problem really is, how it came about
developmentally, and how it is being played out and
causing symptoms and problems in his current life.

—Edward Teyber, *Interpersonal Process in*
Therapy: An Integrative Model

OUR PHILOSOPHICAL FRAMEWORK
FOR HEALING & TRAINING

We use a "developmental-constructivist" framework in our clinical practice and in training mental health practitioners. We believe that clients and students construct their own Internal Working Models of reality that dictate how they learn about themselves, other people and the world around them.

Constructing Internal Working Models and making meaning of relational experiences, in our view, happens through a specific kind of dialogue process. It avoids ideological, economic, physical and institutionally based constraints, celebrates the differences and plurality of values and beliefs in this relational crucible. It also avoids value judgments, and acknowledges that clients and students bring essential elements for both healing and training to the shared field of energy.

The experiential component of our therapeutic and training model asks participants to "deconstruct" outdated aspects of their Internal Working Model and "reconstruct" new aspects of their emerging Self. This process expands their capacities for inner work practices, and builds skills in self-reflection, self-correction, self-directedness, self-authorizing and self-authoring. The outcome is a person with a more complete self-identity and more coherent life narrative who can function effectively in attuned, attachment-based, healing-oriented relationships.

Our training model also emphasizes the need for trainees to understand and heal themselves prior to and while working with clients. Our motto, "do onto yourself before doing onto others," confirms that the personal healing of the trainee is a primary goal and outcome of our training program.

This self-healing model protects therapists from the risk of counter-transference issues that might interfere with their effectiveness. In addition to providing a personal focus to the content, trainees are encouraged to seek additional therapy as an adjunct to their training.

OUR PRACTICAL FRAMEWORK FOR HEALING & TRAINING

While we have actively been using our systemic model of healing and training for over 30 years, only recently have we encountered scientific paradigms and language that adequately describe and validate how and why it is effective. For this we feel immensely grateful, as we now have both scientific models and our own heuristic research experiences to make what has been invisible become visible.

We use a two-part practical framework to describe both how we conduct our clinical practice and how we train mental health practitioners. The two parts of this practical framework are 1) "the field," which serves as a safe container or crucible where the healing and learning happen, and 2) the "healing," which uses energetic practices that facilitate the learning and healing.

The Field and the Container. Think of the "field" as a "container" of the therapeutic environment, and everything that contributes energy to psychotherapy and to learning. Because it is energy, the field is invisible to the human eye, but quantum sciences tell us it is there. Sensitive and aware people are able to sense and feel (also known as proprioception) the energy in the field. Based on our own experience, we know that the more we focus on our proprioceptive abilities, the more available they become as resources.

In both psychotherapy and learning, the container is the physical space—the office or classroom, including the decorating, aesthetics, sound, lighting and external environment (including Nature or lack of it). The container also includes the energy field of therapists and teachers—their attachment styles, beliefs, life experiences, sense of individuated Self (including congruency and ability to hold space), and their connection to Source energy.

Think of the container as a bowl that holds the field of energy. This field occupies the bowl's physical space and contains the energy of the therapist/teacher. Therapists and teachers who are attachment-informed and trauma-informed are able to create safe containers for both students and clients. They use a very specific lens for their work.

Primarily, they are able to recognize and respond empathically to the impact of traumatic stress on students and clients. They consciously avoid anything that might re-traumatize them. They infuse their clinical and teaching frameworks, practices and policies with attachment and trauma awareness, knowledge, and skills.

Being also attachment-informed, they routinely screen for attachment style, trauma exposure and related symptoms, and use culturally appropriate assessment tools to identify attachment and trauma-, shock-, and stress-related therapy issues. They provide support and resources to clients and students who have been exposed to trauma or get triggered during the therapy or learning, while also working to strengthen their resilience.

Attachment- and developmental trauma-informed teachers and therapists consciously merge their sense of Self, including their personal and professional intentions, beliefs and philosophies, with the container itself. This is a critical factor in determining the quality of the field's energy. It also determines the effectiveness of the healing and learning that happens inside the container.

Let's imagine, for example, the quality of the healing and learning energy inside a classroom or therapy office facilitated by a teacher or therapist who is the parent of young children, and that this container sits adjacent to a rail yard where regular trains run. Now contrast this with a classroom or therapy office that looks out onto a glassy lake and is facilitated by a long-time meditator. Sensorily, you can imagine yourself in both these containers and predict how well you might be able to heal and learn in each of these settings.

The most critical factor in determining the quality of energy in the container is therapists' and teachers' personal energy field or "Presence." It is constantly influencing the larger field, and plays a critical role in determining the quantity and quality of learning and healing that happens inside the container.

Clients and students also contribute energy to the container, but have a less central role. For students and clients to grow and evolve, the container must be created and held by therapists and teachers who have a more developed Self and a more organized attachment. Their more stable and more congruent personal energy creates a safe environment where clients and students can deconstruct their old beliefs and selves, and construct new beliefs and expanded selves.

Think of the process in which snakes outgrow and shed an old skin as they expand into a new and larger skin. Ever wonder if they are afraid when their skin splits and cracks open, worrying that there will be a new skin emerge to "catch" the new Self? Do snakes fear they might explode into a million pieces and disappear? We think the primary role of teachers and therapists is to create safe containers and hold space for students and clients while they expand, split open, and reorganize themselves at a higher level of evolution.

What happens inside the crucible or container is a process of evolutionary change known as transformation. Healing and learning are virtually identical at a process level: a human organism has a relational experience that supports, encourages and facilitates the deconstruction of a no-longer-functional Internal Working Model (breakdown) and the reconstruction of a new-and-more functional Internal Working Model (breakthrough).

Healing and learning happens partly because the teacher or therapist has consciously created a safe and supportive container to surround and "hold" students and clients. While it's invisible and often imperceptible, the energy in the container is working all of the time to support learning and healing. Think of this process as a passive experience of "being" rather than "doing."

Healing and learning also happens because the teacher or therapist consciously provides active "doing" processes for the student or client. Constructivist therapists and teachers have identified specific cognitive, behavioral, relational and evolutionary outcomes, and have developed a menu of self-awareness inventories; developmentally based experiential and interactive activities, exercises and processes to help students and clients achieve these outcomes.

Healing has very specific outcomes that are based on a model and comes out of our own personal experiences of wounding and healing. This includes our 33+ years in a conscious and committed relationship, and our 30+ years of working together as therapists and teachers. Therefore, these are our outcomes. From a constructivist perspective, they work for us.

Speaking as constructivists, we recognize that the outcomes you feel are important might be different from ours. You've had different experiences of wounding and healing, other kinds of relational experiences, and may need a very different model for healing yourself and others.

Therefore, we offer these outcomes for your consideration, as examples that you can use to clarify, articulate and define your own. The outcomes that we identify in healing developmental trauma are:

- Learning to self-regulate shock, trauma and stress states
- Creating an integrated and coherent life narrative
- Transforming the traumas of attachment trauma into meaningful "gifts" that open students & clients to their life purposes
- Completing the psychological birth
- Individuating from the family- and culture-of-origin to create an authentic Self
- Living a self-directed lifestyle

HOW THERAPISTS CAN HELP CLIENTS COMPLETE THEIR PSYCHOLOGICAL BIRTH

The current state of human evolution indicates that hardly anyone has successfully completed psychological birth. This means that most people who are seeking psychotherapy or other kinds of counseling services need help in this area. If you agree with your clients when they make their spouse, child or boss "bad" or "wrong," you likely will not be able to help them complete this process. You have to stay neutral and support the client's feelings without agreeing with them when they make someone bad or wrong. This helps the client complete the essential developmental processes of the Counterdependent Stage and paves the way for individuation to develop. It also stops the "splitting" that caused a cognitive stuckness in the separation process

The outcomes list above is a helpful help guide for working with clients who have not completed their psychological birth and unconsciously needing help in this. Likely, they will not come to therapy knowing this is what they need, so it will be up to you to support them.

CREATING INTIMATE, INTERDEPENDENT RELATIONSHIPS

Your clients should determine the timing and sequence in which these outcomes emerge during the course of your work with them. The first few meetings focus on attuning with them and beginning from wherever they are, which helps to create a safe container where healing can happen. The list above is more of a "check list," and doesn't necessarily happen in sequence.

This is particularly true for clients who have Disorganized Attachment. In these situations, we must help our clients become more "organized" through our relationship with them, while simultaneously following and supporting their often chaotic process. This rather paradoxical experience can be quite challenging for beginning teachers and therapists, who prefer nice tidy lesson and treatment plans.

Our constructivistic clinical and teaching models help us stay attuned with students and clients. We focus less on what people say and more on identifying and healing the unconscious, traumatic, intergenerational behavior patterns they reveal through their stories.

We are very attentive to the nonverbal signals coming from a client's body. Our training many years ago with Arny Mindell in what is now called Global Process Work made us forever sensitive to body language, body cues, and the mind-body connection in psychotherapy. We value the body's role as a doorway to identifying and healing developmental trauma and dysfunctional relationship patterns. We also value clients' intractable relationship conflicts as doorways for identifying and healing unresolved developmental trauma and changing their Internal Working Model of reality.

While it is possible to teach developmental psychotherapy as a science, with many components and nuances, practicing it is really an art. No two therapists can work with a client in the same way. This is because the client-therapist relationship creates the critical container that holds their shared field of energy, which is where transformation happens. We have seen this process at work many times during our co-therapy sessions with couples. What Barry experiences in working with one of the partners is very different from what Janae experiences in working with the same person. The best that we can do is offer our students and trainees guidelines and principles to follow that help them create a safe, effective container. Here are some guiding principles for using a developmental approach to psychotherapy.

- Clients have an innate template that guides them towards wholeness. The therapist's job is to help them discover this innate template.
- All human behavior is an attempt to discover this wholeness no matter how unskilled or dysfunctional the attempts appear.
- Because all human behavior represents an unconscious attempt to heal or correct something, there is always something "right" about it. Clients are already in some phase of their healing process when they come for therapy. This principle helps people reframe the meaning of their

experiences and avoid self-shaming, self-judging and splitting against the Self.

- The primary barriers to intimacy in relationships are unmet developmental needs from early childhood. These needs emerge in intimate relationships as intractable conflicts when there is enough intimacy.

- All current intractable conflicts, health issues and relationship problems are the result of unhealed developmental shocks, traumas and stresses.

- Intractable conflicts are anchored in experiences of shock that occur during the first year of life attachment trauma. These early shocks get reinforced during the second and third years, creating dysfunctional relationship dynamics that retraumatize people and lead to degenerative diseases later in life.

- The primary task of intimate relationships, including therapeutic relationships, is to help people change their Internal Working Model of Reality and their attachment style by helping them become more organized at the level of Self.

- Therapists must attune to their clients' energy and pace the work using sensory and right-brain synchrony. Pacing with clients leaves the power in their hands and keeps the therapist in a facilitative role rather than a directive role. This Self-Other attunement creates a shared field of energy between the client and the therapist where the "healing work" happens. Often "doing less is more."

- While following the client's pace, therapists must also stay in touch with their own internal process. This prevents their personal issues from interfering with the client's process and pace.

- The client is always in charge of the therapeutic process and dictates the speed at which it moves. This empowers clients and keeps them out of the victim role. It prevents therapists from countertransference related to their own unhealed attachment issues or roles. It also prevents them from playing into the Drama Triangle dynamic.

- It is possible to slow down a client's healing process, but not to speed it up. Hurrying clients has to counterproductive consequences. The first is skipping important developmental issues that will cause them to "recycle." The second is overwhelming clients' nervous systems with too much information too fast and re-traumatizing them. These are professional breaches of the profession's trauma- and attachment-informed ethics to "do no harm."

- Current illnesses, chronic body symptoms and repetitive relational behavior patterns provide important therapeutic doorways related to the somatization of developmental traumas, particularly those related to Disorganized Attachment.
- Teaching clients to self-regulate emotions anchored in developmental shock, trauma and stress states fosters MindBodySpirit awareness, helps rewire the brain, and heals dissociated somatic memories that can emerge as illness.
- The therapist functions as a protector whose foremost task is to provide a safe, nurturing and empathic space where clients can recall and heal their developmental shocks, traumas and stresses, change their attachment style and modify their Internal Working Model.
- Therapists attract clients who have experienced similar kinds of developmental shocks, traumas and stresses. This mutual attraction can serve as a catalyst for both to heal their developmental shocks, traumas and stresses. It means, however, that ethical therapists must have identified their own their attachment strategy and the developmental shocks, traumas and stresses associated with it.
- Ethical therapists must always be actively working to heal their own developmental wounds to prevent countertransference in the client-therapist relationship.

HEALING VS. TREATING DEVELOPMENTAL TRAUMA

Most of the traumatology literature focuses on how to change clients' symptoms of anxiety, stress and trauma. This typically includes using tools such as cognitive behavioral therapy (CBT) and medication, both of which are typical of the Western medical model. The goal of the Western treatment paradigm is to reduce, relieve or eliminate symptoms. The optimal outcome is helping people live normal lives in which they are able to "cope" with whatever stress and trauma they have.

This medical paradigm is really a diseasing model, one that leaves people feeling bad about themselves—flawed, broken, helpless, hopeless, powerless VICTIMS! When clients have negative experiences with negative, self-blaming messages, the likelihood of even reducing their symptoms is small!

Table 9-1. Treatment vs. Healing Models

Treatment Model	Healing Model
Therapeutic goal is coping and *symptom reduction*.	Therapeutic goal is *transformation*, creating an Internal Working Model of reality based on "selfness."
Diagnosis-oriented, "what's wrong with this person?"	Relationship-oriented, "what happened or didn't happen to this person?
Focus is on following standard clinical procedures and protocols; more likely to use cognitive-behavioral clinical tools and approaches.	Focus is on building relationship between client and therapist and using the clinical relationship to help resolve experiences of relational trauma.
Short-term, therapist-directed.	Process-oriented approach that follows clients' needs and timing.
Mental, behavior, and mind-focused.	Heart-focused and relational emphasis.
Based on more masculine values and practices.	Based on more feminine values and practices.
Customers are seen as "patients" who are sick and disempowered.	Customers are seen as "clients" who seek support and empowerment.
Professionals are considered experts who know more than the patient.	Professionals are considered experienced facilitators who assist clients in making their relationships and lives function more effectively.
Emphasizes techniques, tools and a more mechanical approach.	Emphasizes social and emotional interactions between client and therapist and more artful approach.
Uses a more medical and mechanical framework for addressing the presence of clinical issues.	Integrates new information about the role of epigenetics in identifying the source of trauma and healing it.
Emphasizes the use of evidence-based practices in clinical practice.	More likely to use of practice-based evidence approaches in clinical practice.

HOW A HEALING PARADIGM WORKS

A healing paradigm is quite different from a treatment paradigm. Its goal is to identify the underlying causes of anxiety, stress and trauma, and then address problems at the source. The outcome of a healing paradigm is transformation. Transformation uses a systematic approach to help clients leave their coping, suffering, and victim consciousness, and to create a new Internal Working Model of reality that is based on strengths and mastery.

We think of healing anxiety, stress and trauma as an "archeology" process in which people work through their issues and problems in layers—like peeling an onion. This systematic approach, of course, takes time and patience. It's also complex because it involves a "deconstruction" process that involves changing neurobiological and behavioral programs, gradually re-wiring the brain, and building a stronger sense of Self.

Diving into memories of early childhood trauma and reprocessing them is a delicate operation, one that needs to be done gently, slowly, in a client's own timing. Otherwise the healing process can just re-traumatize clients and do harm, not only violating mental health professionals' code of ethics, but also the core principles of Trauma-Informed Care.

THE EXPLOSION OF AWARENESS ABOUT THIS HEALING PARADIGM

Awareness about the healing paradigm is growing exponentially, for several reasons. The first is due to the explosion of information about trauma, particularly developmental trauma and other kinds of adverse childhood experiences. The more that we know about trauma, the more that the data indicates that anxiety, depression and panic disorders and the freak-out episodes are NOT diseases or mental illness.

The research shows that these issues are caused by trauma, particularly childhood or developmental trauma. Trauma is about "what happened (or didn't happen) to you" rather than the medical "what's wrong with you." So, there's no shaming, no diseasing and no stigma—just a need for support and caring, and targeted tools that help clear the trauma from the nervous system and to rewire the brain.

The second reason for the expansion of the healing paradigm is the growing number of effective tools that really can clear the trauma from the nervous system and rewire the brain. A third reason is that research now indicates that relational trauma is the primary cause of the trauma, and that most of it is anchored in a child's attachment with the mother during the first year of life.

The acceptance of attachment research has increased the focus on the importance of the client-therapist relationship. A few leading developmental researchers and clinicians such as Alan Schore and Dan Siegel have written extensively about how to use the client-therapist relationship as a crucible for healing relational trauma. Their work, which describes how to use the clinical relationship from both the scientific and artistic perspectives, provides a solid theoretical foundation for healing developmental trauma.

We really appreciate the work of these men and the scientific foundation they are creating for clinicians. It provides a framework for explaining *why* the things that we have been doing in our clinical work for the past 30 years are effective. Their work has helped the practice of mental health gain acceptance as both a science and an art. Many of our professional colleagues who use the healing paradigm in their practices feel the same appreciation.

ELEMENTS OF A DEVELOPMENTAL MINDBODYSPIRIT HEALING APPROACH

Mental health practitioners need a developmental, MindBodySpirit approach for both the clinical assessment and the healing of trauma. This integrated approach helps clients understand the following:

- The critical role of early relationship experiences, attachment strategies and the development of affect regulation and dysregulation, on clients' overall mental and physical health.
- The long-term effects of trauma, including abuse, neglect and disruption of the attachment process, on a person's brain and the three parts of the central nervous system: the sympathetic, parasympathetic and social engagement nervous systems.
- How trauma is transmitted across generations and the need for trauma-specific healing interventions for adults and children.
- How the immediate and long-term effects of stress affect immune system functioning; the need for healing interventions that reduce neurophysiological arousal and increase the individual's ability to self-soothe and self-regulate.
- How unhealed early trauma affects character development.
- How childhood victimization can increase the risk of being re-victimized and also becoming a perpetrator of violence.
- What are the effects of early traumas on the individual's capacity to process sensory input, store memories, regulate emotions and organize his/her thoughts? This includes understanding how to use language to help clients make sense of or integrate traumatic experiences. How trauma is stored in their body, mind and spirit. Finally, practitioners need to know

about specific healing interventions that help restore wholeness to their mind, body and spirit.

- The historical, systemic and collective impact of stored trauma in individuals, couples, families and society as a whole, including the self-perpetuating relationship between trauma, aggression and violence.

TEN PERSISTENT MYTHS IN THE MENTAL HEALTH PROFESSION ABOUT HEALING DEVELOPMENTAL TRAUMA

The Myth: Therapy must be long-term in order to be successful. **The Truth:** *You can use a series of 3-6 solution-focused, short-term sessions to successfully treat many developmental traumas.*

The Myth: There is no diagnosis in the DSM-5 that allows clinicians to be reimbursed for treating developmental trauma. **The Truth:** *The DSM-5 contains several possible diagnoses, depending on the presenting symptoms. These include PTSD, Preschool Subtype, Acute Stress Disorder, Adjustment Disorder (now seen as a stress-response symptom) and Reactive Attachment Disorder.*

The Myth: EMDR is the best treatment option available for healing developmental trauma. **The Truth:** *EMDR is not effective in healing the relational elements of developmental trauma, particularly those associated with Disorganized Attachment.*

The Myth: People cannot accurately remember what happened to them as a child without hypnosis. **The Truth:** *There are volumes of research indicating that children are super-sensitive to everything that happens to them in childhood and that their nervous systems record it all.*

The Myth: Children often make up childhood trauma and abuse to impress others, or are describing memories that were implanted by therapists. **The Truth:** *Most of children's self-reports about what happened to them are accurate.*

The Myth: If people had adverse childhood experiences, the best they can hope for is forgetting them and moving on with their lives. **The Truth:** *With the right support, it is relatively easy for people to heal their childhood traumas.*

The Myth: Whatever happened to children during their early childhood gets left behind when they grow up. **The Truth:** *People bring everything left incomplete with them when they grow up, and it continues to recycle at every major life transition.*

The Myth: "It's all in the genes." Your genetic make-up pre-determines the course of your life, including relationship and health issues. **The Truth:** *Research shows that genetics contributes only a small fraction of the long-term effects of developmental traumas. It affects temperament more than anything else.*

The Myth: People use developmental traumas as excuses for not taking responsibility for their actions and things that happen to them. **The Truth:** *Unhealed developmental traumas can be a reason why people do not take responsibility for their life, but it is possible to heal these traumas and become responsible.*

The Myth: It's impossible to change the brain's faulty wiring due to early childhood trauma. **The Truth:** *Research has shown that the brain is malleable and can change quite easily. When you help your client identify his/her developmental traumas and connecting them to the disruptions in his/her adult life, this actually rewires the brain.*

HEALING ON THE TRAUMA CONTINUUM

In Chapter Two we described the Trauma Continuum and its shock, trauma and stress states and the corresponding parts of the brain, the parts of central nervous system, the time orientation, and the behaviors that are active with each. In this section, we identify therapeutic interventions for working with each of these specific states.

In our model, it is irrelevant whether emotionally overwhelming events are acute or chronic, whether they happen through observing or directly experiencing an event, as are the exact circumstances of an event. What is relevant is how people look, what they feel, how they behave, how they communicate during these experiences, and how they remember these experiences.

These behavioral characteristics indicate which part of the brain is active, which part of the autonomic nervous system is operating, and the person's orientation to time. Only after evaluating these behavioral, biological, and temporal cues is it possible to determine a person's state of awareness and the appropriate treatment intervention. Differentiating among these criteria and using them to determine the most appropriate intervention appears to be little known or used in the field of traumatology.

Healing Shock. Dissociation, a shock state, is one of the hallmarks of Disorganized Attachment. Infants who experience fear because they perceive their mothers or primary caregivers as scared or dangerous, find their brains in a double-bind situation. The limbic or mammalian part of their brain tells them to go to an attachment figure when they are in danger.

When their attachment figure is the cause of the fear, their brain stem or reptilian part of the brain tells them to flee the source of danger. The inability to resolve these two conflicting brain signals literally shorts out the brain, causing it to freeze and the child's nervous system to go into shock. At this point, the child dissociates and causes his or her awareness to go out of the body.

The primary goal in healing shock reactions is helping clients re-embody after experiences of dissociation, and to mobilize the regulating and balancing action of the parasympathetic nervous system. Because shocked clients are functioning in the oldest and most primitive part of their brains, they have little access to language and are unable to socially engage. For these reasons, it is important to avoid analysis, catharsis, and asking the client to look into the past or future and instead to focus on what is happening in present time. It's helpful to ask questions that help them focus on the here and now. Even asking them to take a couple of deep breaths can be useful, because in a dissociative state their breathing usually slows down.

Therapists can support shocked clients by helping them track their urges to withdraw further into dissociation, using nurturing, comforting, and protective language to hold clients in a *therapeutic embrace* while they gradually return to their bodies.

It is also important to help clients withdraw from shock states, explore empowering options for restoring their sense of Self and to gradually encourage their expression of feelings. This work must be slow and incremental and follow the pace by which that client's nervous system is able to process overwhelming memories and experiences.

Healing Trauma. The primary goal in healing trauma states is helping clients interrupt the adrenaline cycle and modulate the overactive responses of their sympathetic nervous system. During therapy sessions, the use of nurturing, comforting, and protective language holds clients in a therapeutic embrace while they clear the multiple dimensions of a traumatic experience or memory. Outside the therapy setting, music, quiet, focusing, and awareness-stilling practices such as journaling, walking, and spending time in nature are excellent ways to quiet the sympathetic nervous system and to detoxify the body of any excess cortisol.

Developmental trauma interventions must bring the MindBodySpirit into present-time reality. This involves clearing any confusion between past and present events that are a normal part of trauma-induced regressions. As clients are able to experience themselves in the present, it becomes possible to identify the emotions related to the trauma reaction, and to process any intense or abreactive emotional experiences by feeling, witnessing, and surviving them.

Over time, clients learn how to transform traumatic emotional experiences into sequential and meaningful narrative memories; to develop integrated thinking by holding dualities, opposites, and paradoxes; to develop comfort with eye contact; and to create and maintain clear personal boundaries.

Healing Stress. The primary goal in helping clients heal developmental stress is communicating effectively with them to keep them socially and emotionally engaged. This is particularly important during the first phase of therapy, as it offers clients time to develop safety and to attune with the therapist.

This also prevents the therapy process from moving too quickly before clients have effective tools for braking against a potential slide into more primitive brain states that are associated with trauma and shock. Another goal of stress-related interventions is helping clients develop bodily awareness of unconscious and involuntary internal biological states and helping them gain voluntary and conscious control of their internal biological states.

Once clients recognize the first cues of developmental stress, they can consciously become more relationally engaged. This redirects the autonomic nervous system's impulse to slide into trauma and shock states. It is very common for people who have had high levels of shock and trauma to develop a highly sensitive autonomic nervous system.

In such cases, a stressful situation or issue that is mostly about feeling discomfort can easily become a perceived safety issue, and trigger a trauma reaction. It can also escalate into a perceived survival issue that causes a collapse into a shock reaction. Teaching clients how to discern the difference between comfort, safety, and survival issues is a critical clinical task in healing developmental shock, trauma, and stress.

Because all experiences of shock, trauma, and stress interfere with human development, we classify them as "developmental." Because all humans have experiences of unrecognized and unhealed developmental shock, trauma, or stress, by definition we are all developmentally delayed—individually, systemically, and as a species. Some of us are delayed more and some less, depending on the amount of developmental shock, trauma, or stress that we have experienced, how it was or was not addressed at the time it happened, and what we have done to heal it. It is important, however, to use the right intervention with each different problem. Healing shock with trauma interventions will not work and could do harm.

Here are the components of developmental trauma that we believe need to be healed in the therapy process, and requires specific interventions.

- Desensitizing sensory system triggers (visual, auditory, proprioceptive and kinesthetic).
- Changing distorted beliefs.
- Learning emotional self-regulation.
- Reclaiming dissociated parts of the Self caused by intra-psychic splitting.
- Changing dysfunctional Self-Other relational dynamics.
- Integrating MindBodySpirit memories.
- Reconnecting to the Ground of Being

We know of no single intervention or technique that helps clients heal all of these components, so we have listed the ones that either we have used for each component, or the ones the research suggests could be effective with each component.

We suggest you choose trauma interventions in which you have been trained. Please be aware that you will need to use multiple intervention tools to help clients heal all the components of developmental trauma.

Table 9-2. Interventions for Healing Shock, Trauma, and Stress[121]

SHOCK	TRAUMA	STRESS
• Levine's Somatic Experiencing	• Trauma Elimination Technique (TET)	• Trauma Elimination Technique
• Emerson's Shock Resolution Techniques	• Sensory Integration Therapy (SIT)	• Betrayal Clearing Exercise
• Castellino's Prenatal and Birth Process Therapy	• Eye Movement Desensitization & Reprocessing (EMDR)	• Weinholds' Corrective Parenting Technique
• Mines's TARA Approach	• Levine's Somatic Experiencing (SE)	• Weinholds' Model for Creating Conscious, Committed Partnership Relationships
• Rothschild's Somatic Trauma Therapy	• Emerson's Relational Shock Clearing Therapy	
• Weinholds' Corrective Parenting Techniques	• Mines's TARA Approach	• Sensory Integration Therapy
• Energy and Herbal Medicines	• Rothschild's Somatic Trauma Therapy	• Eye Movement Desensitization & Reprocessing (EMDR)
	• Weinholds' Corrective Parenting Technique	• Levine's Somatic Experiencing
	• Sculpting Exercises	• Empathy & Compassion Training
	• Emotional Freedom Technique (EFT)	• Gestalt Techniques
	• Tapas Acupuncture Technique (TAT)	• Reframing
	• Rebirthing-Breath Work	• Bioenergetic Exercises
	• Holotrophic Breathwork	• Psychodrama Techniques
	• Somatic Experiencing	• Reclaiming Projections Exercise
	• Bioenergetic Exercises	• Completion Process with Your Parents
	• Movement Therapies	• Belief-changing Exercises and Activities
	• Expressive Arts	• Reclaiming Projections Exercises
	• Sculpting Exercises	• Active Imagination Exercises
	• Art & Play Therapy with Young Children	
	• Meditation	
	• Diet & Nutrition	
	• Energy and Herbal Medicine	

SHOCK	TRAUMA	STRESS
		• Partnership Conflict Resolution Skills
		• Rebirthing-Breath Work
		• Holotrophic Breath-work
		• Yoga
		• Top-Down Yoga
		• Tibetan Yoga
		• Movement Therapies
		• Body Therapies (Rolfing, massage, cranio-sacral work)
		• Virginia Satir's Sculpting Exercises
		• Art & Play Therapy with Young Children
		• Energy Medicine
		• Biofeedback
		• Diet & Nutrition
		• Energy and Herbal Medicine
		• Exercise
		• Relaxation Activities
		• Aerobic Exercise
		• Social Engagement Activities

THE ROLE OF EPIGENETICS IN DEVELOPMENTAL TRAUMA

So, what is epigenetics? Why is it important in healing? Epigenetics is now recognized as inherited or ancestral trauma. It studies intergenerational trauma at the level of genes, looking at how genes are able to express themselves in a variety of ways without actually changing their basic genetic code. The field draws language and concepts from the quantum sciences, such as energy, resonance, synchrony and attunement. The field of epigenetics is exploding with new research findings, stirring the age-old debate about nature vs. nurture and whether genes are "set" and create our destiny, or are "fluid" and changeable.[122]

Genetic code can be thought of as "potential." It's a library of possibilities, a "software bank" from which we can download what we need to survive or thrive. Think of newborn infants as computers. They come with an operating system (OS) called "human nature," along with a host of "human nurture" software programs that are available for activation.

The "nurture" experiences in an infant's environment energetically identify which software programs to activate—multiple languages, music, engineering, martial arts, mechanics, childrearing, affection, surviving violence or abuse, sports, art, deprivation, abundance, or adversity. The infant gets a steady stream of "nurture" energy and information from the environment indicating which genetic "nature" software programs are needed for surviving or for thriving.

The genes cooperate by downloading or expressing the appropriate software. This invisible process happens through an exchange of energy and information between the child's cells and what is being received from the cultural and family-of-origin environments.

Language and concepts from epigenetics are very useful in describing and explaining how people learn and change in therapy. Both are the result of epigenetic exchanges of information and energy between people inside the containers that therapists and teachers consciously construct. This invisible interplay is happening all of the time and at an unconscious level. Well, it has been unconscious, and it can be made conscious.

Let's begin by looking at the role epigenetics plays as a causative factor in trauma, neglect and abuse. Nurturing experiences have a primary influence on how genes express themselves. Nurture is everything that happens in the environment—attachment; parenting; family-of-origin experiences, including ancestral influences; and environmental factors such as radiation and air pollution.

Nurturing experiences create an "environmental influence" on children's health, their ability to learn and remember, and their responses to stress. Nurture is the fabric of the lives of our parents and grandparents, from their diet to their education, and includes the quality of the parenting they received. It also includes the traumas they suffered, and perhaps many other experiences that left their legacy written inside our DNA as "instructions for interpretation."[123]

Epigenetics explains the ancestral relevance of Jews whose great-grandparents were in concentration camps, Chinese whose grandparents lived through the ravages of the Cultural Revolution, young immigrants from Africa whose parents survived brutal civil wars and genocidal massacres, and adults who grew up with alcoholic or abusive parents. They all carry more than just memories. These ancestral memories and experiences of our forebears are never gone, even if they have been forgotten. They become a part of us, a molecular residue on our genetic scaffolding. The DNA remains the same, but many psychological and behavioral tendencies are inherited.[124]

An epigenetic experiment unintentionally took place in the Netherlands during World War II. The "hunger winter" was a very cold period from November 1944 to the late spring of 1945 during which a German blockade forced the Dutch people to survive on less than a third of their regular caloric intake. For decades afterwards, Dutch and British scientists studied the children who had been exposed to this famine in-utero. These children grew smaller than the Dutch average and their children were also smaller. They also turned out to be more susceptible to diseases of metabolism including diabetes, obesity and cardiovascular disease.[125]

PRESENCE AND ITS ROLE IN A HEALING PARADIGM

Presence, according to Dan Siegel, is "the bare awareness of the receptive spaciousness of our mind." Our mind's receptive awareness receives whatever arises as it arises.[126] It can be viewed as a state of open awareness to what emerges in the flow of conscious experience, moment by moment. It is a here-and-now experience of being in present time, of being sensorily present, attuned and in synchrony with another person or with a small or large group of people.

Presence is especially important in interpersonal attunement, whether within personal relationships or in a clinical setting. Presence is largely the ability to express the most authentic and least automatic relational response possible.

In a state of Presence, a person is intentional, receptive and flexible to what is emerging in the shared field of energy with others. Being present means gently reining in this natural tendency to be unintentionally preparing for the next thing in order to simply "be" with what is currently happening. We refer to this as "following the process."

With practice, experiences of Presence can become sensorily palpable, meaning that it is possible to feel them proprioceptively. You come to "know" when you are attuned, in resonance and in synchrony with your client. Your body learns to recognize when you are in this state of awareness, and you become skilled in creating, sustaining and following the flow of this field of shared energy.

In a state of Presence, you find yourself connected to a larger field of energy. Some people refer to this as Source. Buddhists and Christian philosopher Paul Tillich call it the Ground of Being. The Mayans called it Hunab Ku. Many contemporary religions refer to it as God or the Divine. Whatever name you give this sensory integration of MindBodySpirit, it is a sacred space in which it is possible to feel reverence and connected to something spiritual and larger than oneself.

Concepts such as Presence can seem complex, abstract and nebulous, like the concept of "God." The challenge is making these concepts concrete. Therefore, I (Janae) want to share a story with you about an experience I had at a three-day training on Disorganized Attachment with Dan Siegel, Mary Main and Erik Hesse in May of 2015.

During our training, I heard Dan say that what changes Disorganized Attachment and the dissociation commonly associated with it is "another person having a felt experience of them." When I heard him say this, I immediately understood that it's not possible for me to do this for a client unless I've also had this experience and therefore know how to create this space for a client. But this was just me processing his idea internally. During a Q & A session on the last day, I was able to ask Siegel a question about his statement.

Dan and the other two speakers were sitting on a stage not too far in front of me, and I was able to make eye contact with him when I asked my question. When I was handed the microphone, I repeated his statement back to him and then asked my question. "So how can I have a felt experience of my clients if no one has had a felt experience of me?" I have no memory of the words he used to answer, though I know he replied rather eloquently for a few minutes.

What I will always remember, however, is him having a felt experience of me. The whole time that he was speaking, I felt as though he was transmitting a beam of light that centered on me but encompassed our group of 300. This stream of light felt like a wave of pure and unconditional love beamed from Source that held me in timeless suspended space. The whole room became quiet and still as he spoke and projected energy directly from his Being. The words became waves of sound that transmitted Source energy into the audience.

I knew immediately that I was having a pure experience of Presence, and that it was both very personal and very impersonal. If I were to see him and mention this moment, I doubt that he would remember it.

We have had similar experiences with Presence. When we make love, we go there. Janae has experienced it regularly teaching students and working with clients during her visits to Ukraine. We've also had it with many American clients while doing what we call "soul-work," exploring wounds and suffering that contain distorted beliefs, intense emotions, and experiences of regression. These moments of holding space feel so fragile and so sacred, places that require absolute and total focus and MindBodySpirit integrity.

Interestingly, we've also discovered that it's possible to have Presence experiences over Skype. Janae always has it while meeting with her colleagues and students in Ukraine, and with her long-time friend in Australia. In quantum field theory, there is no "distance," all experiences are "local." It just requires an open heart and a sensory and Soul attunement for it to happen.

PRESENCE AND EPIGENETICS

The phenomenon of Presence has actually been researched by Elissa Epel at UC-San Francisco, in an effort to determine how meditation impacts DNA. First, a little lesson on DNA.

The ends of human chromosomes are known as telomeres. They serve as protective caps similar to the plastic tips on shoelaces, and shield the ends of our chromosomes each time our cells divide and the DNA is copied. With each cell division, the telomeres wear down over time and fray. When telomeres fray and get too short, cells lose their ability to divide in integrity. This phenomenon is now recognized as a key factor in aging and chronic disease.

In the 1980s, researcher Elizabeth Blackburn, discovered an enzyme called *telomerase*, and that it protects and rebuilds telomeres.[127] Telomerase helps maintain the integrity of the telomere caps, even to repair them, as the research study above indicates.

In 2012 Elissa Epel extended Blackburn's research with a study that examined telomere length in relation to self-reported Presence using a large sample of healthy, relatively low-stress women. She and her colleagues found that greater Presence of mind was related to longer telomere length.[128] Conversely, more negative mind wandering—thinking about other things or wanting to be somewhere else—was related to shorter telomere length.

Drawing from Epel's findings, we can say it is possible for therapists and teachers who are able to hold Presence in the shared energy field while counseling and teaching. This shared field impacts clients and students, according to Epel's research. She found that experiences of Presence can help people increase their production of telomerase, heal their damaged telomeres, and help them "rewrite" the epigenetic impact of adverse childhood experiences on their MindBodySpirit.

Epel's research supports our belief that aware therapists can heal developmental trauma by creating resonant, attuned, synchronized fields of Presence between them and their clients. Through subtle epigenetic exchanges of information and energy between them and the container, clients are able to modify their Internal Working Model of Reality, their attachment strategies, and the expression of their genes.

In order to successfully create and hold Presence in the shared field of energy, therapists must have cleared enough of their own trauma, neglect and abuse to avoid getting triggered by their clients. Therapists' personal Internal Working Model of Reality and attachment strategies must be more evolved and more stable than their clients in order to help them advance in their development.

It's great to finally have scientific frameworks that can help explain how adverse childhood experiences involving trauma, abuse and neglect are able to shape a person's MindBodySpirit. In addition, we now recognize that therapy, learning and other Presence experiences can help transform it.

These quantum paradigms are useful in constructing, making sense of our childhood experiences, and accepting how our adversities have helped to shape us. They are also useful in constructing clinical models for healing ourselves and helping others heal. We have done this both personally and professionally, and now we want to share our own successes in healing developmental trauma.

HEALING DEVELOPMENTAL TRAUMA

Clients' developmental traumas are usually visible in their body language, which most therapists tend to ignore. It's important to recognize body signals, as they contain doorways to healing. This body-oriented approach to healing is far different from the medical model of therapy that defines healing primarily as a short-term, therapist-directed process that uses specific treatment techniques on compliant patients with little regard for their developmental histories.

Healing developmental trauma can be a short-term process when the therapist is skilled at constructing attuned, trusting relationships with clients. Timing is everything when making client interventions. Healing must avoid impulses to speed up clients' processes, as this likely will cause resistance and can actually slow them down. The client's verbal and nonverbal cues will literally invite the appropriate intervention when it is timely.

Healing developmental trauma shifts the focus from "diagnosing" the problem to look for the "prescription." That is, the very act of identifying a developmental issue creates potential solutions to it. For example, "diagnosing" someone with attachment trauma during the codependent stage of development indicates an active parasympathetic nervous system and the need for interventions that address shock and dissociative states. This client-based approach also circumvents the treatment model and some of the limitations associated with it.

Individuals with Disorganized Attachment, which is approximately 80 – 90 percent of those who seek counseling, can heal developmental trauma with the right kind of therapeutic support. Early childhood memories are often disorganized, chaotic, and filled with misperceptions that contain deeply held beliefs. Healing involves a step-by-step process that begins by making sense of their early developmental history and ends with the construction of a new narrative.

One of the most effective tools to use in this sense-making process comes from the work of attachment researchers Mary Main and Erik Hesse. Their Adult Attachment Interview can be adapted for use by therapists.[129] The questions in this interview are designed to elicit responses that open memories of Developmental Trauma.

The next step involves helping clients reorganize early memories into a coherent narrative. They must also confront and feel the full pain of their experiences, so that they can move beyond their unhealed trauma and loss. Hiding from the past or burying unexpressed emotions by trying to "rise above" them isn't effective either. This causes any unhealed painful feelings to get triggered and projected during moments of stress.

Psychological help for resolving early trauma can take many forms. The most important step is finding a person with whom clients can form a safe, healthy relationship that continues over time. This relationship, which can be with a romantic partner, a friend or a therapist, allows a person to develop trust and modify his or her Disorganized Attachment. Breaking the cycle of relational losses and disconnects associated with the Disorganized Attachment requires creating a trusted relationship with a person who is fully present and able to hold Presence.

According to Dan Siegel, Presence allows a person with DA to consolidate fragmented parts of Self into a more integrated whole. Presence, as a part of a phenomenon that he calls Interpersonal Neurobiology,[130] allows cellular functions, multiple parts of the brain, and the MindBodySpirit to more fully integrate. This MindBodySpirit integration becomes visible in people's behavior—expressions of kindness, compassion, wisdom, connection and grace. These qualities are at the heart of individuation and wholeness.

Physical help for resolving developmental trauma requires that clients get information and physical support for their stressed adrenals, including diet, nutrition, exercise and hormone rebalancing. When one part of the endocrine system, such as the adrenals, becomes stressed, it drains energy from other endocrine organs—the liver/gallbladder, testes/ovaries, thymus, hypothalamus, thyroid and pancreas. The longer that the endocrine organs are stressed, the higher the chances of both emotional and physical dis-ease. Only an integrated trauma- and attachment-informed healthcare model can truly help people heal the long-term effects of Disorganized Attachment on human evolution.

(This page intentionally left blank)

CHAPTER TEN

HEALING DEVELOPMENTAL
TRAUMA IN INDIVIDUALS

*Support has no direction. Our plan is to hold the
patient - to strengthen the container - until the patient
develops his own container-strengths or until the contents
settle down. We do not know just how or when all this
ought to happen. Worse we do not have a particularly
cogent rationale for limiting our own actions.*

—Peter D. Kramer, *Moments of Engagement: Intimate
Psychotherapy in a Technological Age*

THE IMPORTANCE OF THERAPISTS HEALING
THEIR OWN DEVELOPMENTAL TRAUMA

Therapists who want to avoid countertransference issues with their clients
must identify and heal their own developmental traumas. This is particularly important for honoring mental health practitioners' "do no harm" ethic.
Here are some ways that therapists can do their personal healing work.

Self-Assessment. Do your own personal archeology to connect the dots between early developmental trauma and issues you have in your adult relationships. Take all self-quizzes in this book yourself before you use them
with your clients. This will not only help you identify any of your unhealed
developmental traumas, it will give you an empathic understanding of how
your clients might feel when they take the self-quizzes.

Get in therapy. Therapists who work on their own incomplete developmental processes are less likely to get triggered by their clients' issues and are able
to successfully avoid the sticky and complicated countertransference issues

with their clients. It is important to work with a mental health professional that is competent in both attachment-informed and trauma-informed therapy. When you interview them, ask if they have done their own trauma work. If they haven't, keep searching.

Read professional publications, take online classes, and participate in live seminars and workshops. Our online course, *Freaked Out 101*, can help you and your clients connect the dots between any unhealed developmental traumas and any conflicts or problems in present time.

Get supportive clinical supervision. Clinical support is critical for helping you and your clients work through the shock states associated with Black Hole memories. A good supervisor can hold space for you, and help you increase your capacity for holding space for your clients. Having high quality supervision is really important for therapists who are re-patterning the "scary mother," distrusting aspect of their Disorganized Attachment strategy, and also working with clients who are doing the same.

HELPING CLIENTS HEAL DEVELOPMENTAL TRAUMA

While there aren't specific clinical protocols, standardized techniques or formal methodologies for attachment-based psychotherapy, there are some general maxims that have emerged informally for bringing attachment issues deeper into your clinical work. There are four maxims or conditions for therapeutic change that most attachment-oriented therapists would agree on.

1. Insecure, ambivalent, avoidant, or disorganized early attachment experiences are real events that can substantially and destructively shape a client's emotional and relational development (clients' adult problems don't originate in childhood-based fantasies).
2. The attachment dynamics learned in early childhood experiences will play out in psychotherapy.
3. The right brain/limbic (unconscious, emotional, intuitive) interaction of the psychotherapist and client is more important than cognitive or behavioral suggestions from the therapist; the psychotherapist's emotionally charged verbal and nonverbal, psychobiological attunement to the client and to his/her own internal triggers are critical to effective therapy.
4. Reparative enactments and experiences of early attachment experiences that are co-constructed by therapist and client are fundamental to healing.

Healing developmental trauma isn't for the fainthearted. Therapists must stay present, not only to the client's emotions, but also to their own. This goes beyond transference and countertransference issues. It calls for something more challenging than performing cognitive activities. Attachment-based therapy requires that therapists stay in their right brain and empathically experience the client's feelings, no matter what comes up for them or what raw emotion gets triggered from their own history.

Attachment therapists aren't observers of their clients' emotional journeys or disinterested guides. They are fellow travelers, resonating with their client's sadness, anger, and anxiety. Rather than recoiling from the intensity of their clients' emotions, attachment therapists provide stability through their voice tone, eye contact, expression, posture, and language. This keeps clients feeling not only understood, but safely held and relationally supported.

This kind of work is emotionally demanding, more than more cognitive and behavioral modalities, and requires therapists to have their own internal work organized. Perhaps the APA clinicians and academicians who rejected adding the DTD diagnostic category to the DSM-5 realize how much it would change the clinical game.

California clinical psychologist David Wallin, author of *Attachment in Psychotherapy*, is very clear about this. "If in childhood a certain quality of expression such as anger cannot be felt or experienced, then we cannot relate to this expression in a patient." Wallin says, "We are the tools of our trade, the primary creative instrument with which we do the work."[131] Our ability to use our Self effectively in this intense work is therefore inhibited by our own core emotional vulnerabilities.

A SYSTEMS APPROACH TO HEALING DEVELOPMENTAL SHOCK, TRAUMA, AND STRESS IN INDIVIDUALS

It is important for developmental therapists to understand the individual as a system, and to recognize the interconnectedness of body, mind and spirit. The biological human contains several subsystems—a nervous system, a digestive system, a circulatory system, a skeletal system, a respiratory system, and a reproductive system.

Each of these subsystems contains smaller subsystems. The circulatory system, for example, consists of veins, arteries, and the heart. The heart is composed of cells, and the cells are composed of cellular subsystems. For the body to be healthy, all subsystems must function effectively and cooperatively. If the heart does not function properly, for example, the other subsystems (and the human) are radically affected.

Many experiences of developmental shock, trauma, and stress are caused by neglect related to energetic disconnects during the first year of life, rather than abandonment and abuse. It is very difficult to recognize the presence of emotional, physical, spiritual, or psychological neglect because nothing happened. Abandonment and abuse are easier to recognize and recall, because something happened.

It's also easier for people to remember acute events that involve shock, trauma, or stress caused by growing up in an abusive family, living in a war zone, losing a loved one, or surviving natural disasters or terrorist attacks. Because developmental shock, trauma, and stress impact the brain structure and function, personality, character structure, and body, effective therapeutic modalities must have the capacity to access the deeper, long-term effects of developmental shock, trauma, or stress. They must be able to access much deeper layers of the MindBodySpirit, even down to the miasmic level. The miasmic level is an energetic imprint of an experience or trauma that gets passed inter-generationally through ancestral or cellular memory, and often treated with homeopathic remedies.

Our clinical model for helping people heal symptoms of long-repressed developmental shock, trauma, or stress tends to be slower, more complex, and deeper. It works like peeling off the layers of an onion, and processing the unhealed developmental shock, trauma, or stress stored in each layer.

This process happens gradually, through intermittent series of 4-6 sessions that allow clients to regulate themselves and continue functioning in their daily lives. Going slowly and following clients' process and timing also helps build trust in the therapeutic relationship. This allows clients to strengthen their egos, and helps them solidify their sense of Self. By the time clients reach the "core of the onion," the issues emerge that are anchored in developmental shocks, traumas, or stresses from the critical first three years of development.

Although we have tools that help clients get to their core developmental shocks, traumas, or stresses rather quickly, we found some limits that require honoring. For example, moving faster than clients' nervous systems can process and assimilate the information in each memory layer can re-shock, re-traumatize, or re-stress them, and slow down the healing process. For this reason, we focus on staying attuned and synchronized with our clients at each step of the healing process.

This not only helps to anchor and stabilize clients at an emotional level, it also provides them with a sense of safety and security. It also strengthens and heals the intrapsychic fragmenting caused by disorganized caregiving.

PROFESSIONAL SKILLS FOR HEALING DEVELOPMENTAL SHOCK, TRAUMA AND STRESS[132]

Developmental therapists operate from a framework containing the goals and philosophical principles presented in Chapter 9, and use specialized skills that build on their core counseling skills. Our framework provides a clinical lens to help identify clients' patterns of early childhood experiences containing unhealed developmental shock, trauma, and stress. It also uses developmental interventions for healing the effects of these shocks, traumas, and stresses, particularly when they surface as intractable conflicts. The clinical session uses a process model that follows the client's signals and cues until the underlying issues emerge.

Developmental therapy focuses on identifying the client's attachment strategy and any distorted parent–child dynamics anchored in it. It also examines the prenatal, birth, infancy, and early childhood experiences to find the sources of current intractable conflicts, relationship problems and health issues.

We use developmentally based inventories to help clients identify shocking, traumatic, and stressful experiences from early childhood. We help them correlate these experiences with their adult symptoms of shock, trauma, stress, recurring intractable conflicts, illnesses, and degenerative diseases. This helps clients identify and re-pattern distorted relational dynamics caused by disorganized caregiving that might be impairing their ability to create and sustain healthy relationships.

We also create behaviorally-based goals as part of our therapy contracts that stress the need for safety, and support an attuned and empathic client-therapist relationship based on genuineness, compassion, and unconditional love. We also identify the roots of current relational difficulties in past relationship disturbances that are anchored in attachment and separation trauma.

Developmental therapy helps clients reconstruct their Internal Working Model of reality through their real-time relationship experiences. This provides the missing emotional resonance and attunement in their experiences of being parented as children.

In addition to responding attentively to clients' verbal cues and non-verbal behavior while attuning with clients, developmental therapists must be skilled in following the flow of sensory information during a therapy session. This skill involves following shifts in people's nervous systems as clients move from their unconscious to their conscious minds. Sensory system flows include two levels of processing: internal and external. The internal flow of information is divided into four sensory channels:

- Auditory
- Visual
- Proprioceptive (intuition, emotions and physical sensations)
- Kinesthetic or movement

The external flow of information is divided into additional two channels:
- the relationship channel (two persons)
- the family channel (three or more persons)

The primary task of developmental therapy is to follow the flow of communication as it moves through the client's sensory channels during the session and respond to the client in language that mirrors the part of the sensory channel the client is using to describe the presenting problem.

For example, when the client is recalling a past trauma through their visual channel ("I have this picture in my mind of the time my mother hit me and knocked me down.") the therapist might respond, "I can see how traumatic this must have been for you. Your face looks sad right now. Are you feeling sad?" At this point, the client closes her eyes, lowers her head, and she begins to shed tears. The shift from the visual channel to the proprioceptive or feeling channel has allowed her to access and express the emotions associated with her trauma.

At this point, the sensory-attuned developmental therapist can continue to work on the emotional level or switch to the relationship channel by saying, "This experience with your mother must have had a lasting effect on your ability to trust not only her, but also other women."

Dividing the sensory system into internal and external channels provides a structure for working with issues in more detail. The internal sensory channels relate to individual issues and processing, while the relationship and family channels reveal the systems context in which they operate.

Since developmental shock, trauma, and stress happen in the context of relationships with parents and other bonded caregivers, sensory theory provides a verbal and nonverbal structure that therapists can use to help clients connect their internal experiences with their external world.

During developmental psychotherapy, the therapist determines which intra-psychic parts of the client are visible and conscious, and which are invisible and unconscious. The visible or conscious parts of the client's thought process emerge in the client's presenting issues and are usually stated as though they have conscious ownership of that part ("I feel angry when she yells at me like that"). This response indicates that the client is more identified with parts that use fight and flight responses to stay defended and protected.

An unconscious part would be active in a statement such as, "I get yelled at a lot by my mother." This statement shows little ownership of the conflict and represents a victim identity, and a frozen or dissociated response to the problem.

Developmental psychotherapy helps clients approach the boundary between the conscious and unconscious parts of their awareness, and provides a safe container for this very deep and sacred work. The therapist's intention is to help clients to identify both the invisible or unconscious self-parts that have been split-off because of unhealed shock, trauma, or stress. A split-off part might be an inner protector part, an assertive adult part, a nurturing parent part, or a child part that fears failure.

A client can also speak through a split-off unprotected child part that needs adult support and parental nurturing, or as the powerless child part wanting to feel capable and strong. The next step is helping the client connect these unconscious parts to an earlier experience involving unhealed developmental shock, trauma, or stress.

Once this part is identified and present, the therapist affirms the client's presenting problem and supports the parts of the self that are conscious. This, again, involves using language that matches the client's active sensory system:

Visual system = visual language
"I see why you might have this perception."

Auditory system = auditory language
"I hear how difficult this was for you."

Feeling system = emotional language
"I can feel how sad you are about this."

In Chapter 9, we suggested specific clinical interventions for healing shock, trauma and stress that involve different parts of the brain and nervous system. We recognize that this is a partial list of tools and modalities.

INTERVENTIONS FOR HEALING DEVELOPMENTAL SHOCK, TRAUMA AND STRESS[133]

1. CLEARING SENSORY SYSTEM DISTORTIONS (VISUAL, AUDITORY, PROPRIOCEPTIVE AND KINESTHETIC MEMORY):

TET: The Trauma Elimination Technique is the primary tool that we use to help clear the sensory system of distortions caused by developmental trauma and stress. After becoming trained in several trauma treatment modalities, we developed TET by synthesizing elements of Tapas Fleming's (n.d.) Tapas Acupressure Technique (TAT), Francine Shapiro's (1997) EMDR (Eye Movement Desensitization and Reprocessing), and Roger Callahan's (2001) Thought Field Therapy (TFT). We use TET as an adjunct to our DPW, which focuses on clearing and re-patterning the relational elements of developmental shock, trauma and stress. We found that the combination of TET and DPW treat all seven elements of developmental shock, trauma, and stress.

Our experience in using TET revealed that it not only clears trauma from present-life experiences, but also from other realities such as past lives, when people are consciously seeking this level of clearing. While this may seem like a very simple tool, it is quite powerful. For this reason, prior to using this technique with clients, we strongly suggest that readers use it on themselves first, preferably with a therapist or trusted colleague or friend.

Step 1: Learn the TET holding pose (See Figure 10-1).
  a. Use one hand to hold three points on your face. Touch the points lightly. Touch your thumb lightly just above and adjacent to the inner corner of one eye.
  b. Place the end of your ring (4th) finger just above and adjacent to the inner corner of the other eye. Place the end of your middle finger on the indentation in the middle of your forehead about 1/2" higher than your eyebrows.
  c. Place your other hand palm down with fingers together at the back of your head just below the bump at the bottom of your skull (the occipital ridge), centering it at the midline.

Figure 10-1. The TET Pose

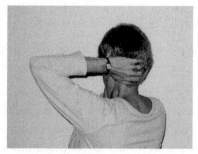

d.   Once you have learned this pose, go directly to Step 2.

Step 2: Identify the trauma you want to work on. The earlier the trauma you identify, the better the results, although start where you have a clear memory of the trauma situation. Identify a single incident or isolated memory of a trauma, rather than one that recurred over time.

- Focus your attention on a picture about this particular trauma.
- Notice what thoughts accompany this picture.
- Identify the belief about yourself that goes with this picture.
- Notice what emotion you feel when you see this picture.
- Feel your feelings, think your thoughts, and remember the belief you had about yourself in this situation.

Step 3: Simultaneously hold your picture, thoughts, belief, and feelings while doing the TET holding pose. Remain in this pose until you feel something happen internally. This can be different for each person. It may be a subtle shift of energy, a feeling of relaxation, a deep sigh, or a change in your breathing. Hold this pose for one minute or until you feel a shift, whichever comes first.

Step 4: Notice where you have been holding tension in your body related to the picture/thoughts/belief/feelings. Focus your attention in this place in your body while continuing to hold the TET pose. Again, remain in this pose until you feel a shift or for one minute, whichever comes first.

Step 5: Return to your picture of the trauma you began with and zoom in close to review it as if with a magnifying glass, looking for *hot spots* or things about the picture that still upset you.

Step 6: Zoom in on a hot spot where you still have a reaction to some part of the picture. Again, focus on the picture/thoughts/belief/feelings. Do the TET holding technique until you feel a shift. Focus on the *storage place* in your body where you hold tension related to this memory while using the TET holding technique for one minute or until you feel a shift.

Step 7: Continue returning to the original picture and reviewing. Repeat this process until no more hot spots remain in your picture.

Step 8: Do the process one more time to see whether you can review the picture of the trauma and have a different response to it. You should be able to see the trauma but not have the reactions you first had to the incident. You may sense a calmness or peacefulness in your body–mind.

Step 9: Drink a glass of water immediately after completing a session. Be sure to drink another eight glasses in the next 24 hours to help the toxins released by the TET procedure to leave your body.

EMDR: Eye Movement Desensitization and Reprocessing is a psycho-therapeutic approach, developed by Francine Shapiro, to resolve symptoms caused by exposure to a traumatic or distressing event and to treat PTSD. It involves moving the eyes side-to-side or using other lateral cues while re-calling a trauma. While it is effective in clearing sensory elements of event trauma, it does not clear the intra-psychic splitting and relational elements of developmental trauma.

EFT: Emotional Freedom Technique is a body-oriented therapy developed by Gary Craig that involves specific patterns of tapping on the body's energy meridians. EFT includes more emphasis on clearing the emotional aspect of trauma but also addresses the role of trauma in disease.

SIT: Sensory Integration Therapy is designed to correct Sensory Integration Dysfunction, a neurological disorder involving difficulties with processing information from the five classic senses (vision, auditory, touch, olfaction, and taste), the sense of movement (vestibular system), and the positional sense (proprioception). Because of unhealed developmental shock, trauma, and stress, sensory information is accessed normally but is perceived abnormally. This is not the same as blindness or deafness, because sensory information is sensed but tends to be analyzed by the brain in an unusual way that may cause pain or confusion.

The most common form of sensory integration therapy is a type of occupational therapy that places a child in a room specifically designed to stimulate and challenge all of the senses. During the session, the therapist works closely with the child to provide a level of sensory stimulation with which the child can cope and to encourage movement within the room. Sensory integration therapy is driven by five main principles:

- **Just Right Challenge**. The child must be able to successfully meet the challenges that are presented through playful activities.
- **Adaptive Response**. The child adapts his or her behavior with new and useful strategies in response to the challenges presented.
- **Active Engagement**. The child will want to participate because the activities are fun.
- **Child Directed**. The child's preferences are used to initiate therapeutic experiences within the session.
- **Desensitization**. A child with lower or hyposensitivity may be exposed to strong sensations such as brush strokes, vibrations, or rubbing. Play may involve a range of materials to stimulate the senses such as play dough or finger painting.

Breathwork Techniques also called *Pranic Breathing, Conscious Breathing,* or *Transformational Breath Work*, is a branch of alternative medicine postulating that specialized breathing techniques may have therapeutic benefits. Leonard Orr created Rebirthing-Breath Work, so named because he began having memories of his birth during his early experiments with connected breathing. The client makes a connected breath without a pause between inhale and exhale of the breath or between the exhale and inhale of the breath. The inhale part of the breath is very deep, filling both the belly and the top of the lungs. Total relaxation during the exhale part of the breath is critical for avoiding unpleasant body sensations like stress, tension, or even muscle cramps.

We use a version of this tool with clients who have difficulty feeling their emotions in their bodies. It also helps them experience what it is like to temporarily shed a level of developmental stress they are carrying around in their hypervigilant avoidance of developmental shocks, traumas, or stress.

Holotropic Breath Work™ was developed by Stanislav Grof, MD, together with his wife Christina, as a substance-free means of discovering the healing power of human experience in non-ordinary states of consciousness. It is a safe and simple way to trigger experiences of non-ordinary consciousness that open us to psychic depths and spiritual understanding. It can help people recover memories of developmental shocks, traumas, or stresses from their personal history, experiences from their birth, and archetypal and cosmic phenomena that become available to them in holotropic awareness. It can help people re-regulate their emotions and transcend the constraints of their ordinary thoughts and habits.

2. INTERVENTIONS FOR CLEARING MIND–BODY MEMORIES:

TET: (described previously)

EFT: Emotional Freedom Technique (described previously)

Somatic Experiencing (S.E.) S.E. is a short-term naturalistic approach developed by Dr. Peter Levine for resolving and healing trauma. It is based upon the observation that animals in the wild utilize innate mechanisms to regulate and discharge the high levels of energy arousal associated with defensive survival behaviors. These mechanisms provide animals with a built-in immunity to trauma that enables them to return to normal in the aftermath of highly charged life-threatening experiences.

While humans are born with virtually the same regulatory mechanisms as animals, the function of these instinctive systems is often overridden or inhibited by the rational portion of our brains. This restraint prevents the complete discharge of *the stress hormones from our blood stream* and does not allow the nervous system to regain its equilibrium. The un-discharged survival energy remains stuck in the body and the nervous system. The various symptoms of trauma result from the body's attempt to manage and contain this unused energy.

Somatic Experiencing uses the awareness of body sensations to help people *renegotiate* and heal their traumas rather than relive them. With appropriate guidance with the body's instinctive *felt sense*, individuals are able to access their own built-in immunity to trauma, allowing the highly aroused survival energies to be safely and gradually discharged. When these energies are discharged, people frequently experience a dramatic reduction in or disappearance of their traumatic symptoms. Levine's therapeutic work is available to both professionals and non-professionals.

Bioenergetics. This is a set of body psychotherapy tools that helps people identify places in their bodies where the energy is blocked and to release the chronic tension that is stored in these blocked places due to developmental shocks, traumas, or stresses. After identifying a developmental trauma, it is necessary to help people release the body memories connected to it. Where appropriate, a skilled therapist can help a client to release body memories very quickly and easily. We use bioenergetics tools in our training workshops.

Yoga. It is a system of physical and mental practices that originated in India. It includes a number of variations, such as Hatha Yoga, Karma Yoga, Bhakti Yoga, Nada Yoga, Raja Yoga, Tantra Yoga, Bikram Yoga, Kundalini Yoga, Kriya Yoga, and Iyengar Yoga. Most of these schools emphasize bringing the mind–body into balance through the use of the breath and different poses or asanas to help strengthen the body and manage stress.

Tibetan Yoga. This is also known as the Five Tibetan Rites. Reportedly, over 2,500 years old, it is based on a series of five movements that are each repeated 21 times. Practiced over a period of time, the rites rejuvenate the body and help keep it in energetic balance. We utilize this form of Yoga and sometimes teach it to our trainees or clients.

Movement Therapies. These help clients release stuck places where they have stored body memories connected to a developmental shock, trauma, or stress. This tool is often part of our training workshops for therapists.
Body Therapies (Rolfing, massage, craniosacral work). These therapies all work to realign the body's bones, muscles, and connective tissue. Some, such as craniosacral therapy, also work with the cerebrospinal fluid. These deeply transformative therapies are very useful for restoring the body to its natural state after shocking, traumatic, or stressful experiences have distorted it.

Art & Play Therapy with Young Children. They help children to access unconscious processes related to shock, trauma, or stress. There are various kinds of art and play therapy, and we employ an assortment of tools from these modalities in our trainings.

Sand Tray Therapy is a form of expressive therapy that is sometimes referred to as sand play. It was developed by Margaret Lowenfeld, Goesta Harding, Charlotte Buhler, Hedda Bolgar, Lisolette Fischer, Ruth Bowyer, and Dora Kalff. This type of therapy is often used with children, but can be applied to adults, couples, families, and groups as well. Sand tray therapy allows a person to construct his or her own microcosm using miniature toys and colored sand. The scene created acts as a reflection of the person's own life and allows him or her the opportunity to resolve conflicts, remove obstacles, and gain acceptance of self.

Energy and Herbal Medicine. This includes interventions include homeopathic remedies such as Bach Rescue Remedy and Perelandra products,[134] (flower remedy therapies such as aromatherapy, herbs such as valerian, hawthorne and kava kava, which are some of the more well known. Because homeopathics and herbs are powerful substances, they are best used with the support of trained professionals.

Biofeedback. This involves the use of sensors that are stuck to a person's head and/or hands. The sensors are attached to an electronic device that emits different frequencies that alter brain wave signals. The relaxation frequencies are typically in the alpha and theta ranges of 5–11 Hz. A wide range of technological devices is now available for home biofeedback use. Neurofeedback is being used to help train the brain to relax and re-regulate emotions.

Diet and Nutrition. This is a critical component of a stress-reduction regime. Food intake should be rich in a variety of whole grains, vegetables, and fruits, with a minimum of processed foods, alcohol, caffeine, and tobacco. Ideally, foods should be produced organically, as nonorganic foods often contain toxins that cause the body to have a trauma reaction. Foods containing high fructose corn syrup should be avoided because they are very hard on the liver and kidneys.

Formal and Informal Support Groups. A support group is a gathering of people who share a common condition or interest for specific issues such as weight loss, bereavement, addictions, and health conditions; informal and unfacilitated support groups such as men's, women's, parent's, and couple's groups. They can also be facilitated therapy groups; and extended family networks. Support group members can share their personal journeys with each other and offer comfort and moral support, and they may provide tips and advice based on their own experiences.

There are now many online support groups, which are very convenient for helping people who have rare or unusual conditions connect with each other. Social support is a critical component healing of shock, trauma, and stress, as it provides the important emotional connection that was missing during experiences that caused developmental trauma. These kinds of social engagement activities help people resist the urge to withdraw into regressive and dissociative states associated with recent traumas and shocks.

3. INTERVENTIONS FOR CHANGING DISTORTED COGNITION AND BELIEFS:

TET. (described previously)

Trauma-Focused CBT. Trauma Focused Cognitive Behavior Therapy is a manualized, evidence based, treatment approach developed in Pennsylvania at the Allegheny General Hospital's Center for Traumatic Stress in Children and Adolescents by Judith A. Cohen, MD. The treatment synthesizes trauma- sensitive interventions with cognitive behavioral principles to target the emotional and behavioral problems that children develop in the wake of traumatic events. The development of a trauma narrative is central to this model of treatment.

Working–at-the-Edge. This involves helping the client to work on a problem without actually diving into the heart of it. Sometimes clients need to go to the edge and look over it before jumping into the heart of the problem. A skilled therapist can help provide the safety a client needs to explore the problem before deciding to work on it.

Belief-Changing Exercises: Breaking Free of Your Personal Law. We developed this exercise to help people uncover unconscious beliefs about themselves that were formed as part of a developmental shock, trauma, and stress, and are still causing them to create unpleasant experiences in their life. Start by identifying your personal law, which is the bottom-line most negative belief or thought you have about yourself.

It is the basis of self-hatred and usually shows up in the self-talk that you engage in when you make a mistake or do something that does not turn out the way you want. See Appendix I for the protocol for this exercise.

Reframing techniques.[135] Reframes are communication tools that help clients assign a different meaning or context to a life experience. We use them to help clients change distorted beliefs they have about what happened to them during their childhood, and put them in a different context. For example, an adopted client entered therapy with us believing that her birth mother rejected her because she was unlovable. After reading books we suggested that were written by mothers who relinquished their babies, the client began wondering whether her birth mother still thought about her and grieved her loss. We had two adoptee clients who sought and eventually met their birth mothers after they read these books. Afterwards, both women experienced a deep gratitude to their birth mothers for relinquishing them and giving them the adoptive parents and the lives they had led with them.

Betrayal Trauma Clearing Exercise. If clients have experienced a break in primal trust with their parents, it caused developmental shock, trauma, or stress. They will need to heal this developmental shock, trauma, and stress in their close relationships as a way of completing this essential developmental process of the codependent stage of development. The need to recreate primal trust also involves developing an "all good" view of the therapist with whom a person is healing this trauma.

Clients perceive this person as kind, loving, and available to meet their needs. This is actually an internal split because the other side of this projection is the "all bad" therapist. For more information about betrayals and our experiential tools, see our book, *Betrayal and the Path of the Heart.*[136]

CHAPTER ELEVEN

HEALING DEVELOPMENTAL TRAUMA IN COUPLES

The level of differentiation is the single most important aspect distinguishing a therapist from a technician. Differentiation is the ability to maintain a non-anxious presence in the face of another's anxiety. It does not mean being uninvolved or indifferent. It is the ability to tolerate pain for growth.

—David Schnarch

ADVANCED SKILLS FOR WORKING WITH COUPLES

In this chapter, we describe the framework we use in couples therapy. We begin by creating short-term contracts of three to six sessions with them that are spread over the course of several months. We've discovered that higher functioning couples can learn how to work cooperatively to heal their traumas in this structure. During this period, we also teach them how to work cooperatively to heal their mutual traumas. In these next sections, we describe other components of our couples' therapy framework.

CONSCIOUS, COMMITTED, COOPERATIVE RELATIONSHIPS

We encourage people to create conscious, committed, cooperative relationships with those they are close to. This may be in a variety of forms—friends, business partners, parents and children, or romantic couple relationships. While "commitment" can be defined in several ways, the most common aspects include the following:

- A willingness to stay engaged in the relationship and not run away when the unhealed developmental traumas and dysfunctional relational patterns emerge;
- An agreement to close the "exits" partners have used in the past to avoid resolving these issues. This includes using threats of leaving each other while they are in an active therapy contract where the relationship considered as a source of healing;
- A willingness of both people to support each other's efforts to change;
- A willingness of both people to be emotionally honest; and
- A willingness for each person to ask for what he or she wants from the other 100 percent of the time. While it may not be necessary to ask that often, only to be willing to help avoid getting caught in the role of helpless victim.

Now for more specific definitions of the words used above. *Consciousness* refers to the degree to which people are aware of their behavior and are able to understand what motivates them to do what they do. *Cooperative* means a willingness to help each other in the healing process. Many relationships are competitive rather than cooperative in nature. They compete to see whose needs will get met, often operating out a "scarcity" framework. In a cooperative relationship, people freely teach and learn from each other, rather than withholding information or using it to manipulate and control their partner.

Conscious, committed relationships provide an ideal relational crucible for healing developmental trauma. We believe this is love and intimacy at its highest and most pure. Most people define intimacy as only the warm, close, maybe sexual times that are blissful and serene. Our experience is that helping each other heal our core traumas has opened us to a deeper kind of intimacy. This agreement to work cooperatively to heal these wounds rewires the brains and nervous systems of each partner so they can move forward in their individual and couple development. Both experience greater compassion, empathy and love for each other.

The goal of successful couple's therapy is to grow into the interdependent stage of relationship. This stage can look codependent, counterdependent, or independent. The critical component is that both partners consciously negotiate their time together and their desired amount of intimacy.

When connected with another person at a deep level, a new dance with many moves emerges, allowing for the free flow of energy between partners. When two people become separate, whole, autonomous people, they no longer need to protect themselves from each other. In an interdependent relationship, each person is free to be themselves. Each is able to experience being loved for who they really are, not for some false or artificial self.

Intimate relationship partners dance and weave in and out of deep connection, are not always physically together, still can fight and argue with each other, but do it fairly and with respect for each other's needs and feelings. This structure is possible because of their commitment and more advanced consciousness.

Characteristics of Conscious, Committed, Cooperative Relationships

- Both partners recognize that each of them brought unhealed traumas from childhood into the relationship.
- They agree that the primary focus of the relationship is to help each other heal the long-term effects of core traumas and re-pattern the behaviors associated with them.
- Each person commits to staying engaged with conflicts when they get triggered into reenacting unhealed traumas until personal awareness and resolution occur. They may need a short "time-out" to reregulate their emotions before trying to resolve the conflict.
- The relationship has a therapeutic function. The word "therapy" comes from the Greek word *therapea* and means "doing the work of the whole." The relationship itself functions as a healing *and* a "wholing" crucible.
- The relationship is a discovery process. Each person's intent is to discover, understand, and change themselves and not to try to change their partner.
- Each person works to develop self-trust rather than primal trust. Rather than believing that the other will or won't hurt you, each learns to trust Self more. This means each person will be less hurt by their partner, and that they will feel less responsible for hurting the other person. If one says or does anything that the partner says hurts them, the other can trust the partner to ask for what he or she wants in order to assuage any hurt feelings.
- Each partner sees the other as a mirror. This helps each recognize their deepest parts and any parts of the other that they might have avoided seeing. It also assists both partners in rewiring their brains.
- Each partner focuses on a relationship with himself or herself. Partners agree to cooperate and support the development of the other person's relationship with himself or herself.

- Both partners recognize that children are their greatest teachers. Children can help them each become more self-aware and deepen their ability to love themselves and others.

- Conflicts with children get resolved in ways that support their search for personal autonomy. As parents, both partners give up trying to control their children and get to know them and learn from them instead.

- Both partners recognize that these principles apply to all relationships, including student-teacher, employee-employer, friend-colleague, and nation-nation relationships. The goal is to help humankind learn to live together in peace and love.

Nourishing vs. Toxic Relationships.[137] Not everyone is ready for a conscious, committed partnership relationship. It's important to assess when working with couples where they are in their relationship, and start where they are. There is a spectrum of consciousness and commitment in relationships that extends from highly nourishing to highly toxic. The five levels are as follows:

A **highly nourishing relationship** is characterized by a high level of both consciousness and commitment. Each partner contributes greatly to each other's growth.

A **mildly nourishing relationship** has a lower level of consciousness or commitment in some areas. This impairs the contribution each partner can make to the other's life.

A **non-contributing relationship** entails little consciousness and commitment to growth and learning, and so makes little or no contribution to the partners' personal development.

A **mildly toxic relationship** incorporates so little consciousness and commitment that each partner feels slightly diminished as a person, and the relationship interferes with their enjoyment of life.

A **highly toxic relationship** involves no noticeable commitment to growth and, instead, entails excessive demands, intimidation, repression, hostility, and verbal or physical abuse that depletes both partners

If you personally are in a relationship that is toxic, or less nourishing than what you want, you must determine if it is possible to make it more cooperative and supportive. You must also determine the other person's willingness to cooperate with your vision for the relationship. If this strategy proves to be unsuccessful, then you must find the courage to end this relationship — and any others where you cannot get your needs met.

CREATING NEW FORMS OF RELATIONSHIP

It's also important to release the things that no longer work in a relationship and find ways to create new relationship structures. Releasing begins with identifying and healing any codependent and counterdependent behaviors.

Tools for Working on Yourself Alone. Sometimes it's necessary to take a time-out in the middle of a conflict in order to get emotionally re-regulated so you can think through your reactions and options. Here's an activity to give you more clarity.

Think of three things you don't like about your partner that you want him or her to change. Write them on a piece of paper. Then ask yourself, "How am I like that?" and "When do I do these same things?" Write your answers on the paper. Then ask yourself, "Am I willing to change these things in myself?" If the answer is "no," then what right do you have to ask your partner to change these things?

If you *do* change these undesirable things in yourself, the other person may be encouraged to change as well. This is the only way to change your interactions with others—by first changing yourself. Remember that the ultimate state of stuckness is waiting for someone else to change before you can feel better.

ADVANCED TOOLS FOR COUPLES THERAPY

Couples therapy presents a unique challenge and opportunity. It is sometimes necessary to do individual therapy with each person in a couple so they do not bring so many of their personal traumas into the relationship for healing.

We encourage couples to take our Freaked Out online courses before or early in therapy. Here they get basic information about the long-term effects of developmental trauma, and learn a common framework to use in their communication. It is important for a couple to have a common framework and language while they are in therapy.

We use the Sculpting Exercise below as part of a contract for working with couples. The sculpting usually reveals the core unhealed childhood traumas that are currently recycling in this couple relationship.

Sculpting Diagnostic Exercise for Couples.[138] We use this diagnostic sculpting exercise to help a couple see how their traumatic histories interlock, and even have a kind of "cosmic perfection" to them. We explain briefly the process and tell them that we will guide them through it.

If possible, we videotape the couple's sculpting to use as a reference in our work with them, and let them take it home with them after we have seen it. When they get stuck in unraveling their individual pieces of their dynamic, they can refer back to the dynamics displayed in their sculpting.

Work with one person at a time. They decide who will be the "sculptor" and who will be the "sculptee." The sculptor looks at his/her part of the dynamic first.

Step #1: Identifying the link between the past and the present.

- The person feeling the most intense emotions is usually the first to volunteer. If we have an intuitive hit on which one we think should go first, we sometimes make this suggestion.
- Say to the sculptor: "Remember the very worst conflict you have had, one where you hit the wall and left you feeling hopeless about finding a resolution to it—perhaps you thought about leaving the relationship."
- Ask the sculptor to make a freeze-frame kind of photo of this conflict, using no or very few words.
- Ask the sculptor to show what this conflict looks like to him or her by shaping the partner into body/body language/facial expressions that illustrate how the person appears during their conflict.
- Ask the sculptor to position him or herself to show the body/body language/facial expression reaction he or she has when the other person goes into this body posture.
- Ask the sculptor, "When you go into this interaction with your partner, what feeling do you feel?"
- Ask the sculptor,
  o   What is your earliest memory of feeling this feeling?
  o   How old do you feel?
  o   Describe what was happening in the past memory?
  o   Where do you feel this feeling in your body?
  o   Focus on this body feeling and breathe into it, so that you can feel it more deeply.
  o   Who in the past event does your partner represent in present time?
  o   What did you need from this person in the past conflict that you believe would have resolved it for you?

Step #2: Clarifying the vision of the couple's future.

- Say to the sculptor: "If you could work through this conflict in present time, what would your future together look like?" (This question helps determine whether the couple is working more on individuation issues or if one member of the couple is really invested in getting divorced. This is important in determining the course of counseling with this couple.)

- Make a sculpted picture of your vision of the future. Shape your partner and then shape yourself in relationship to him/her.
- Ask each person how this vision feels, beginning with the sculptor. (If you notice one partner is less accepting of their partner's vision, you may need to see how they would sculpt the future when it is their turn). If their visions are fairly different, this could mean their future together is in doubt.

Step #3: Using the future vision of the relationship to resolve the present-time conflict.

- Have couple resume sculpting postures created in Step #1.
- Tell the sculptor that s/he is 100% responsible for changing his/her part of the conflict by changing his/her behavior during the conflict.
- Usually there has to be some internal shift that the sculptor needs to understand.
- The internal shift usually involves:
  o Recognizing that they are in a regression and that their present-time partner is not at the source of the conflict.
  o Initiating some proactive behavior to reregulate themselves and return to an adult state of consciousness.
  o Then using a step-by-step process to re-connect non-verbally with your partner using micro-movements and NO words. (In this process, the sculptor makes a physical move and then waits for their partner to respond and make a corresponding move).
  o Identifying what they needed from the other person in the past conflict that would have resolved it for them.
- Have them share this information with their partner.

Step #4: Summarizing the sculptor's traumatic history. Help them see they are reenacting unhealed developmental traumas. Look at the projections that they are placing on the other person and not seeing them as they really are. We often say to them, "You have been in relationship with your mother as much as you have been in relationship with your partner. He/she does something just enough to remind you of what your mother did, provoking memories and emotions that cause you to reenact your trauma with her."

Step # 5: Reverse roles. The other person now goes through the same steps as their partner did. Look for how their unhealed traumas fit together. You usually see that when one partner needs something from the other partner, it triggers the other and they are not able to provide it and vice-versa. Comment on the compatibility of their visions of the future. If they are not very compatible, it is a sign that the couple may not want the same things for their future.

THE CHALLENGES OF COUPLES WORK

We work as co-therapists when we work with couples so that both partners feel supported, and to prevent any Drama Triangle dynamics from emerging in the therapy. Working with a co-therapist in couples work is really important, if you begin by seeing one half of a couple first and develop a stronger relationship with this person.

Working with a couple without a co-therapist also increases the likelihood of countertransference issues emerging, given that we attract clients who have issues similar to ours. If it's not possible to have a co-therapist to work with you in couples' counseling, then it's important to have clinical supervision to help you keep your personal issues and triggers separate from your clinical work with couples.

CHAPTER TWELVE

HEALING DEVELOPMENTAL TRAUMA IN FAMILIES

*The overall goal [of counseling] is to help family
members become 'systems experts' who could know
[their] family system so well that the family could
readjust itself without the help of an expert.*

—Murray Bowen

HEALING DEVELOPMENTAL TRAUMAS IN FAMILIES

The healing of developmental trauma in families follows our developmental
model, and parallels that of individuals and couples. Adults bring into their
family system all their unresolved conflicts and issues anchored in developmental traumas from their families of origin and their individual and couple
systems. This relational baggage primarily surfaces as drama triangle conflicts within the larger family system.

We define a family system as a structure containing three or more individuals, whether they are parents and a child, three friends, or three coworkers. Most people do not understand that a dramatic shift occurs in relational dynamics when the structure of a system shifts from two to three
people.

You may notice that the word "dramatic" contains the word "drama."
This is no coincidence. As soon as three people become engaged, there are
sufficient players to physically fill all the roles in the drama triangle. These
dynamics, however, often do not appear until a group of three has developed
sufficient trust and intimacy. Once this foundation of security is in place,
the combined force of the three persons' unhealed developmental histories
eventually surface. For this reason, conflicts involving relationships of three

or more tend to be some of the most intractable, because they involve issues anchored in people's unhealed developmental histories.

Staying aware and clear in a family can be quite difficult, as members' unhealed developmental issues are unconsciously seeking resolution. The success of family or three-way relationships depends on the degree to which each person has healed his or her developmental issues. Individuals must also know how to stay clear of drama triangle dynamics and have resolved the issues from the splitting phase of the counterdependent stage of development.

When each individual member of the system, including the parents' couple relationship, has healed their developmental histories, the family system can evolve to the next stage of development. This evolution is mapped below as to the essential developmental processes that need to be completed in each stage.

The four stages of family development, like those of individuals and couples, are the codependent, counterdependent, independent, and interdependent stages. Table 12-1. illustrates the essential developmental processes for each stage.

Table 12-1. The Essential Developmental Processes of Families[139]

Developmental Stages	Essential Developmental Processes of Family Evolution
Codependent: Bonding	• Create secure bonding experiences in the family between parents and children • Establish primal trust of family members with each other • Establish healthy emotional communication & social engagement skills among family members • Establish an identity as a family
Counter-dependent: Separation	• Parents and children learn to assert their individual needs and have them supported by other family members • Use of fair, equitable and non-shaming methods of limit-setting and discipline • Resolve conflicts effectively between needs of parents and needs of children

Developmental Stages	Essential Developmental Processes of Family Evolution
Independent: Mastery	• Develop individual and couple autonomy within the family structure • Develop core values and beliefs as a family • Achieve object constancy as a family • Bond with nature as a family (hiking and camping)
Interdependent: Cooperation	• Build consensus in decision-making skills among family members • Family members learn to cooperate with each other so all get important needs met • Create rituals that sustain a spiritual dimension in the family • Create divisions of labor based on individual interests and abilities • Family members cooperate to help each other to heal their developmental shocks, traumas and stresses • Family members cooperate to develop each member's fullest potential as a human being

A SYSTEMIC APPROACH FOR HEALING DEVELOPMENTAL TRAUMA IN FAMILIES

To be effective in working with families, developmental therapists need to understand the uniqueness of family counseling and be able to conceptualize family problems systemically.[140] This means that they must be able to recognize the family as a functioning human system connected by relationships, history, and shared emotional experiences.

Effective family therapists must be able to conceptualize the family system as the client and as the focus of treatment. In addition, they need interpersonal skills that allow them to attune with each family member and to offer interventions that impact the entire family system.

DEVELOPING A FAMILY SYSTEMS PERSPECTIVE

It is important for family therapists to understand that systems exist at many levels. The image below illustrates a systems perspective that begins with the individual and expands to include the whole human species.

Figure 12-1. A Systemic Perspective

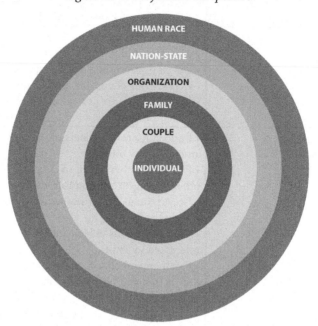

The individual human is a subsystem of a couple system, which is part of a larger living system called the family. The family is part of a living system called the community. The community is part of a larger system, known as the state, which is also part of a larger system, and so on. Our developmental approach says unhealed developmental traumas ripple out into the next larger systems, and impacts their long-term development through a process we call "leaky margins."

This concept is especially important when a counselor or social worker treats a family in which the problem seems to reside primarily in one of the members. Family systems therapists recognize that, although an individual exhibits the presenting problem, it may be maintained by behaviors of other family members. Furthermore, the systems counselor or social worker recognizes that the problem behavior affects the behavior of other members of the family system.

Most family theorists and researchers were initially schooled in models of psychotherapy that emphasized treatment of the individual. These models focused on problems of an intra-psychic nature—problems that resided within the mind of an individual. Each of these theorists sought to understand the nature of problem formation in a more inclusive theoretical orientation.

Rather than viewing the client's problem as being intra-psychic in nature, they came to view the psychological problem as a symptom of dysfunctional patterns in the identified patient's family system.[141] Thus, they presented a new way of conceptualizing problem formation. With this new conceptualization of problem formation came new models and strategies for problem resolution. This shift in problem formation formed part of the foundation for our systemic model.

The movement from an individual perspective to a systems perspective of problem formation and resolution is recognized as a paradigm shift, a term frequently used in the family therapy literature.[142] To most effectively employ systems-based counseling interventions, counselors must experience this paradigm shift and learn to understand how an individual's symptoms are one aspect of a family's interactive sequences of behavior and may serve to stabilize and maintain the current family system.

A classic example of this concept is the case of a child whose symptoms divert the focus of the parents from their marital problems and thoughts about divorce to the problems of the child. By manifesting psychological symptoms, the child has preserved, at least temporarily, the unity of the family system through the symptomatic behavior.

The parents rarely dwell on their marital problems when they are needed to help their child. The result of the child's symptomatic behavior is the preservation of the larger system, the family. Thus, the symptoms of the child can mask a larger problem with the family system.

SOURCES OF DEVELOPMENTAL SHOCKS, TRAUMAS, AND STRESSES IN FAMILIES.

The birth of the first child creates a shift from couple to family system dynamics. The change in dynamics becomes most visible when the child and mother or primary caregiver are actively separating during the counter-dependent stage of development. This stage, characterized by an increase in conflict, is the time when adults must learn to cope with the frustration of the splitting and oppositional and defiant behaviors that are characteristic of this stage.

When a parent is directive and authoritative, the child may become oppositional. This can set off a power struggle that triggers the parents' unhealed developmental shock, trauma, or stress.

Family conflicts are complicated because two parallel levels of dynamics are happening simultaneously. The first level is occurring between the child and parents in present time. The second is occurring inside of each of the parents in past time with their own parents. Psychodynamic psychology recognizes that adults often unconsciously regress to the chronological age of their child and reenact unprocessed feelings, and traumas.[143]

This psychological phenomenon, known as *regression–progression*, stimulates the unconscious restaging or reenactment of parents' own unresolved developmental trauma. This restaging provides the parents with a venue where they unconsciously reprocess the shock, trauma, or stress related to same-age experiences from their own childhood. In essence, parent child conflicts function as an unconscious "therapeutic" mechanism for the parents.

Parents can be expected to replay their own unhealed developmental shock, trauma and stress through each stage of their child's development, particularly during the counterdependent stage of development. Each parent becomes psychologically vulnerable to regression-progression experiences during family conflicts, especially when the other parent or caregiver is in conflict with the child. The parents' symbiotic bond and strong identification with the child trigger their own unhealed developmental issues, activating latent feelings and behaviors related to their own struggle for separation.

In short, the boundaries between the parent's experiences of the past and their experiences with their children in the present become blurred. Similar to a post-traumatic flashback experience, the past feels as though it is still happening in the present. Parents experience exaggerated feeling states that relate more to their past than the present.

For example, when the mother is in conflict with the child, the father may identify with the child as the victim and perceive the other parent as the persecutor. This symbiotic identification with the child triggers rescuer behavior in the father and activates the dynamics of the drama triangle between the two parents and the child.

In another common parent–child drama, a parent sees his or her child as an enemy. For example, the father perceives that the mother is more attentive to the child than to him. This triggers his memories of unresolved family-of-origin sibling rivalry issues, provoking him to criticize his wife for "spoiling" the child. Unable to identify his own unmet needs for nurturing, the father attempts to diminish the strong bond between the mother and the child. Parenting provides a stage upon which both parents can unconsciously or consciously play out their developmental trauma. The recycling of trauma through family dramas is a major cause of intractable family conflicts.

REGRESSION-PROGRESSION IN FAMILIES

One of the most fascinating aspects of family conflict is the regression–progression phenomenon. While it sits on a foundation of love-based symbiosis between parent and child, conflict can suddenly shift into a hate-filled situation in which the parent perceives the child as an enemy. The realization that a young child could appear threatening to adults indicates they are projecting.

Projections involve splitting between past/present, self/other, and us/them are prevalent in family conflicts. Parents' inability to separate past-from-present and self-from-other can suddenly trigger a small present-time conflict to erupt into a life-threatening episode of family violence that triggers parents' deepest emotions. The parents' loss of reality and accompanying emotional dysregulation indicates symptoms of either unresolved shock or trauma, both critical causes of intractable family conflicts.

The problem with the regression–progression restaging is that it allows adults to unconsciously use children as projective or "therapy" objects to purge themselves of their feelings anchored in their own unresolved developmental shock, trauma and stress. Rather than working consciously on these issues through counseling or parenting classes, parents simply reenact their trauma with their children. This reenactment is the primary cause of intergenerational patterns of child use and abuse.

The solution to regression–progression is conscious parenting in which adult family members use external resources such as therapy or support groups to clear themselves of their unresolved developmental traumas. This applies not only to parents rearing children but also to all adults who provide custodial care for children, such as childcare personnel, schoolteachers and officials, athletic coaches, and church supervisors and teachers.

Parents who are intentionally curtailing their practice of regression–progression typically have done extensive personal work in therapy and support groups to resolve their developmental issues. Most significantly, however, these parents learned to redefine the nature of their wounds. Rather than seeing themselves as "broken," we help them reframe their problems as "developmental delays."

This helps them de-pathologize their dysfunctional behaviors and to accept their projections and episodes of emotional overreactions as cues for looking at their own developmental histories. This reframing helps create a vision for complete healing of developmental shocks, traumas and stresses and the full realization of their potential.

Acting out through regression–progression, some parents lay traps, lie, threaten violence, manipulate, withdraw their love, humiliate, distrust, scorn, ridicule, coerce, terrorize, and commit violence against their children. Doing this to their children is a way that parents unconsciously prove that their own parents really loved them. This denial and repression of abusive and traumatic experiences is a major force in the replay of conflictual family patterns.

INTERGENERATIONAL FAMILY PATTERNS

One of the best ways to identify developmental shocks, traumas and stresses is looking for the fractal patterns a family uses to transmit them inter-generationally. This shows how the same developmental shocks, traumas and stresses flow from one generation to another when there is no external intervention in the family system's behavior patterns. Most people experience a moment of frightening awareness when they see that a family pattern and developmental issues begin showing up in their children and grandchildren.

In his book, *Breaking Free: How to Identify and Change Your Addictive Family Patterns*[144] Barry lists twelve common behavior and relational patterns that are transmitted inter-generationally that contain unhealed developmental shock, trauma and stress. The Appendix in the back of the book has two self-inventories from this book describing how to identify these intergenerational family patterns and the developmental shocks, traumas and stresses associated with them.

Table 12-2. Interventions for Completing the Essential
Developmental Processes of Families[145]

Stage of Development	Essential Developmental Processes of Families	Interventions for Completing These Processes
Codependent	• Creating secure bonding experiences in the family between parents and children • Establishing primal trust of family members with one another	• Help reestablish consistent parenting practices for the children. • Teach family members how to give and receive unconditional love.

Stage of Development	Essential Developmental Processes of Families	Interventions for Completing These Processes
Codependent (cont.)	• Establishing healthy emotional communication and social engagement skills among family members • Initiating a healthy family vision and inducting family members into it •Establishing a healthy identity as a family	• Create a process for parents to exchange nurturing touch and talk between parents and children and between siblings. • Help the family establish effective rules and roles (Family Sculpting can be used). • Initiate activities to help create common interests, values, beliefs, and goals among family members.
Counter-dependent	• Parents and children learning to assert their individual needs and have them supported by other family members • Using fair, equitable, and non-shaming methods of limit setting and discipline • Parents being able to set effective limits for themselves and their children • Resolving conflicts between needs of parents and needs of children effectively	• Encourage parents and children to individually explore interests outside the family. • Help parents learn to recognize the unique characteristics and life path of each child. • Help parents identify their needs and the needs of the children. • Help parents build appropriate boundaries between children and parents.
Independent	• Supporting development of individual initiative in family members • Developing individual and couple autonomy within the family structure • Setting limits on children, selves, and extra-family involvement, to preserve couple relationship/couple autonomy within the family structure	• Have parents provide children with independence training in managing time, money, school, extracurricular activities. • Help parents develop a consequence-based method of discipline for children. • Teach parents to establish and maintain boundaries between adult activities and interests and parenting activities.

Stage of Development	Essential Developmental Processes of Families	Interventions for Completing These Processes
Independent *(cont.)*	• Developing core values and beliefs as a family • Achieving object constancy as a family • Bonding with nature as a family (camping or being on the water)	• Help the family learn to achieve a balance between adults and children's needs. • Help parents to support children's development within and away from the family. • Help the family experience constancy of family relationships and structure during times of stress and/or conflict.
Inter-dependent	• Building consensus in decision-making skills among family members • Teaching family members to cooperate with each other so all get important needs met • Creating rituals that sustain the spiritual dimension of the family • Creating divisions of labor based on individual interests and abilities • Cooperating to help each other heal their developmental shocks, traumas, and stresses • Cooperating to develop each member's fullest potential as human being	• Teach parents how to manage family affairs through regular family meetings. • Help family members to value and keep agreements between family members. • Help parents to set limits on children, selves, and those outside the family. • Help family members to use power equitably between adults and adults, adults and children, and between children and children. • Help the family to create a high level of physical, mental, emotional, and spiritual resources for all members.

A DEVELOPMENTAL SYSTEMS APPROACH TO COUNSELING FAMILIES

To be effective in working with families, therapists need to understand the unique concepts of family therapy and to conceptualize family problems systemically. This means that the counselor or social worker must be able to recognize the family as a functioning organism connected by relationships, history, and shared experiences. They must also be able to make effective interventions in the powerful intergenerational fractal patterns that lock families into dysfunctional behaviors and relational structures.

How Family Therapists Can Prevent Burnout. Again, the key for the trauma therapist to prevent burnout is doing his or her own personal work and getting effective clinical supervision. In addition to these practices, it is imperative that you monitor your level of involvement with your clients and make sure you are not working harder than your clients in healing their problem. This "rescuing" is a common problem for therapists, one that must be avoided. If you don't pay close attention to the amount of work you are doing with your clients, you will quickly start resenting them for expecting too much from you.

The other important way to prevent burnout is to monitor carefully any countertransference issues or cues that trigger you in your counseling with families. Working with families is bound to bring up memories of any unhealed developmental shocks, traumas, or stresses for you to heal. Working with families therefore provides the counselor with a unique opportunity to identify his or her own developmental shocks, traumas, and stresses and use the tools that he or she has to heal them.

CASE EXAMPLE USING INTERVENTIONS IN COUNSELING WITH A FAMILY[146]

The following example shows how we used DPW interventions with a family. As you read the description below, see if you can identify the key DPW principles.

Leonard, a single professional father with five children, came to us with his fiancée, Melanie, for couples counseling. The two of them had been dating for about a year and were beginning to experience recurrent conflicts. Some of the conflicts were related to their couple relationship, but the most difficult ones involved family issues.

Leonard had been divorced for 4 years and recently had gained custody of his children through a lengthy legal battle. Their mother was unhappy about her loss of custody and was filing a countersuit. Melanie, a single woman with no children, had been spending a lot of time with Leonard and his family and saw problems within the family system.

The children, whose ages ranged from 3 to 14, were exhibiting signs of developmental trauma due to both their parents' Disorganized Attachment, including bedwetting, fighting, dependency, and poor academic performance at school. Leonard had hired a housekeeper to provide childcare, cleaning, and laundry services for the family. The housekeeper sometimes brought her own two children with her to work.

Melanie actually made the therapy appointment for the couple and identified several concerns that she felt needed to be addressed in their counseling. First, she mentioned a conflict between her and Leonard regarding the children's need for therapy to help them adjust to their new home and school environments. Second, she cited the number of recurring intractable conflicts between the two of them.

These conflicts had been present prior to the children coming to live with Leonard, but had increased after they arrived. The third concern involved problems with the housekeeper bringing her children with her to her job at Leonard's home and the regular conflict between her children and Leonard's. The fourth issue related to the stress created by Leonard's former wife's attempt to regain custody of their children.

This complex case involved several levels of work. After the initial session with Leonard and Melanie as a couple, we counseled them separately to look at the individual issues they were bringing into their relationship. We did an intake of their personal history and administered a series of diagnostic inventories to assess their individual development. After discussing the results of these assessments with them, we helped each of them understand the role of Disorganized Attachment in creating the developmental shocks, traumas, and stresses inherent in the intractable conflicts with each other, their children, and the housekeeper.

This was a rather difficult task, as both Leonard and Melanie preferred to see Leonard's former wife and her parenting as the source of all of their family problems. It took a lot of patience and empathy to mirror and validate the impact of their Disorganized Attachment in causing the childhood shocks, traumas, and stresses in their current conflicts and problems.

Initially, we rotated between individual counseling with Leonard and Melanie and conjoined couples counseling. We also administered the diagnostic inventories for couples and helped them see how the conflicts in their relationship mirrored unhealed individual issues from their childhoods. We also spent a considerable amount of time helping them recognize the traumatized parts of each other and develop compassion for each other's wounds.

This helped them identify their childlike behavior that emerged when they regressed during conflicts. They began to work cooperatively to help each other heal the effects of their developmental shocks, traumas, and stresses and get some of their unmet developmental needs met. This skill increased the level of intimacy between them and strengthened their relationship sufficiently to make the next level of intervention.

We gave Leonard a number of books on parenting to read and then began a series of family counseling sessions. Because of the size of Leonard's family, we conducted these sessions in his home. We have found home visits to be extremely effective. The children tended to behave more spontaneously, without the kind of constraints that office visits create. This allowed us to see family dynamics very quickly.

We helped Leonard design and implement a format for family meetings that would help build a more democratic family structure. This was the first experience for Leonard in parenting these children, as his former wife had been the children's primary caregiver. In one of the first family meetings, we suggested that Leonard ask all the children to present their perspectives on the problems in the family, while he took notes.

During these meetings, we were able to observe more closely the children's behavior and the relationships between them and with Leonard and Melanie. From these interactions, we were able to see their unmet developmental needs, incomplete developmental processes, and determine their levels of development. The children participated in problem-solving family issues that involved them, such as conflicts between siblings, laundry, homework, and kitchen cleanup.

One of the most poignant moments of our family intervention came during a family meeting and involved the children giving Leonard feedback about how they appreciated his efforts to be a father and make a loving home for them. Leonard had just shared his feelings of discouragement about their fighting and lack of cooperation.

While we saw how much the children loved their father, we also saw how he was seldom able to see beyond the struggles he was having. We encouraged the children to speak their love and appreciation directly to him one at a time. As they did, Leonard's eyes welled. By the time the last one finished, he was sobbing uncontrollably. This authentic encounter with his children bolstered his sagging confidence as a father.

Once the family meeting structure was firmly established in the system to address their day-to-day problems, Leonard invited the housekeeper and her children to participate in a family meeting. As we observed the dynamics between her and Leonard's children, it was clear that her job in Leonard's home was very stressful for her.

While she was able to perform the physical aspects of housekeeping, the child-care component was complicated by the presence of her own two children. We recommended that she find separate childcare for them, which she did for a while. She eventually decided to terminate her position with the family, and Leonard hired a new housekeeper without children to take her place.

The behavioral problems with Leonard's children continued, however, in spite of our efforts. We eventually recommended individual therapy for those exhibiting the most problems, including attachment therapy for one of the younger children. We consulted periodically with the therapists of these children regarding the family situation and gave them feedback after our family meeting sessions.

On several occasions, we also went to school and consulted with the counselors regarding the developmental issues of the children who were not in therapy and made recommendations to their teachers regarding possible interventions. We also went to court and testified as expert witnesses during a custody hearing.

The complexity of the problems in Leonard's household overwhelmed Melanie. Though she struggled to ride the regular waves of family chaos and conflict, she found her experiences there kept her flooded with post-traumatic stress symptoms. She undertook an earnest program of personal counseling to help her cope. While she did free herself from many of these symptoms, she eventually decided that she was not physically or emotionally able to be a full-time stepmother to Leonard's children.

She continued to be friends with Leonard and his children for a while and then entered a new relationship. Leonard continued in individual therapy for a while to help him adjust to this loss. He also continued to provide for some individual therapy for his children.

Our experience with this family was a great laboratory for expanding our clinical skills as systemic developmental psychotherapists. This example illustrates the complexity of working with large systems and the amount of perseverance required to address the complexity.

It also presents a realistic picture of the interface between individual development and couple, family, and social systems, as well as the limitations in changing larger systems when the individuals who comprise them are restricted in the internal resources that are needed for transformation.

This case also helped us develop patience and realistic expectations about working with large systems. Change does not happen overnight and the effects of interventions are often not visible in the short term.

CHAPTER THIRTEEN

HEALING DEVELOPMENTAL
TRAUMA IN ORGANIZATIONS

*In most organizations, change comes in only two flavors: trivial
and traumatic. Review the history of the average organization
and you'll discover long periods of incremental fiddling
punctuated by occasional bouts of frantic, crisis-driven change.*

—Gary Hamel

HOW ORGANIZATIONS CAN HEAL TRAUMA

This chapter describes the principles necessary for healing developmental
traumas in organizations. They help people develop skills that support them
in becoming more confident, capable, and individuated in their work settings. These skills include "both-and" and I'm okay/you're okay" thinking
strategies that encourage the clear communication and transformative relationship strategies that are essential in an environment where people can
heal their developmental traumas.

Organizational structures are complex and often disorganized because
people unconsciously bring their unhealed developmental traumas to the
workplace. These early developmental issues eventually surface during
workplace conflicts as drama triangle dynamics. When you see people over-
reacting during workplace conflicts, they probably have been triggered, and
are regressed reenacting an unhealed developmental trauma. Rather than
judging or criticizing them, respond to them with compassion and empathy.
This is not only the appropriate trauma-informed care response, it is also
the most effective way to heal developmental trauma. If you get triggered in
workplace conflicts, it is also important to develop a compassionate attitude
toward yourself.

Traditional organizational structures are often rigid, which make it difficult for people to heal their old traumas and resolve present-time conflicts in the workplace. Corporations, businesses, and other organizations have formal horizontal and vertical structures that are designed to accomplish the primary goal of the organization: making money.

Quantum science and chaos theory both suggest that the informal and invisible self-organizing structures actually determine how an organization operates. Chaos theory says that "strange attractors," or organizing forces, create predictable patterns that invisibly structure an organization.

One of the most common strange attractors in organizations is Disorganized Attachment. We believe that it actually operates as an organizing force, which is paradoxical. Perhaps it's more accurate to say that "DA serves as a *disorganizing force* in organizations, and that many workplaces function more as "dis-organizations."

We remember attending several executive committee meetings in a company where we served as Developmental Process Consultants (DPCs). During one of these meetings, we noticed a small group that regularly discounted the manufacturing vice president's comments. The executive committee members ignored him at breaks, cut him off when he was speaking, and tried to disempower him by interpreting his words. It was clear that they saw him as weak and passive, and reinforced their perceptions in as many ways possible. They had him in a "category."

We voiced our observations regarding this man's treatment during an executive committee meeting, and then waited to see if they changed their behavior. After our third executive meeting, we asked the vice president how he was feeling. He said that he was feeling ignored. He confronted his colleagues, telling them he felt hurt about the way they ignored him and that he wanted to speak more freely in meetings. He admitted to becoming a bit reluctant to speak at meetings as a result of being discounted or ignored. Our support and encouragement helped him give feedback that was both honest and direct, and helped to change the family-like group dynamics.

Once he was able to express his feelings and needs, he became more confident and assertive. The group discovered that he had many good ideas and that he was not weak and passive as they had previously believed. His colleagues implemented some his suggestions and found them to be helpful, and he was gradually seen as a valuable resource in meeting discussions.

People's unresolved internal and interpersonal conflicts can affect the morale, productivity, and wellness of an organization once there is sufficient safety and closeness for family-of-origin issues to surface. An effective way to address this is to create a workplace structure that enables the organization to operate more like a functional family. In her excellent book, *Family Ties, Corporate Bonds* by Paula Bernstein, she holds such a vision:

> *"Tomorrow's corporate family will be headed by a man or a woman— not necessarily in the old-fashioned father or mother role, but more an adult friend, a protector, and advisor to his or her adult children, cousins, siblings, and stepchildren. We will be grown-ups working with grown-ups, but still fulfilling our own individual, special emotional needs."*[147]

THE DEVELOPMENTAL STAGES OF ORGANIZATIONS

According to the tenets of developmental systems theory, the evolution of organizations follows a developmental process similar to that of individuals, couples, and families. The four stages of organizational development are codependent, counterdependent, independent, and interdependent. The essential developmental processes of each stage are listed in Table 13-1.

Table 13-1. The Essential Developmental Processes of Organizations[148]

Stage of Development & Primary Tasks	The Essential Developmental Processes	Methods for Completing These Processes
Codependent *(Bonding)*	• Build trust with employees. • Create a secure financial foundation for your organization. • Build customer base. • Help create work standards and organizational identity. • Meet basic needs of self and employees. • Build good social relationships with employees. • Create supportive work relationships. • Maximize direct, face-to-face, wide bandwidth communication.	• Set fair wages/benefits for employees. • Establish a customer network to ensure growth of your organization. • Provide work time to build trusting relationships with employees. • Decisions are made at level of implementation. • The organization has minimum number of hierarchical levels. • Utilize regular group rituals to enhance social engagement skills.

Stage of Development & Primary Tasks	The Essential Developmental Processes	Methods for Completing These Processes
Codependent *(Bonding)* *(cont.)*		• Identify personal and employee feelings and needs, and build structures to meet them.
Counter-dependent *(Separation)*	• Identify each employee's unique contributions. • Foster personal development in self and employees. • Resolve conflicts between organizational needs and the needs of employees. • Promote practices that move employees away from drama triangle dynamics. • Encourage employees to take more ownership of their jobs. • Provide more opportunities for social engagement.	• Create flexible job descriptions, differential workloads, and work schedules; utilize employee input. Provide training in conflict resolution for all employees • Encourage new and innovative ideas of employees. • Utilize minimal rules and fair methods of enforcement. • Eliminate employee power plays to get needs met. • Teach dialogue skills to help employees understand and accept differences.
Independent *(Mastery and Autonomy)*	• Build a work culture that fosters personal integrity. • Support mastery of job skills. • Encourage employees to be the inventors of their work. • Reward self-initiating, self-correcting, and self-evaluating employees. • Support autonomy, creativity, and innovation. • Offer specialized training and development to enhance individual contributions to employees and the organization.	• Reward individual initiative of clients and coworkers. • Create flexible work situations. Encourage direct communication of feelings and needs by employees. • Reward personal growth and personal mastery. • Support independent actions by employees. • Train employees to recognize and heal developmental traumas that interfere with work performance.

Stage of Development & Primary Tasks	The Essential Developmental Processes	Methods for Completing These Processes
Inter-dependent *(Cooperation and Negotiation)*	• See the organization as a tool for self-actualization. • Create transformational tools for employees. • Develop consensus team-building. • Foster methods that expand consciousness of employees. • Allow employees to be guided by their own visions at work.	• Determine goals and visions through collective processes. • Develop work teams to accomplish organizational and personal goals. • Practice partnership conflict resolution methods with employees and customers. • Make personal growth a priority. • Train key employees in developmental process consultation skills to help foster organizational evolution.

SOURCES OF DEVELOPMENTAL TRAUMAS IN ORGANIZATIONS

An organization provides a working environment in which individual employees can complete the essential developmental processes and heal their traumas. This kind of organization is described in Table 13-1 showing how it can evolve to more conscious and individuated stages of development. Organizations are living systems with interrelated developmental processes that determine the system's developmental health.

Managers who facilitate the system's steady movement to higher stages of organizational development, make a conscious effort to address employees' work-related developmental traumas and unmet developmental needs. This includes helping employees recognize and process traumatic events that get triggered at work and resolve workplace conflicts. Otherwise Drama Triangle dynamics get activated, employee morale falls, productivity declines, and the company stagnates.

Understanding the essential developmental processes of an organization, and where and how the organization might be stuck in its evolution, is fast becoming an important focus of organizational development consultants. Below is a description of the developmental processes in each stage of organizational development.

THE CODEPENDENT STAGE OF AN ORGANIZATION

In this stage of development, management is able to help employees bond securely with the organization. This involves paying fair wages and offering real benefits, as well as attending to employees' unmet bonding needs. Managers provide opportunities for employees to have meaningful social interactions with one another and with the organization's managers.

Bonding activities can include intramural sports activities in which employees can play recreational sports. It can also involve employees in group decision-making, and personal and organizational goal-setting, and valuing their opinions. Employees may also participate in revenue-sharing activities such as owning stock or stock options and sharing in the future success or failure of the organization.

Employees want their needs to be taken seriously and respected. They need encouragement to express their feelings and needs directly by asking for what they need from the organization and their fellow employees. It is important to have many face-to-face meetings involving a wide bandwidth of communication that includes expressing feelings and needs. Some organizations overuse emails and telephone calls, which tend to be narrow, impersonal bandwidths of communication with fellow employees.

THE COUNTERDEPENDENT STAGE OF AN ORGANIZATION

This is a pivotal stage in the evolution of an organization. Many organizations fail at this stage because they either have not laid the solid foundation for this stage in the codependent stage, or they fail to provide interventions that address resolving the conflicts and unmet anchored in unhealed developmental trauma that predictably will surface in this stage.

The counterdependent stage parallels the separation stage of individual development. Employees who are striving for personal autonomy in the workplace can cause conflicts when an organization is too rigid, micromanages its employees, or doesn't give incentives or rewards for creativity and self-initiation. Repressive or rigid organization rules and regulations can trigger employee memories of not receiving emotional support when they were becoming independent in their families. The organization's policies and procedures may feel too similar, and trigger reenactments of unhealed developmental traumas from their childhood.

Providing employees with choices regarding flexible job descriptions and work schedules and organizational structures encourages self-initiation, innovation, and creativity. This approach at an organizational level can provide a systemic environment that helps them heal separation issues from their families of origin.

We have gotten a lot of feedback from our TIC participants about how our unique Trauma-Informed Care training model has supported them in resolving some of their developmental issues in their workplace. They tell us that the information about Disorganized Attachment has been particularly helpful in communicating more effectively at work, particularly in avoiding Drama Triangle dynamics. This kind of professional support can help employees become more aware of the sources of their relationship conflicts, both at work or at home. They no longer use manipulation or power plays, or become victims, to get their needs met.

We once worked with a client who got regularly triggered at work. Once she was able to connect the dots between her workplace traumas and her childhood traumas, we taught her how to use the Trauma Elimination Technique (TET) described in Chapter 9. We had not trained her workplace peers in this technique, so she went to the restroom and used TET privately when she got triggered. She felt very relieved that she was able to disrupt her triggering reactions, and felt increasingly more secure about going to work each day.

In addition to helping employees heal early developmental traumas that get triggered at work, employees need support in learning better communication and social engagement skills. We advocate the use of dialogue rather debate communication to help people better understand and accept differences between them and their fellow workers. This strategy helps employees feel closer to others with different values or beliefs and creates more workplace harmony.

THE INDEPENDENT STAGE OF AN ORGANIZATION

This stage builds on the previous two stages of development and provides organizations with new opportunities for growth. At the independent stage the challenge is to structure the organization in ways that allow employees to develop mastery of their work skills and become even more independent and differentiated. This requires providing rewards for mastering job skills and innovative ideas. It may mean getting additional training in recognizing unhealed developmental traumas at work and learning ways to assist one another in the healing of traumas and resolving the conflicts that are associated with them. It also means encouraging employees to become the inventors of their work.

THE INTERDEPENDENT STAGE OF AN ORGANIZATION

This stage builds upon a constructivistic foundation created by employees who successfully healed their developmental traumas and the conflicts related to them. The interdependent stage requires a structuring of the workplace so that it becomes a place where people can transform their lives. Teaching employees such transformational tools as TET and utilizing the skills of in-house developmental process consultants can help them transform the organization. Both employees and the organization can grow and thrive on the energy created by a constructivistic work environment. Employees who can co-create within the organization find their personal evolution supported at the same time they are supporting the evolution of the organization. At this stage of development, personal growth of employees becomes the highest priority. Work is no longer just a job, it is an exciting place where people grow and self-actualize.

Because the organization operates through the collective effort of all its employees, there is never any question about their loyalty to the organization. There is also very little turnover and when someone does leave the organization, they are applauded for making choices that support them personally.

CAUSES OF DEVELOPMENTAL TRAUMA IN AN ORGANIZATION

Some organizations do a good job of creating an organizational identity that help its employees bond with it. They may have a logo, motto, mission, objectives, and goals that employees can identify with the organization. Such organizations might offer fair wages and good benefits, but they still may not provide ways for employees to bond personally with each other or with the management. The workday may be filled with tasks that prevent much interpersonal interaction between employees or with management. On the surface this might look very efficient and productive, but what is wrong with this picture? If there is not enough opportunity for meaningful social engagement in which people feel safe to express their feelings and needs directly, employee morale may slowly erode.

Low morale at work often causes people to change jobs. Employee turnover and the loss of friendships affects the corporate esprit de corps, as well as people's sense of security and safety. Most corporate environments, unfortunately, do not help people cope with workplace losses. Unprocessed grief from lost workplace relationships, even though the people who left were not known well, can trigger memories of employees' previous personal losses. This can distract them from the present-time focus needed in order to stay productive.

The Need/Obligate System. Unless organizations encourage employees to express their feelings and needs directly, they will use indirect ways to communicate them such as the drama triangle dynamics. These dynamics emerge in organizations through the good old boy/good old girl social structures, and are anchored in unspoken codependent agreements involving mutual but invisible dependencies. One person rescues another, who is then obligated to rescue the first person at some point in the future. This mutual rescuing agreement creates an ideal dynamic that encourages each person to act out the traumatic elements of his or her personal psychodrama via the drama triangle.

Here are some typical good old boy/girl network interactions:

- Employee A needs something from employee B but doesn't ask for it.
- Employee A does something for employee B without getting permission.
- Employee B then feels obligated to do something in return for employee A; employee B must guess what employee A needs, and provides it without asking permission or checking it out.
- Employee A rescues employee B to reciprocate.

This need/obligate system keeps both persons stuck in codependency. Both participants keep score to make sure that the tally stays equal. The problem with this system is that each person invariable ends up feeling used by the other.

For example, Sally usually arrives first at work because her husband drops her off on his way to work. She makes the coffee for everyone, even though this is Milly's job. When Milly gets to work and finds that Sally already has made the coffee, she feels conflicted. She likes to make the coffee her way, which is a little stronger than the way Sally makes it. Milly also feels uncomfortable because she believes that she now owes Sally a favor. When Sally asks Milly to cover for her so she can leave work a little early, Milly doesn't want to do this but feels obligated to do so because Sally made the coffee for her. Their inability to be direct with each other causes strained relations between them. Then a conflict erupts at the copy machine because Milly is using the copy machine for a big job and Sally wants to leave work early. The conflict is not about the copy machine but about the need-obligate dynamics they are caught in. Unless they can sort out their communication dynamics and the need/obligate system, it will be difficult to resolve it effectively.

Another common way that people get caught up in the Drama Triangle at work is from the Victim role. For example, an employee, John, is often late or absent. No one says anything to him, so his behavior continues. A female employee eventually complains to their supervisor (triangulation).

Here is how the dialogue goes from there: "I don't see why John gets away with being late. Nobody seems to care. Maybe I'll just start coming in late, too." The supervisor (Persecutor) decides to make an example of John and his tardiness and issues him an ultimatum: "If you are late one more time, you will be fired." John (Victim) feels angry with his boss and asks one of his colleagues (Rescuer) to intervene. The colleague defends John's behavior with his boss, discovers the name of the woman who complained about John's tardiness, and then confronts her for John (Persecutor). The woman feels guilty when she finds out that John was given an ultimatum about his job. She then goes to their supervisor and pleads John's case (Rescues): "But he was only late three times, and then by just a few minutes." The supervisor (Victim), who is tired of hearing about this problem, finally says: "Since you are the one who caused this problem in the first place, maybe I should fire you instead" (Persecutor).

This game can go on forever until someone refuses to be a victim and begins asking directly for what he or she needs without any expectation from others. Remember, the best way to break the power of the drama triangle is by making agreements in which all people get their needs met by asking directly for what they need and by negotiating any conflicts of needs.

Dysfunctional Employee Behavior. Bolton[149] wrote about the impact of dysfunctional employee's behavior on more functional employees. He describes how some people carry an "emotional plague" that undermines the effectiveness of those who are working constructively in the organization. Dysfunctional employees with Disorganized Attachment can keep a workplace in constant turmoil through drama triangle dynamics. It is important to recognize the source of these dysfunctional workplace games and to correct the problems at their source. In most organizations, it isn't easy to recognize drama triangle dynamics until you find yourself deep in the middle of them.

Most people spend more than one-third of their lives in workplaces embroiled in recycling conflicts. The only formal structures in place for resolving these conflicts are established grievance procedures. Most employees avoid using them because of their adversarial and confrontational nature. Without corporate-endorsed structures that protect employees who get caught in conflict, most people develop avoidant or indirect means of communication such as the drama triangle to cope with their conflicts.

If all employees had skills in conflict resolution and a work environment that supported healing traumas, organizations would not only save enormous amounts of time and money they would greatly increase employee productivity. We wonder why companies don't invest more in training employees in basic communication dynamics. Some of the more enlightened ones do, but most do not recognize the benefits.

For example, a middle manager of a large high-tech company to which we proposed employee conflict resolution training said with great seriousness, "Our employees don't have conflicts at work, they leave them at the door." We rolled our eyes at each other, recalling the company's reputation for high levels of alcoholism and dysfunctional family-like dynamics. We also wondered if these employees were carrying their work-related conflicts and traumas home to their families their families.

Unfortunately, this situation represents a still too common attitude among corporate leaders and managers. They simply do not understand the economic impact of unresolved workplace conflicts and unhealed personal traumas.

Triangulation and the Gossip Mill. One of the most destructive forms of communication in an organization is the gossip mill, which typically involves drama triangle dynamics. It involves triangulation, a form of splitting that creates divisiveness and a lack of trust inside organizations.

It can be very tempting to engage in gossip in the workplace, particularly when people aren't bonded to each other and don't feel safe. People fear going directly to the people with whom they have conflict because they anticipate repercussions. Gossip transactions sound something like this: "Do you know what she did? Well, let me tell you." This indirect expression of anger during a conflict can cause repercussions that escalate into a major drama triangle episode. One employee can become the organizational scapegoat or cause the sudden departure of someone from the organization.

The best way to avoid these dysfunctional relationship dynamics is to refuse to participate in triangulation dynamics. This requires a commitment to resolving your conflicts directly with those who are involved. If someone comes to you to talk about another person, here's what to do:

- Refuse to get in the middle of a conflict between other people. Direct a triangulator to talk directly to the other person involved.
- Inform triangulators that you do not want your relationship influenced by a third person or by their perceptions of the conflict situation, that you wish to stay neutral.
- You can offer to act as a mediator in the conflict, if both people agree.
- Agree to serve as a mediator, only if both persons involved agree that they want your assistance and will ask you directly for it.

Teaching employees how to effectively resolve their conflicts and how to recognize their developmental traumas are good management practices. Bernstein writes that when she interviewed employees, the conversation always returned to one theme: the lack of good management, the need for it, and how much the employees hungered for it. The employees she interviewed longed for fairness, leadership, and justice, and for simpler, less convoluted, and more straightforward conflict-free (trauma-free) relationships.[150]

HOW TO IDENTIFY DEVELOPMENTAL TRAUMA IN AN ORGANIZATION

Before deciding how to best facilitate the completion of employees' essential developmental processes in an organization, you need to determine how much developmental trauma and conflict is present in that organization. Litvak[151] found that the potential for conflict is greater in centralized, highly bureaucratic organizations than in organizations with less centralized processes or structures. Likert and Likert[152] developed a method for rating organizational processes on a continuum between rigidity and flexibility.

The most effective organizations are those that are open to adapting to changing conditions and needs. The following criteria, based on our research on developmental systems theory and the work of the Likerts, can help you determining how well an organization is set up to complete the essential developmental processes that foster its evolution.

1. A minimum of rules and regulations. The openness of a system can be determined by identifying the number of rules and regulations and how long these have existed. Most open systems have very few rules and use a set of operating principles for each subsystem of the organization. These principles need to be determined by the group or the team most directly involved in implementing the rules or regulations.

2. Decision making at the level of implementation. Another quick way to assess a system's openness is to check the number of levels any decision must pass through before it can be implemented. In an open system, all important decisions are made at the level of implementation.

3. A minimum number of hierarchical levels. An open system is relatively flat in organizational structure. The more levels that information and decisions must pass through, the more chances of error or misperceptions, and the more opportunities for conflict.

4. Maximum data flow with external systems. To determine this, notice how the system exchanges information, resources, and data with the systems that are contiguous to it. In open systems, established methods ensure a reciprocal flow of information, resources, and data.

5. Collectively determined goals and purposes. Identify how goals and purposes are determined. In an open system, they are determined collectively by those directly involved in the process. Input is also sought from members of the larger contiguous system to accommodate changing needs and purposes.

6. Direct, wide-band, face-to-face communication. In closed organizations, communication tends to become indirect (memos, voice mail, e-mail). Open systems use more direct, face-to-face, wide-band (information and feelings) communication. This offers some potential for group decision-making. By checking the transmission of information, it is possible to assess the openness of a system. There is also a need for structures that encourage the expression of both positive and negative feelings.

7. Neutralized power. Power plays are common in organizations. In open systems, power is distributed through all levels. There is no one–up/one–down power moves and no win–lose decision-making or conflict resolution. A good way to check the openness of an organization is to look for evidence of misuse of power.

8. Flexible processes. The processes (work schedules, flexibility of hours, curricula) in open systems are very flexible and dynamic. They can easily be changed in response to the changing needs of those involved. In less open systems, curriculum guides or job tasks are rigidly enforced and time schedules allow few opportunities for change.

9. Open, permeable, system boundaries. Instead of operating as an enclave, the open system extends its boundaries into the next larger system. The goals, purposes, and processes of the organization are completely visible. Open systems seek to blend their information, resources, and data flow with the next larger system. Open schools, agencies, and corporations operate as integrated, rather than separate, systems that enfold the daily lives of the people involved.

10. Flexible role definitions. Job descriptions and rigid role definitions can affect the degree of openness in an organization. In an open system, the roles that people are assigned or choose to play are flexible and able to change.

A good way to assess the openness to change of any organization is to administer our "Openness to Change Inventory." This inventory is in the Appendix at the end of this book. It is based on the Likerts research, which found that more rigid organizations manage conflicts poorly and control people to prevent the reenactments of unhealed developmental traumas.

They also found that the personality and methods of the managers and supervisors make a difference. If it is not possible to administer the inventory all employees, ask the managers and supervisors to take it. Less defensive managers who are able to receive feedback and were naturally supportive of others, tended to prevent conflict and were willing to be supportive of employees when developmental traumas appeared.

The leadership style of the managers and supervisors sets the tone for conflict management. Those with good communication skills, supportive attitudes toward those they supervise, and the ability to facilitate the resolution of conflicts generally have fewer conflicts and typically encounter fewer reenactments of unhealed developmental traumas in the workplace.

The culture of the organization can also play a part in managing conflict and developmental trauma. Organizations with competitive, win–lose, everyone-for-themselves cultures have more conflict than those with a spirit of cooperation for achieving the organization's goals. Punitive attitudes also tend to trigger more reenactments of relational traumas, particularly those involving issues of competition. Some organizations unwittingly create a competitive climate because of authoritarian, petty, and divisive organizational policies and procedures. These kinds of policies trigger employees into reenacting their family-of-origin traumas. They gnaw at morale, erode productivity, affect the health of employees, and ultimately impair the organization and its productivity.

An organization's stability is an important factor in healing developmental traumas, particularly the number of employees with Disorganized Attachment. Organizations experiencing high levels of change trigger internal stressors associated with chaos and uncertainty. Chaotic organizational practices and policies can destabilize employee morale, increase their stress and trigger more reenactments of developmental trauma. Organizations experiencing rapid change can handle stress better by going slowly and creating a supportive social and emotional climate that includes conflict resolution and time for processing emotions. When this isn't available, conflict can ripple through the company and increase the chaos.

HOW UNHEALED DEVELOPMENTAL TRAUMA IMPACTS ORGANIZATIONS

Anytime you find yourself interacting with three or more people, there is a high probability you may unconsciously get triggered into reenacting developmental traumas from your family-of-origin experiences. Why? Three people recreate a family system and our formative relational dynamics. It is natural for humans to unconsciously recreate situations where they can heal their early relational wounds.

Bosses may resemble your father or mother and trigger family dynamics and unresolved conflicts related to them. This is why certain coworkers may irritate you. They may be activating early memories involving traumatic family experiences.

Organizations are a great stage for playing out old family patterns. It is quite common for founders and presidents and employees to unconsciously engage in the reenactment of family-of-origin issues and dynamics. For example, one of our clients was an employee at a large company the engaged in endless replays of developmental trauma from the founder's alcoholic family. Our client eventually recognized that company policies such as avoiding conflict, keeping secrets, rigidly defining the roles of subordinates, using unpredictable decision-making strategies, and throwing lots of high-alcohol parties was a recreation of the founder's alcoholic family.

Such unrecognized family patterns can be a major factor in the failure of family-owned businesses. Their internal dynamics can become so chaotic and intertwined that corporate productivity and decision-making dictate the "story line" of the company's progress. The typical pattern of small companies is a period of initial rapid growth, followed by a stabilizing and leveling off period, and then a decline in productivity that may lead to the company's demise.

Jongeward[153] stated that a company story line "may depict a comedy, a saga, a tragedy, a farce, or a dull plodding drama going nowhere." She said that the family-patterned story line determines the company's cast of characters, their dialogue, the themes carried out, the dramatic actions taken, and the ultimate fate of the company.

Company policies are one of the most common places for the recycling of family patterns and drama triangle dynamics because the rules often resemble the structure from the company founder's family of origin. For example, if the founder's family avoided conflict, it is likely that the company will also act to help its employees avoid conflict. In some companies, the founder runs the organization like an authoritarian parent whose word is law and decisions are unquestionable. In a company with a non-collaborative leader, the boss often stays distant from the problems inside the business and employees are afraid to provide the boss with information about changing markets, the company's position in those markets, and other critical management issues.

HOW TO DIAGNOSE THE NATURE OF DEVELOPMENTAL TRAUMAS IN THE WORKPLACE

Employees often view their bosses as the good parents they always wanted, hoping the corporation or organization will take care of them better than they were in their family-of-origin. The family patterns of employees and those of the company are often remarkably congruent, providing a stage upon which can trigger everyone's unhealed developmental traumas.

You may choose a role at work that is different from the one you played in your family of origin; however, it is likely to be a role that was played out by someone else in your family. If an abusive mother or father persecuted you, for example, you may assume the persecutor role at work when you are promoted to a supervisory position. The reasons for doing this are always unconscious, but it is usually an attempt to heal victimization wounds by victimizing others.

You may find yourself using your position at work to discharge repressed feelings of anger and resentment about your family-of-origin experiences. Some people find it safer to act out their repressed feelings in the workplace than at home. If you do find yourself reenacting your family-of-origin conflicts in your workplace, be compassionate toward yourself. Just focus on identifying what triggered you so that you can identify the reenactment pattern and the unhealed developmental traumas, and work outside the office to change the pattern.

If your organization doesn't provide you with a safe forum for clearing your family-of-origin issues (and few companies do so), you run the risk of re-traumatizing yourself via workplace conflicts. This vulnerability can affect your job effectiveness. Without an awareness of the triggers that activate your developmental traumas, you may be unable to prevent their replay at work. This can have a significant impact on your career because it may contribute to chaotic employment history.

FUNCTIONAL FAMILY POLICIES IN ORGANIZATIONS

Perhaps the organization of the future will create "functional family" policies. The traditional corporate model not only lacks the perspective of the family, but often forces employees to sacrifice their family lives the company. Some corporations understand that this policy is destructive in the long run, and really don't care. More employees are now demanding changes in corporate structures that make the workplace more humane and family friendly.

In order to keep their employees, some corporations are providing benefits for employees that demonstrate appreciation. Some companies are also providing more work-site policies and programs, such as flexible work hours, recreation programs, and on-site childcare facilities. These innovations facilitate a family-like atmosphere at work and provide a functional family structure. In this time of unsettled social conditions, rising divorce rates, and single-parent families, the workplace can be a stabilizing force for many individuals and families.

The self-inventory "Intergenerational Family Patterns in Organizations," found in the Appendix, will help you identify developmental trauma, family-of-origin patterns, and conflicts in your workplace.

Our vision of the corporation of the future as a functional family can become a reality if you learn how to use your corporate or work-family traumas and conflicts as a valuable source of information. When you do, you will be able to move forward in your personal development and also function more effectively in your work environment.

HOW TO HEAL DEVELOPMENTAL
TRAUMA IN ORGANIZATIONS

At the core of our systemic model for healing developmental traumas in organizations is the assumption that it is possible to move them forward in their development. We have developed two self-inventories to assess where your organization is stalled and how to correct the problem. These self-inventories are also in the Appendix of the book.

An important assumption of our systemic approach is that every person, couple, family, or organization is in a process of evolving. It is possible for any system to move forward when people understand how it operates and know how to facilitate movement. Once they truly understand and personally experience this, they can become partners in the process of evolution.

Healthy organizations periodically review their structures to determine how well they are supporting their mission and objectives. Here are the key human interactions where conflicts containing developmental trauma appear:

- Communication
- Roles and functions in groups
- Group problem solving and decision-making strategies
- Group norms and group growth
- Leadership and authority
- Intergroup cooperation and competition

Woven through all of these conflicts and policies are opportunities for resolving them through specialized consultation services. The person who specializes in identifying and healing developmental trauma in organizations is known as a Developmental Process Consultant (DPC). This approach expands the process-consultation model long recognized in organizational development circles and as an effective tool for organizational change. The DPC helps members of an organization gain insight into the source of their conflicts and problems, and teach managers, supervisors, and employees about the developmental principles inherent in their intrapersonal, interpersonal, and intergroup relationships. Below are listed the steps that a DPC might use when consulting with an organization:[154]

STEP 1: ESTABLISHING FIRST CONTACT
WITH AN ORGANIZATION

A member of the organization, usually an administrator, seeks your help in addressing a specific problem. We find the most difficult part of this step is encountering a hierarchical orientation that gives us "expert" status as an outsider. This approach ignores the inherent wisdom of people who work within the organization regarding the causes of the problem and workable solutions for it.

During face-to-face meetings between us and organizational representatives, we advise them to consider a different approach. We begin by outlining our alternative consultation approach that draws on organizational experience and wisdom. In some instances, there may be a lack of compatibility between this approach and their culture. In these cases, we decline their offer to retain our consulting services.

If we find an organization receptive to our ideas, then we define our relationship via a formal contract stating how we will be paid, the exact nature of services we will provide, the time frame for providing services, and the outcome goals for the contract. It is very important to make the outcome goals as explicit as possible.

STEP 2: OBSERVING THE ORGANIZATION'S DEVELOPMENTAL PROCESS

We recommend attending key meetings to learn more about the organization and its processes. Here you can observe how the organization functions and what developmental components should be targeted for further study. Observe top-level meetings first because these meetings reveal most about the organization and its functions. Provide a context for your presence in these meetings to help people know you and you to know them. You may also choose to first interview some key people, not to gather data, but to help them know you better. Once they know and trust you, they are more likely to cooperate when you recommend interventions.

Attending key meetings is a great way to identify developmental processes to address at subsequent meetings. We once participated in a strategic planning process for a small company that was part of a large corporation. One activity asked employees to list their personal goals for the next year. Then employees were to compare their personal goals with the branch company's goals, and then with the corporation's goals. One employee after another wrote his or her personal goals on a large piece of newsprint. It was interesting to discover that each employee actually presented not only personal but organizational goals ("I am going to increase my attendance at supervisory meetings," and "I am going to work late to keep the paperwork from piling up"). Their work goals did not focus on their own needs ("I am going to work towards a promotion by the end of this year," and "I am going to join the company bowling team and spend at least one evening a week having fun").

What we saw was pretty amazing: a reversal process. Employees in this company focused on supporting the company rather than themselves inside the company. Through interviews and questionnaires, we confirmed that many employees had Disorganized Attachment in their histories. These employees grew up caring for their parents' and other adults, with few experiences of having their own needs met. They were unaware not only of having this pattern, but also of bringing it with them to work. When we disclosed this observation in our reports from the data-gathering phase of our consultation, the management decided to implement policies that encouraged more balance between the welfare of the company and the needs of the employees.

STEP 3: CONDUCTING COLLABORATIVE DATA-GATHERING ACTIVITIES

Unlike other consultation models, the DPC model does not rely exclusively on consultants' expertise to diagnose the organization's problems. Instead, the DPC consultant suggests activities designed that actively involve everyone in the organization in identifying and remedying its problems.

There are basically three kinds of data-gathering strategies in process consultation: observation, interviews, and questionnaires. The most effective approach is using a combination of all three. Having everyone fill out questionnaires will help reveal the problems and their developmentally related components that block the fulfillment of organizational objectives. There are two self-inventories in the Appendix that can be used in data-gathering activities.

In addition, the DPC should conduct structured interviews with key people who represent a cross section of the organizational structure. Even in situations where the organizational objectives and goals have been jointly determined, it is best to have everyone identify the developmental processes that are needed to achieve corporate goals and objectives. These interviews should also identify what might prevent the organization from reaching its goals and objectives.

STEP 4: ANALYZING THE RESULTS OF DATA GATHERING

Once you have analyzed the results of your data-gathering activities, report your findings back to the organization. This prepares the organization for implementing any interventions you suggest. All organizational members should have access to a written report of your findings. This step sets the stage for future developmental interventions. Your report should provide information about the six main processes of organizations that we identified earlier.

STEP 5: EFFECTIVE ORGANIZATIONAL INTERVENTIONS

There are three primary ways to intervene as a developmental process consultant:

- Observe key meetings and provide process feedback to help people change dysfunctional behaviors and processes.
- Train employees in key skills that can change the developmental patterns of the organization (i.e., conflict resolution training, counseling, or coaching for individuals and/or groups). These interventions should be part of your contract with the organization.
- Give process feedback to groups you observe by allowing time for process analysis at the end of the meeting. You can use key questions to focus this analysis. For example, if you observe any nonverbal reactions to a decision made during a meeting, you might ask: "How did all of you feel about how the decision was made about topic X? Did you feel that you had enough input into the decision in order to carry it out effectively?"

Giving process feedback to individuals or groups often leads to coaching or counseling sessions with the people involved. When given feedback about the ways their behavior is affecting others, people ask, "What can I do to change this behavior?" As a DPC, you can help key people identify how their family-of-origin patterns and unmet developmental needs may be reenacting and then help them find ways to address them more effectively.

Create trainings that come out of your consultations based on the results of your data-gathering activities. Structure them around specific issues or problems such as drama triangle dynamics, communication skills, and conflict resolution. Perhaps you can offer basic training courses for everyone and more advanced methods for the key employees or executives.

STEP 6: EVALUATING THE RESULTS

The goal of a developmental process consultant is to improve an organization's effectiveness and functionality. The most important outcome is helping people effectively resolve their conflicts, and learn how to separate their personal history from interpersonal events happening in the workplace.

It is also helpful to teach skills that enable members to identify developmental traumas and to resolve associated conflicts within any system: individual, couple, family, and group. One of the best indicators for success is that the company begins allocating time to and creating structures that include it reviewing and analyzing itself. The long-term goal is supporting an organization so that it becomes self-renewing by using reflective coaching sessions, conducting focus groups, or designing questionnaires where the members can suggest self-renewing strategies.

SUMMARY

The most effective ways to help heal developmental traumas in the workplace are:

1. Teach everyone about the dynamics of the Drama Triangle. This is where some of the unhealed developmental traumas will get acted out.
2. Get consensual agreements requiring that everyone ask directly to get their needs met. This is the most effective way to break free of the Drama Triangle.
3. Educate the organization about the destructive power of triangulation and gossip.
4. Train everyone in conflict resolution skills. This training should be very experiential and provide opportunity for extensive skill practice.
5. Have the whole organization become Trauma-Informed. This will help them have a framework for identifying the signs of any developmental traumas that show up on the job and how to react to them.
6. Train all employees in how to identify signs of developmental traumas at work and how to effectively intervene to help heal them with each other.

Our approach to Developmental Process Consultation works well in the workplace because it teaches skills in resolving three different kinds of conflicts:

1. conflicts of wants and needs,
2. conflicts of values and beliefs, and
3. conflicts that involve unhealed developmental traumas.

People can learn how to recognize the symptoms of developmental trauma and then consult with professionals in an employee assistance program who are trained in helping people heal their personal traumas. Healing traumas is not possible at a workplace unless the organization has supportive company structures and policies.

Most companies can create structures to help identify the symptoms of developmental traumas that show up on the job and then refer to others to do the healing work. Other small companies may be able to create a safe, nurturing environment where just coming to work in that kind of an environment can have healing effects. Refer back to the table showing the developmental processes needed to be put in place in organizations to facilitate the healing of developmental traumas.

(This page intentionally left blank)

CHAPTER FOURTEEN

THE GIFT IN DEVELOPMENTAL TRAUMA

Compassion asks us to go where it hurts,
to enter into the places of pain, to share in
brokenness, fear, confusion, and anguish.

Compassion challenges us to cry out with those in misery, to
mourn with those who are lonely, to weep with those in tears.

Compassion requires us to be weak with the weak, vulnerable
with the vulnerable, and powerless with the powerless.

Compassion means full immersion in
the condition of being human.

—Henri J.M. Nouwen

TRAUMA AND THE SEARCH FOR MEANING

In this Chapter, we focus on the positive aspects of developmental trauma, and how it can become an asset in people's relationships, even a force for personal and collective evolution. We also present our vision of what the world would be like if we could really heal developmental trauma, and even prevent it. We believe it is important to understand the potential for transformational change. Yes, developmental trauma is both a game-changer and a gift.

It was Victor Frankl's remarkable story about surviving imprisonment in a Nazi concentration camp that first showed the modern world that it is possible to make meaning of personal trauma and adverse life experiences. In his book, *Man's Search for Meaning*,[155] Frankl observed that the prisoners who were able to retain a sense of meaning in their experiences were the most likely to survive the horrifying conditions. From this observation, he theorized that the search for meaning is a primary human motivation that enables individuals to retain hope in the face of adversity.

Most of the research on coping with adversity has focused on personal traumas such as spinal cord injury, bereavement, illness, violence, and incest.[156] Within this literature, theorists have argued that what makes traumatic events so distressing is that they violate many of the basic assumptions people have about themselves and the world. Several theorists have proposed that people hold deeply ingrained beliefs that the world is benevolent, predictable, and meaningful and that the Self is worthy. These beliefs offer individuals a sense of security and invulnerability and instill coherence into their lives.

Traumas and other adverse experiences profoundly challenge these deeply held beliefs. One of the major tasks that traumatized individuals face is reconciling the harsh reality of adversity with previously held, more benign assumptions about themselves and the world. In the context of direct personal traumas, the challenges to people's "assumptive worlds" trigger a search for meaning. Searching for meaning often involves seeking answers to questions such as, "Why did this event happen to me?"[157]

In adult survivors of childhood incest experiences, nearly 90% still reported searching for meaning up to two decades after the abuse stopped. Frequently, survivors' attempts to make meaning are accompanied by substantial emotional distress. Among incest survivors and the bereaved, those who most actively searched for meaning also reported the highest levels of distress.

HOW FRANKL MADE MEANING OF HIS TRAUMA

Prior to his imprisonment, Frankl was a Jewish psychiatrist and director of the Neurological Department of the Rothschild Hospital in Vienna, Austria. During World War II he spent 3 years in various concentration camps, including Theresienstadt, Auschwitz and Dachau, where he worked five months as a slave laborer.

Therefore, Frankl entered captivity with both educational advantages and psychological tools that he was able to use in his efforts to make meaning of his captivity. His book about his experiences and learning, *Man's Search for Meaning*, was published in 1963, has sold more than 10 million copies and been translated into 45 languages.

During his captivity, Frankl identified three psychological reactions that all inmates experienced: (1) shock during the initial admission phase to the camp, (2) apathy after becoming accustomed to camp existence, in which the inmate valued only that which helped himself and his friends survive, and (3) reactions of depersonalization, moral deformity, bitterness, and disillusionment if they survived and were liberated.[158]

Frankl came to believe that the meaning of life is found in every moment of living; life never ceases to have meaning, even in suffering and death. In a group therapy session during a mass fast inflicted on the camp's inmates trying to protect an anonymous fellow inmate from fatal retribution by authorities, Frankl offered the thought that for everyone in a dire condition there is someone looking down, a friend, family member, or even God, who would expect not to be disappointed.

Frankl concluded from his captivity experiences that a prisoner's psychological reactions are not solely the result of the conditions of his life, but also from an internal sense of freedom of choice that is always available, even during severe suffering. He believed that a prisoner's relationship to his spiritual Self requires having hope for the future, and that once a prisoner loses that hope, he is doomed. Irving Yalom, who had studied Frankl's work, believes that **the lack of meaning is the paramount existential stress**, ultimately it becomes a crisis of meaninglessness.[159]

Making meaning of experiences that involve developmental trauma during the first three years of life is a critical component of healing them. The most effective tool for doing this is known as creating a "coherent life narrative." According to Dan Siegel, this narrative is a process of making sense of one's childhood experiences.[160]

Siegel says, "...having difficult experiences early in life is less important than whether we've found a way to make sense of how those experiences affected us. Making sense is a source of strength and resilience. In my twenty-five years as a therapist, I've also come to believe that making sense is essential to our well-being and happiness."[161]

Creating a coherent life narrative requires having a Self and the skill of self-reflection: the ability to witness or observe one's inner world and to question "why" things happen in order to make meaning of them.

Self-witnessing and self-observing requires an individuated Self, one with defined boundaries that knows "this is me/that is not me." This internal sense of self-identity includes one's body, beliefs, personality, needs, history and sense of membership in larger social, ethnic or religious groups. A per-

237

son with self-awareness is conscious of what he/she is feeling, thinking and experiencing in any given moment.

Given that most people who seek psychotherapy have Disorganized Attachment, their lives are often disorganized, chaotic and senseless. They have limited ability to connect *cause* with *effect*, which interferes with their ability to predict the outcomes of their choices. Because the world seems random and unpredictable, much of their life operates through trial and error. Logic is a foreign language, which makes planning and strategic thinking very difficult.

The most important skill for those with Disorganized Attachment is connecting childhood events and experiences with their adult conflicts, issues and problems. This is the primary goal of creating a coherent life narrative, as it helps bring cause-and-effect thinking into their awareness.

The most effective way to determine the coherency of a person's life narrative comes from a research instrument known as the *Adult Attachment Interview*.[162] Developed Mary Main and her colleagues, it contains 15 questions that a trained interviewer asks and often records, then reviews for analysis. The AAI questions, which are designed to "surprise the unconscious, are listed below.

1. Could you start by helping me get oriented to your early family situation and where you lived and so on? If you could tell me where you were born, whether you moved around much, what your family did at various times for a living?
2. I'd like you to try to describe your relationship with your parents as a young child… if you could start from as far back as you can remember?
3. Can you give me five adjectives or words that reflect your relationship with your mother/father during childhood? I'll write them down and when we have all five I'll ask you to tell me what memories or experiences led you to choose each one.
4. Now I wonder if you could tell me, to which parent did you feel the closest, and why?
5. When you were upset as a child, what would you do, and what would happen? Could you give me some specific incidents when you were upset emotionally? Physically hurt? Ill?
6. What is the first time you remember being separated from your parents?
7. Did you ever feel rejected as a young child? Why do you think your parent did those things – do you think he/she realized he/she was rejecting you?

8. Were your parents ever threatening with you in any way --- maybe for discipline, or even jokingly?

9. In general, how do you think your overall experiences with your parents have affected your adult personality?

10. Why do you think your parents behaved as they did during your childhood?

11. Were there any other adults with whom you were close, like parents, as a child?

12. Did you experience the loss of a parent or other close loved one while you were a young child or as an adult?

13. Were there many changes in your relationship with your parents after childhood?

14. What is your relationship with your parents like currently?

Mary Main's colleague, Erik Hesse, says that these questions require clients to engage in simultaneous tasks. They must produce and reflect on memories related to their early attachment experiences, while also maintaining a coherent conversation with the therapist. Because their interview moves along at a rapid pace, while also asking questions that require careful reflection, it creates opportunities for clients to contradict themselves and lose coherence in various ways.

The therapist tracks the coherence of the client's life story, paying attention to how organized or disorganized it is, and to assign it to one of four categories:

- Coherent/secure
- Not coherent/dismissing
- Not coherent/preoccupied
- Disorganized

After asking these questions of clients, therapists are able to determine the coherency of their life narrative and the degree to which they have made sense of their attachment histories. It also shows the therapist the course of treatment for the client, much of which is learning how to create a self-reflective, coherent, emotionally rich and meaningful story about their childhoods.

No matter how neglectful, abusive or inadequate, the goal is to help clients experience the emotional security they missed, to learn how to form healthy adult relationships, and to parent their children effectively. Siegel says, "If you can make sense of your life story you can change it."[163]

Making sense of past experiences and memories is an integrative process. It links together parts of the brain; the mind and body; past, present and potential future; and the elements of thought, feeling, memory and imagination. This integration helps clients organize themselves in ways that make all life experiences meaningful.

Disorganized life stories might be described as chaotic, and lacking understanding of cause and effect. It might be written mnemonically as CAEBD, while an integrated, organized life narrative mnemonically reads ABCDE. Logically, it contains a timeline, order and meaning.

Sometimes known as "re-authoring," narrative therapy helps people move beyond the telling and retelling of stories in ways that reinforce the original traumas and the associated beliefs about hopelessness and helplessness. Re-authoring one's life story reframes the meaning from Victim to Victor, creating a "personal truth" that is empowering and uplifting.

This narrative approach is very similar to Frankl's in that he reframed his adversities into learning experiences that allowed him to develop a new level of mastery. In its new context, his adversity became a foundation for moving to a higher level of self-development and achievement.

Frankl's life became a living demonstration of how he was able to convert the adversity of his imprisonment experiences into a large and very personal laboratory for understanding the impact of trauma on the human psyche. After being liberated from Dachau in 1945, Frankl went on to create Logo therapy, his own Existential approach to psychology, directed the Vienna Neurological Policlinic, lectured on five continents, wrote 39 books, and was granted honorary doctorate degrees to 29 Universities. Frankl might have come to honor and acknowledge the importance of his time in death camps by stating, "Had I not been imprisoned... ."

HAD I NOT BEEN WOUNDED: DEVELOPMENTAL TRAUMA AS A PERSONAL GAME-CHANGER

The "wounded healer" is a term created by psychiatrist Carl Jung. His idea, which stated that psychoanalysts were compelled to treat patients because the analysts themselves were "wounded," may have its origins in Greek mythology associated with the centaur, Chiron, a healer who was wounded.

For Jung, "a good half of every treatment that probes at all deeply consists in the doctor's examining himself... it is his own hurt that gives a measure of his power to heal. This, and nothing else, is the meaning of the Greek myth of the wounded physician."[164]

Alison Barr's research indicated that 73.9% of counselors and psycho-therapists have experienced one or more wounding experiences that lead to their career choice. A famous clinical psychologist, Dr. Marsha Linehan, agrees.

In 2012 Linehan courageously confessed that she suffered from what she believed to be Borderline Personality Disorder all of her adult life.[165] Professor of Psychology, Psychiatry and Behavioral Health at the University of Washington, her self-revelations surprised many of her colleagues. Some questioned if much of her success in working with severely disturbed and suicidal patients came from having faced down and overcome, or learning to live with and manage her own destructive demons. Linehan's breakdown and breakthrough happened in a Catholic chapel, during a spiritual epiphany at the age of twenty-three.

Her transformative experience closely parallels Jung's psychotic break-down that began in his late 30s and lasted until his mid-40s. Although he was never hospitalized like Linehan nor formally treated, he admitted to ex-periencing visual hallucinations, disorientation, depression, massive anxiety, suicidal despair, and was unable to fully function for many years during his prolonged recovery. Jung actually emerged from his painful transformation-al journey a new man, more whole, conscious, better balanced, more spiri-tual, more compassionate, and a psychologically self-aware and insightful person and psychiatrist.[166]

Both Jung and Linehan used their childhood traumas as personal game-changers. While these experiences weren't something that they consciously chose, they served as catalysts for changing themselves from broken, vic-timized people who had difficulties in coping with their lives. Ultimately, their childhood traumas were responsible for more than changing their life games, they also provoked deep transformative experiences that guided them to their life's work as healers.

Jung directly confronted his demons and engaged his unconscious mind. Linehan, however, remained a cognitive-behavioral therapist. Her work avoids and even dismisses the affective and irrational part of the psyche that Jung referred to as the *Shadow*.

Both Cognitive Behavioral Therapy (CBT) and Dialectical Behavior Therapy (DBT) and their practitioners tend to avoid encounters with the unconscious. This is surprising, as unconscious demons are at the very core of Disorganized Attachment, the Borderline Personality Disorder and many other serious mental disorders. The bottom line, from our perspective, is that therapists can best help clients by doing unto themselves before doing unto others.

DOING UNTO MYSELF BEFORE DOING TO OTHERS

Given that up to eighty percent of those who have psychopathology and seek therapy have Disorganized Attachment (DA), there's a high probability that a comparable percent of therapists also have DA. This isn't an issue when therapists are committed to doing their own work—doing unto themselves before doing to others.

There's quite a variation in focus on self-healing among counselor education programs, whether it be for social workers or mental health counselors. In some universities, personal growth work is integrated into the curriculum and monitored—even mandating psychotherapy sessions outside the course work.

In other training programs, personal growth is encouraged, and in some there's no emphasis at all on personal growth. This variation in standards naturally produces a spectrum of mental health professionals who have varying levels of self-awareness and capabilities for working with clients who have experienced early and/or pervasive childhood trauma.

Ethically, mental health practitioners are bound to *do no harm*. Much of the harm that does happen in clinical practice is unintentional, and happens through the mechanism of countertransference. It can also occur through other unethical practices such as dual relationships.

Both are caused by unhealed wounded healers. This phenomenon is often activated by the Law of Attraction in which therapists attract clients who have wounds and issues similar to theirs. For this reason, it is really important that therapists do unto themselves before doing to others.

Much of the personal growth that therapists need to do for themselves involves healing what we call "soul wounds." Soul wounds are injuries that the eyes can't see, the mind can't explain, but that the heart feels. They cause a destructive unraveling in the core of children's being that affects their capacity for healthy adult relationships with others, especially parents and future spouses, and ultimately with God.

Those suffering from unhealed soul wounds find it difficult to be spontaneous and sufficiently open to experience and sustain intimacy in their adult relationships. They may desire intimacy, but the body memories of their soul woundings make them hypervigilant, rigid and controlling in intimate situations. They maintain protective defenses against re-experiencing the pain of the early traumas that interferes with intimacy.

These early relational or developmental traumas create a distorted perception about 1) who I am, 2) what is safe for me to say and do in my relationships with others, 3) what other persons will say and do to me, and 4) what will happen to me if I open to explore the world around me.

This distorted relational template, or Internal Working Model of Reality, consists of early feelings, thoughts and behaviors that are hard-wired into the nervous system by the age of three. Effective therapy seeks to change this template through a shared field of energy that modifies clients' Internal Working Model of Reality.

Change happens when clients are able to "upgrade" this template because the therapist's Internal Working Model is more organized and operates at a higher level of integrity. This requires therapists do the kind of in-depth, game-changing personal work that Carl Jung and Marsha Linehan did.

Having been practicing clinicians for many years, we came to recognize that life is our laboratory. Everywhere we go we find opportunities to work on ourselves. Twice we've lived for extended periods in other countries— once in Switzerland and once in Slovakia.

We also have traveled extensively and exposed ourselves to living in different cultures, a sure way to trigger shadow parts and wounds that are not visible in our home culture. We also moved to a different part of the country to live for eleven years, as a way of shedding old roles and "selves." This move enabled us to see how we coped with being outsiders and newcomers. These experiences revealed a lot of things about ourselves that we could never have seen by staying in the same place and interacting with the same circle of people.

We've also discovered that we are "shadow-busters," repeatedly finding ourselves involved with projects and people where there are shady or unethical things happening. Our "shadow-busting" experiences usually begin with a person or group with whom we have conflict about some practice or event that is questionable. Not being afraid of conflict, we have confronted the group or person directly and discovered that our experience has exposed the tip of a crooked iceberg.

Most interesting, though, was how each of these shadow-busting experiences revealed our own shadow parts. Janae actually wrote a book about this—*Con Job: How to Break Free of Con Artists, Sociopaths & Predators.*[167]

Using the wounded healer context is one way for therapists to work on themselves, seeing each client as a gift, using them as mirrors for parts of themselves. Identifying the mirrored parts early on in the therapist-client relationship is extremely important to avoid doing harm through projections and countertransference. Having a good clinical supervisor can help therapists find their way through these mirrored parts so that they truly heal both themselves and their clients.

DEVELOPMENTAL WOUNDS AS INITIATIONS TO THE MYTHIC REALMS

There often comes a point in people's lives where their suffering from unidentified and unhealed developmental wounds create a life crisis. The energy required to contain the compartmentalized memories, repressed emotions and dysfunctional relational patterns eventually builds to a crisis point. Like a growing snake, the internal tension reaches a place where it becomes intolerable, and the "old skin" of the Self splits. Gradually, the new Self emerges, but not without having a lot of pain, anxiety and fear.

This life crisis often happens around midlife, as it did with Carl Jung. Scholars suggest that Jung's childhood vulnerabilities compelled him to heal his own life.[168] Jung stated that "certain psychic disturbances can be extremely infectious if the doctor himself has a latent predisposition in that direction...For this reason he runs a risk - and must run it in the nature of things."

Further he stated that "it is no loss, either, if [the analyst] feels that the patient is hitting him, or even scoring off him: it is his own hurt that gives the measure of his power to heal."[169] Jung's closest colleague, Marie Louise von Franz, said "the wounded healer IS the archetype of the Self [our wholeness, the God within] and is at the bottom of all genuine healing procedures."[170]

By confronting our developmental wounds, we discover the part of ourselves that is not wounded. This part is whole and free of trauma imprints. Confronting our shadow frees us from being identified with its wounds as well as the victim consciousness associated with them. Yes, this is a bit paradoxical, but it changed our life-game and led us towards conscious awareness that made us more whole and awakened us to our core Self and the world.

Joseph Campbell, an American mythologist, drew on Jung's mythic approach to life, and created an archetypal story called *The Hero's Journey* that mapped what he called "the journey of transformation." Campbell found this journey was imbedded in all of the ancient myths, and considered it a universal experience for people developing conscious awareness.

Campbell's book, *The Hero with a Thousand Faces*, describes this mythic journey. The basic narrative of the journey is as follows:

> "A hero ventures forth from the world of common day into a region of supernatural wonder: fabulous forces are there encountered and a decisive victory is won: the hero comes back from this mysterious adventure with the power to bestow boons on his fellow man."[171]

The mythic journey of transformation has three distinct stages: the Departure, the Initiation and the Return. The Departure begins with *The Call to Awaken*, a situation that summons the budding hero into the unknown, into his unconscious. It is common for the journeyer to *Refuse the Call* because of fear, insecurity, and a sense of duty or obligation or a host of reasons that work to hold the person in his or her current circumstances.

Therefore, the prospective journeyer continues to be walled in boredom, hard work, obligations and victim consciousness, until a catalyzing event causes the dried skin of self to split. This crisis, which catapults the journeyer into the compartmentalized, Shadow parts to confront the unidentified, unhealed developmental wounds, marks the initiation stage.

The Initiation stage takes journeyers into the region of supernatural wonder, where they encounter fabulous forces within the unconscious mind. Like it or not, they have begun the quest for self-knowledge and self-awareness, leading them away from their known Selves and into their unknown, emerging Selves.

The Return stage requires traveling heroes to complete their journey, to bring the wisdom gained in the underworld back into the common day world and accept it as real. The goal is to function in both worlds and to be master of them both. This challenge continues for the rest of the journeyers' lives, as it is an ongoing process.

Therapists have an individual, life-long transformational journey, with many small ones inside the large cycle. Each new client brings information about their shadow parts, and the therapy experience can create full-blown a mini-journey for the therapist.

Experiences of depth psychology can be both very intense and very fulfilling for both clients and therapists. The deeper that therapists can go in clearing their developmental traumas and changing their life-games, the more organized their attachment strategy becomes, increasing their ability to help their clients organize. Most importantly, therapists are able to be present and to hold their connection to Source energy and *Presence*.

HEALING DNA THROUGH PRESENCE

A 2014 study published in *Psychotherapy and Psychosomatics* demonstrated that psychotherapy can heal DNA damage caused by traumatic stress.[172] Previous research has revealed how traumatic stress may damage DNA and DNA repair mechanisms, leading to an increased risk for numerous diseases, including cancer and heart disease.

The authors of the study assessed DNA breakage in cells from individuals with post-traumatic stress disorder (PTSD) and measured the cellular capacity to repair DNA breaks after exposure to radiation. They further investigated the effect of psychotherapy on both DNA breakage and DNA repair. The study concluded that psychotherapy worked not only to reverse the symptoms of PTSD, but also to heal DNA damage caused by traumatic stress. This research provides significant new evidence on the impact of trauma on the body and provides insights into new strategies for helping those suffering from the effects of trauma.

The thing that this study doesn't discuss is exactly *what* in the psychotherapy process causes the damaged DNA to repair itself. We believe that it is the subtle and invisible communication that happens between clients and therapists called *Presence*.

Language from quantum sciences best captures experiences of *presence*: resonance, attunement, and synchrony. These words describe a sensory experience of being connected to or immersed in a field of unconditional love or positive regard. In such experiences, people are open to what's happening as it happens, and feel calm, centered, filled, peaceful and safe. Their bodies relax as their cells open to receive this nurturing energy. Some say they feel connected to the Divine and describe *Presence* as a spiritual communion with God.

People who embody Presence often seem to glow, radiating love and compassion. When they speak, others feel seen, heard and felt. Even when in a large group, they feel this "present person" is speaking to them personally. This is because Presence is an open receptive state in which people can merge energy fields and experience oneness. The most common human experience of Presence comes during encounters with newborn babies who carry the energy and imprint of the Divine. This is why people love to meet and hold newborns!

Presence is a state of being that allows the linking of a wide range of differentiated aspects of our lives into a harmonious and ever-emerging whole.

Presence permits integration to unfold. In addition, integration is at the heart of well-being, even at the level of our cellular functions.

According to Dan Siegel, *Presence* allows a person with DA to consolidate fragmented self-parts into an ever emerging whole.[173] It facilitates the integration of cellular functions, multiple parts of the brain and the Mind-BodySpirit. This integration is visible in a person's expanded capacity to experience and express kindness, compassion, wisdom and connection, as they move towards an emerging sense of wholeness.

So, how do therapists cultivate their capacity for holding and emanating Presence? Primarily by healing and clearing their own developmental traumas. What heals a person, particularly someone with DA, is someone having a "felt experience" of them. Feeling "felt" is a whole-body sensation that comes from another person feeling what we feel—a compassionate, empathic, emotionally attuned experience of communion and connection.

We and many of our colleagues have experienced entering a therapy session and not feeling centered or emotionally balanced, then emerging from it feeling much happier and more whole. We know it is because Presence entered our shared field of energy, and affected us both.

Nature is also a great supplier of Presence. Walking on the Earth, soaking up sunshine, listening to birdcalls, sitting by the beach or in the deep woods, all help to connect us to something larger than ourselves. The silence of Nature quiets our minds and restores our soul.

Spending time in nature and with small children and pets also connects us to Presence. All contain unbounding unconditional love and compassion, opening our hearts and calming our nervous systems.

SURRENDER TO PRESENCE

In spite of the availability of meditation, Nature, children and pets, some people find it difficult to allow Presence in. This is primarily because they have closed hearts because of childhood trauma—hearts that are like doors locked from the inside. What to do? The answer is *surrender*.

Surrender has two sides—a masculine and a feminine. You need skills in both to allow Presence in your life. The feminine side of surrender is your ability to receive energy and information from outside of you without resistance or judgment. It is the ability to listen, see and accept others exactly as they are without resisting any part of them. This means giving up the wish that others would change to make you happy.

It also means accepting a fundamental truth: people are not going to change unless *they* want to. Mastering the feminine side of surrender also requires seeing yourself the same way. If you over-develop your feminine side, you remain open to receiving everything, but cannot use any of what you receive to help you organize and direct your life.

Being open to receive Presence also requires skills in the masculine side of surrender. This is the willingness to take charge of your life without guilt or shame, including taking charge of opening your heart to Presence. It means giving up the fear of being rejected or not loved because you become independent. If you over-develop the masculine side of surrender, you may be able to take charge of your life, but will find it difficult to allow Presence in.

Ideally, you need skills in both of these masculine and feminine forms of surrender, and the ability to use them when you need them. Using your masculine and feminine skills in surrendering creates profound advances in your consciousness that create cooperative, loving, sustainable relationships.

Our clients often ask us when they will know they are through with therapy. We tell them that when they can ask for what they want directly and people they ask are delighted to give them what they ask, they don't need any further therapy. In order to be able to do that, clients need to integrate both the feminine and the masculine forms of surrender.

LIFE IS... WHAT WE MAKE OF IT

One of our favorite fables about making meaning of life is the story of the Chinese Farmer.[174]

> *There is a Chinese story of an old farmer who had an old horse for tilling his fields. One day the horse escaped into the hills and, when all the farmer's neighbors sympathized with the old man over his bad luck, the farmer replied, 'Bad luck? Good luck? Who knows?'*
> *A week later the horse returned with a herd of wild horses from the hills and this time the neighbors congratulated the farmer on his good luck. His reply was, 'Good luck? Bad luck? Who knows?'*
> *Then, when the farmer's son attempted to tame one of the wild horses, he fell off its back and broke his leg. Everyone thought this very bad luck. Not the farmer, whose only reaction was, 'Bad luck? Good luck? Who knows?'*
> *Some weeks later the army marched into the village and conscripted every able-bodied youth they found there. When they saw the farmer's*

son with his broken leg they let him off. Now was that good luck? Bad luck? Who knows?

The moral of this story is that life is an integrated process with immense complexity. Therefore, it's really impossible to know whether an event or experience is good or bad, because it's not possible to know in the moment if the long-term consequences will be good fortune or misfortune. The best that we can do is to trust the process, accept what comes without judgment, and stay open to giving and receiving unconditional love.

(This page intentionally left blank)

CHAPTER FIFTEEN

THE FUTURE OF THE MENTAL HEALTH PROFESSION

We are still the masters of our fate.
The future cannot be predicted, but futures can be invented.
It was man's ability to invent which has
made human society what it is.

—Dennis Gabor

ON PREDICTING OR INVENTING THE FUTURE

It has always been difficult to predict the future because no one has been there yet. What most people do is look at where they are in present time, where they have been in the past, and then try to make some educated guesses about future trends. It does seem that many prognosticators have tried to predict the future over the years. Some have become famous. Think Nostradamus. Maybe it is a wishful endeavor that gives us all some hope for a future that we can all enjoy.

For many reasons, we believe that mental health professionals are in a unique position to invent the future of our profession. One reason for our optimism is that we have more experience in looking back than most people. Barry took his first counseling class in 1957, and Janae took her first mental health class in 1964.

We have also witnessed and analyzed the many changes in the mental health profession over the course of our profession. We also have taken a long where the profession is now, so we are willing to risk predicting the future of the U. S. mental health profession. Let's begin with how the profession started and where it is today.

A BRIEF HISTORY OF THE COUNSELING PROFESSION

The counseling profession is still young. In the sections below, we identify some of the people and events that have helped shape it.

Early History of Mental Illness.[175] Some ancient cultures viewed mental illness as a form of religious punishment or demonic possession. In ancient Egyptian, Indian, Greek, and Roman writings, mental illness was categorized as a religious or personal problem. In the 5th century B.C., the Greek physician, Hippocrates, became a pioneer in treating mentally ill people with techniques not rooted in religion or superstition. Instead, he focused on changing a mentally ill patient's environment or occupation, or administering certain substances as medications.

During the Middle Ages, the mentally ill were believed to be possessed of demons and in need of religion. Earlier in U. S. history, these religious attitudes led to stigmatization of mental illness, and unhygienic (and often degrading) confinement of mentally ill individuals in mental hospitals. While there are still negative attitudes towards mental illness, today in the US, we are making progress on this.

Mental Health Hospitals and Deinstitutionalization. In the 1840s, activist Dorothea Dix lobbied for better living conditions for the mentally ill after witnessing the dangerous and unhealthy conditions in which many patients were forced to live. Over a 40-year period, Dix successfully persuaded the U.S. government to fund the building of 32 state psychiatric hospitals. Although institutionalized care increased patient access to mental health services, the state hospitals were often underfunded and understaffed, and the institutional care system drew harsh criticism following a number of high-profile reports of poor living conditions and human rights violations.

By the mid-1950s, a push for deinstitutionalization and outpatient treatment began in many countries. The closure of state psychiatric hospitals in the United States was codified by the Community Mental Health Centers Act of 1963, and strict standards were passed so that only individuals "who posed an imminent danger to themselves or someone else" could be committed to state psychiatric hospitals.

In place of institutionalized care, outpatient community-based mental health care was developed to include a range of treatment facilities, from community mental health centers and smaller supervised residential homes to community-based psychiatric teams. This also led to the widespread use of psychotropic drugs to regulate the behavior of those diagnosed with a mental illness.

Most counseling sessions consisted of talking as a form of treatment for emotional problems. This was usually practiced in the form of giving advice and information. Early counseling professionals actually called themselves teachers and social advocates. Their areas of focus mostly involved child welfare, education, employment guidance, and legal reform.

Sigmund Freud. The modern approach to counseling actually began in 1896 in Vienna, when the Sigmund Freud, created "psychoanalysis." It began a form of therapy for those with serious internal, emotional conflicts. Psychotherapy at that time focused on a person's unconscious and was based on Freud's belief that mental illness was the result of repressed memories and emotions. The treatment that Freud came up with he called "free association."

He had patients lie on a couch and talk about whatever came into their mind. He believed this helped him access to their repressed memories and emotions. He reasoned that bringing these unconscious repressed memories to conscious awareness by the patient would lead to a cure. As his approach was practiced, patients required long-term therapy in order to bring up all the repressed memories contained in the unconscious.

Early Counseling Pioneers.[176] In the early 1900s, three people stand out as pioneers in the advancement of counseling. The first was Frank Parsons, regarded as the father of the vocational guidance movement. He founded Boston's Vocational Bureau in 1908, which was a major step in the institutionalization of vocational guidance. The second was Jesse B. Davis who created the first systematized vocational guidance programs in public schools which was the precursor to school guidance counseling programs. Finally, Clifford Beers' report of his own battle with mental illness and depression exposed the poor conditions of mental institutions in his book, *A Mind That Found Itself* in 1908. He founded Mental Health America (MHA) in 1909 to help change the poor conditions in mental hospitals.

Setting the Groundwork for The Profession. As the vocational guidance movement began to take root in the early 1900s. There were two important benchmarks that helped spread its practice and legitimacy. The first happened in 1913, when the National Vocational Guidance Association (NVGA) was founded. It was the forerunner of today's American Counseling Association. The second, the Smith-Hughes Act, happened in 1917, and provided funding to public schools for vocational education. In addition, after WWI, several of the psychological screening devices for personnel used by the Army were introduced in civilian populations. This led to a raised awareness of how psychological testing could be used as part of vocational counseling.

Vocational Counseling Evolves with the Great Depression. In 1929, Abraham and Hannah Stone started the first marriage and family-counseling center in New York City. It marked the beginning of a broader approach to counseling during the 1930s when the Great Depression sparked a change in the counseling methods related to employment.

E.G. Williamson, at the University of Minnesota, developed the first theory of counseling to work with students and the unemployed by emphasizing a directive, counselor-centered approach known as trait-factor theory. Finally, in 1939, the U.S. Employment Service was established. They published the first edition of the Dictionary of Occupational Titles (DOT) as a source of career information for vocational guidance specialists.

This theory later spawned a number of tests to diagnose various personality traits in clients. The first was the Strong Vocational Interest Blank (SVIB) developed in 1927 by University of Minnesota psychologist E.K. Strong, Jr. He created it primarily to help people exiting the military find suitable jobs. It was revised later by Jo-Ida Hansen, and David Campbell, one of Strong's students, at the University of Minnesota and published as the Strong-Campbell Vocational Interest Inventory. The modern version is based on the typology of psychologist John L. Holland' called Holland Codes.

Next diagnostic test was the Minnesota Multi-Phasic Personality Inventory (MMPI), first published by the University of Minnesota Press in 1943. It was replaced by an updated version, the MMPI-2, in 1989. A version for adolescents, the MMPI-A, was published in 1992. An alternative version of the test, the MMPI-2 Restructured Form (MMPI-2-RF), was published in 2008. The next instrument created at the University of Minnesota was the Miller Analogy Test, which along with the GRE is still used as part of the admission process for graduate school.

Guidance and Counseling Takes Hold. In 1942, Carl Rogers, at the University of Wisconsin, gained notoriety after publishing his book *Counseling and Psychotherapy*. He emphasized the "personhood" of the client, and a nondirective, person-centered, approach to counseling. His theory was controversial because it was based on a belief that clients could participate in and be held responsible for their growth.

He felt clients would better understand themselves if they felt accepted and heard by their therapists. His theory emphasized the importance of building a relationship with clients in counseling sessions, and created a clear delineation between guidance and counseling. Guidance focused on giving individuals information to help them identify what they value most, while counseling focused on helping clients apply the information so they make changes in their lives.

In 1946, President Harry Truman signed the National Mental Health Act, which created the National Institute of Mental Health and allocated government funds towards research into the causes of and treatments for mental illness. In 1963, Congress passed the Mental Retardation Facilities and Community Health Centers Construction Act, which provided federal funding for the development of community-based mental health services. The National Alliance for the Mentally Ill (NAMI) was founded in 1979 to provide "support, education, advocacy, and research services for people with serious psychiatric illnesses"

WWII Increased Government Involvement in Counseling. Because of the country's involvement in WWII, the U.S. government began to identify counselors and psychologists to train specialists to work with the military. In 1946, the George-Barden Act further promoted counseling by providing funding for vocational education for counseling training institutes for returning veterans. The Veterans Administration (VA) also funded counselor and psychologist training and was responsible for coining the term "counseling psychologist."

1950s: A Profound Decade of Change for Counseling. The American Personnel and Guidance Association (APGA) was founded in 1952. It formally organized groups interested in guidance, counseling, and personnel matters. The APGA Division of Counseling Psychology was also created in 1952 out of interest in expanding the client base of clinical psychologists. In 1953, the American School Counselor Association (ASCA) was chartered.

When Barry first began his career and lived in Pennsylvania, there was an extreme shortage of school guidance counselors. So, the state legislature passed a law that allowed some Teacher's Colleges to offer an undergraduate minor in Guidance Counseling that led to state certification as a School

Guidance Counselor. Millersville State Teachers College, where he got his undergraduate degree, was awarded one of these programs.

Barry was a sophomore studying to become a high school social studies teacher when this law passed, so he applied for and was accepted into the undergraduate guidance counselor minor. He graduated from Millersville State Teachers College with certification as a secondary school guidance counselor in 1959. In 1962, after three years as a high school social studies teacher, he became guidance counselor in the Middle School in the district where he taught.

National Defense Education Act (NDEA) of 1958 increased funding so that school counseling programs could give counselors additional training. This act followed the Soviet launch of the Sputnik satellite. The objective was to train more school guidance counselors so they could "counsel" more students to enter the field of engineering. The so-called "space race" began, and counselors were viewed as part of the launching pad.

NDEA began providing scholarship funding to selected universities to train more school guidance counselors. Barry applied for one of these scholarships and was accepted into an M.A. program at the University of Minnesota in 1963. In 1968, he received his Ph.D. from the University's APA approved Counseling Psychology program.

The Emergence of New Counseling Theories. Before the 1950s, there were four main counseling theories: 1.) psychoanalysis (Sigmund Freud), 2.) trait-factor and directive theories (E.G. Williamson), 3.) humanistic, and client-centered theories (Carl Rogers), and 4.) behavioral theories (B.F. Skinner). In the early 60's new theories began to emerge, such as systematic desensitization (Joseph Wolfe), rational-emotive (RE) therapy (Albert Ellis), transactional analysis (TA) (Eric Berne), and cognitive theory (Aaron Beck).

Counseling Becomes a Developmental Profession. Gilbert Wrenn at the University of Minnesota wrote an influential book *The Counselor in a Changing World* in the early 1960s. It focused the profession on working together to help counselors identify and resolve people's developmental needs, helping it take on a developmental focus.

In 1963, the U. S. government passed the Community Mental Health Centers Act. It authorized the establishment of mental health centers and paved the way for counseling careers in addiction and alcohol abuse counseling. The Education Resource Information Center Clearinghouse (ERIC) on Counseling and Personnel Services was founded in 1966, and became one of the largest, most used resources on counseling trends and activities throughout the world.

Diversification in Counseling. Title IX legislation and the affirmative action and anti-discrimination legislation passed in the 1970's. They provided funding for specialized counselor training so they could better assess and address clients' different needs. During this time period, mental health clinics, hospices, employee assistance programs, psychiatric hospitals, and rehabilitation centers began to employ counselors. Returning veterans from the Vietnam War received counseling for PTSD for the first time. In 1980, PTSD was added as a diagnostic category in the DSM III-R.

In 1973, the Association of Counselor Educators and Supervisors (ACES) was established and set the standards for master's degree programs in counseling. Virginia became the first state to adopt a professional counselor licensure law in 1976. By the dawning of the new millennium, 44 other states and the District of Columbia had followed suit. Virginia initially passed counselor licensure legislation, while counselors in California, Hawaii, Minnesota, Nevada, New York and Puerto Rico were still struggling to achieve recognition.

Judith Ritterman, executive director of the New York Mental Health Counselors Association, worked for 11 years on the effort in New York before a bill passed through the state Legislature in 2002. Now all 50 states, the District of Columbia and Puerto Rico have licensure for professional counselors

In 1976 the American Mental Health Counseling Association (AMHCA) was formed. As a professional association, AMHCA affiliated with APGA (a precursor to the American Counseling Association [ACA]) as a division in 1978; in 1998, AMHCA became a separate not-for profit organization, but retained its status as a division of ACA.

1980s: Standardization of Training, Certification, and Human Development. The National Board for Certified Counselors (NBCC) formed in 1982, and began offering counselor certification on a national level. During this decade, standardized tests were developed that counselors had to pass in order to become a National Certified Counselor.

Counselor training curricula also began to include developmental counseling over the course of the lifespan. It often included Erik Erikson's work on life-stage development. It also expanded to include gender issues, sexual preferences, and moral development. This increased the need for specialized training in working with different cultural groups. We began our study of developmental or relational trauma during this same period.

The Counseling Profession in the 1990s. Counseling was first included in the health care human resource statistics as a primary mental health profession in 1992 by the Center for Mental Health Services and the National Institute of Mental Health. This effectively placed counseling in the same professional categories as psychology, social work, and psychiatry.

During that same year, Derald Wing Sue, Patricia Arredondo, and Roderick J. McDavis established the competencies and standards for multicultural counseling, opening a larger debate about the nature of counseling. Counselors began giving more consideration to the social factors that contribute to mental illness. These factors included, spirituality, family environment, socioeconomic considerations, impact of groups, and overall prevention.

Trends for The Counseling Profession in the 21st Century. After the Columbine Massacre in Colorado, the Oklahoma City bombing, and the September 11 attacks, counselors began to focus on safety and larger social issues from the perspective of prevention and treatment. This increased emphasis on trauma and tragic events continued following Hurricane Katrina, the Iraq and Afghanistan wars, and the Virginia Tech shootings.

The counseling community began creating crisis plans for working with the aftermath of disasters. Counselors received training in how to work with different age groups to provide disaster support and treatment for event traumas. Counselors learned how to properly facilitate grieving and healing interventions, with a renewed emphasis on acute stress disorder (ASD) and post-traumatic stress disorder (PTSD).

Bessel van der Kolk and his team of researchers at Harvard began talking about acute or complex trauma. They were, as we said earlier, not successful in their attempts to get the diagnosis of Developmental Trauma Disorder added to the DSM-5 in 2013.

What Does the Future Hold for The Counseling Profession? Looking to the future, the idea of wellness is gaining traction as a way for counselors to promote a "positive state of well-being." In addition, emerging technology is increasing the profession's community outreach, public policy making, and interactions between counselors and clients.

As a profession, we are in a transition period. Its rather antiquated treatment models are being questioned by therapists themselves. Some of the more conscious practitioners are asking: Is this the best, most efficient and most effective way to treat my clients? Many are saying, "no," but do not have training to do anything else.

Is the Tail Wagging the Dog? Currently, the professional organizations, the accreditation agencies and the actual counselor training institutions are locked in a paradigm that Bessel van der Kolk says, "....is training people to do malpractice."[177] Because the professional organizations also control the accreditation agencies, they dictate to the colleges and universities offering counselor-training degrees the content in these training programs.

There is virtually nothing in the CACREP accredited counselor training curriculum that would make graduates of these programs "trauma-informed," let alone have "trauma proficient skills." This means they are not prepared to meet the challenges that their clients are bringing to them. Most CACREP approved programs offer nothing related to the developmental, inherited or complicated categories of trauma.

The 2016 CACREP Standards require the following to be offered in the area of Human Growth and Development: "effects of crisis, disasters, and trauma on diverse individuals across the lifespan."4 However, most graduates of CACREP Approved Programs who have come to our TIC trainings complain that their training in trauma was too general and lacks depth.

Many counselor training programs emphasize Cognitive Behavioral Theory and therapy because it is the easiest to teach. This means that CACREP approved graduates are more likely use this approach for every problem they encounter, including developmental trauma. This can turn them into being technicians, who have one tool for fixing all problems.

Cognitive behavioral techniques can be useful in helping change distorted beliefs related developmental trauma. While cognitive behavioral therapy is believed to have strong evidence-based research that supports it, a close examination of evidence is not convincing. A review of the CBT research revealed some serious flaws:

- Assessment of the long-term outcome of a randomized controlled study of the use of CBT for anxiety disorders showed that patients with PTSD fared particularly poorly.
- Treatment with CBT had a better long-term outcome than non-CBT in terms of overall symptom severity, but didn't change in clients' diagnostic status.
- Positive outcomes for CBT in the original trial were not supported in follow-up studies.

- CBT costs more than non-CBT treatments, which have slightly higher benefits.
- There was insufficient evidence for the effectiveness of trauma-focused CBT in traumatized populations who didn't have an acute stress disorder diagnosis.
- Many of the studies had large unaccounted-for dropouts of participants.
- Most research studies compared CBT against a wait group that did not receive any treatment protocol.
- Comparison studies showed those conducting the comparison treatments were often not trained to conduct that treatment.[178]
- Almost no research involved treatment of childhood trauma.

The Winds of Change Are Blowing. We have known for some time that young children are acutely susceptible to trauma. The rates of abuse and neglect among this population are staggering. However, there are elements of our adult population that refuse to look at their childhood. The prevailing myth that is still strong today is that you can leave behind whatever happened to you as a child when you became an adult. Back in the 80's the False Memory Society tried to convince us that whatever adults are saying about their childhood is just their imagination.

In the mid 90s we saw the beginning of the ACE research that links later physical and mental health problems to adverse childhood experiences. This is a promising set of over 80 studies showing the link. It helps validate what we found clinically in our work with adults. This research also can provide a strong basis for integrative medicine that combines the treatment of mind and bodies. Next, we have to integrate the spiritual dimension as well.

While the profession has moved past the myths of the past about 'False Memories,' remnants still exist in this country. There also are people who are lumping "re-birthing" and other experimental and experiential approaches to healing early attachment disorders together with more traditional models for treating attachment disorders. The traditionalists reject the experiential and experimental methods for treating and healing developmental trauma. For example, we know several highly trained therapists who use various forms of "holding therapies," and find them highly effective in truly helping adopted children from other countries and cultures with severe attachment disorders.

Despite decades of statistical data, counselors still have limited knowledge about the impact of traumatic events on younger children.[179] Reasons for this disparity in knowledge include an historical resistance to the idea that early childhood mental health is important, and they have concerns about diagnosing young children with mental disorders.

Because most counselors are not trained to treat the long-term effects of developmental trauma, they tend to ignore even the most obvious symptoms. For example, counselors who treat couples involved in domestic violence often fail to ask if they have suffered trauma from witnessing it as children.

The latest evidence that the winds of change are blowing stronger is the attempt by several national organizations including federal government agencies to promote the notion that everybody needs to be trauma-informed. SAMHSA is one of the leading governmental agencies addressing the impact of trauma on individuals, families, and communities.[180] SAMHSA has made many contributions in key areas through a series of significant initiatives over the past decade. These contributions include:

- The development and promotion of new trauma-specific interventions,
- the expansion of trauma-informed care training, and
- the consideration of trauma and its behavioral health effects across health and social service delivery systems.

The National Council on Behavior Health is also promoting trauma-informed care, and other groups such as the National Child Traumatic Stress Network now provide resources in the form of mini-grants, articles and multi-media courses to help educate both professionals and non-professionals on the standards of trauma-informed care.

Here is what NCBH says on its website: "A trauma-informed child-and family-service system is one in which all parties involved recognize and respond to the impact of traumatic stress on those who have contact with the system including children, caregivers, and service providers. Programs and agencies within such a system infuse and sustain trauma awareness, knowledge, and skills into their organizational cultures, practices, and policies. They act in collaboration with all those who are involved with the child, using the best available science, to facilitate and support the recovery and resiliency of the child and family."[181]

NCBH describes a service system with a trauma-informed perspective as one in which programs, agencies, and service providers:

(1) routinely screen for trauma exposure and related symptoms;
(2) use culturally appropriate evidence-based assessment and treatment for traumatic stress and associated mental health symptoms;

(3) make resources available to children, families, and providers on trauma exposure, its impact, and treatment.

(4) engage in efforts to strengthen the resilience and protective factors of children and families impacted by and vulnerable to trauma;

(5) address parent and caregiver trauma and its impact on the family system;

(6) emphasize continuity of care and collaboration across child-service systems.

(7) maintain an environment of care for staff that addresses, minimizes, and treats secondary traumatic stress, and that increases staff resilience.[182]

Another national player is the National Technical Assistance for Children's Mental Health at Georgetown University. They provide resources on their website to help educate the general public on trauma-informed care.[183]

SUMMARY

Based on how rapidly things are changing in the mental health profession, we predict that all states will have statewide trauma-informed initiatives within five years. Like other grass-roots efforts, it will require that consumers of mental health services demand this kind of care. We also believe that counselors and social workers who want to deliver quality mental health services to victims of childhood trauma, will personally seek trauma-informed care training and push their local, state and national organizations to integrate it into their models of service delivery.

NOTES

INTRODUCTION

1. Van der Kolk, B. (2005). Developmental trauma disorder: A new rational diagnosis for children with complex trauma histories. *Psychiatric annals*, 35, pp. 401-408.

2. Schore, A. (2003b). *Affect regulation and the repair of the self*. New York: W. W. Norton.

3. Siegel, D. (2012). *The developing mind* (2nd Ed.), pp. 28 – 29. New York: Guilford.

CHAPTER ONE

4. Scott, W. J., 1990. PTSD in DSM-III: A case in the politics of diagnoses and disease. *Social Problems*. 37 (3).

5. Kral, V.A. (1951). Psychiatric observations under severe chronic stress. *Am. J. Psychiatry* 108: 185–192.

6. Selye, H. (1956). Stress and psychiatry. *Am. J. Psychiatry* 113: 423–427.

7. Fenichel, O. 1996. *The psychoanalytic theory of neurosis*, 2nd ed. London: Routledge.

8. Scott, W. J., 1990. PTSD in DSM-III: A case in the politics of diagnoses and disease. *Social problems*. 37 (3).

9. Herman, J. (1992). *Trauma and recovery*. New York: Basic Books.

10. Ibid.

11. Weinhold, J. (2017). *LOVEvolution: A heart-centered approach for healing developmental trauma*. Colorado Springs, CO: CICRCL Press.

CHAPTER TWO

12. SAMHSA News. (Spring, 1914). Vol. 22, #2. http://www.samhsa.gov/samhsaNews-Letter/Volume_22_Number_2/trauma_tip/

13. SAMSHA. (2014). ZU. S. Department of Health and Human Services, Substance Abuse and Mental Health Services Administration, Center for Substance Abuse Treatment. Washington, D.C.

14. Retrieved August 23, 2015 from http://www.thenationalcouncil.org/topics/trauma-informed-care/.

15. Retrieved August 23, 2015 from http://www.thenationalcouncil.org/topics/trauma-informed-care/.

16. Retrieved August 23, 2015 from http://gucchdtacenter.georgetown.edu/TraumaInformedCare/.

17. Retrieved August 23, 2015 from https://www.google.com/?gws_rd=ssl#q=trauma-informed+care+state+initiatives.

18. (2014).Trauma-Informed Care in Behavioral Health Services, *Treatment Improvement Protocol (TIP) Series, No. 57*, Center for Substance Abuse Treatment (US). Rockville, MD.

19. Weinhold, B. & Weinhold, J. (2008a). *Breaking free of the co-dependency trap.* Novato, CA: New World Library.

20. Weinhold, J. and Weinhold, B. (2008b). *The flight from intimacy.* Novato, CA: New World Library.

21. Feletti, V., Anda, R., et. al. (1998). Relationship of childhood abuse and household dysfunction to many of the leading causes of death in adults: the adverse childhood experiences (ace) study. *Ma. J. Prev. Med.* 13(4). Pp. 245-256.

22. Centers for Disease Control and Prevention, (2010). "Adverse Childhood Experiences Reported by Adults --- Five States, 2009." *Morbidity and Mortality Weekly Report.* Atlanta, GA.

23. Weinhold, B. and Weinhold, J. (2010). *Conflict Resolution: The Partnership Way.* Denver: Love Publishing, pp. 115-136.

24. Weinhold, J. (2017). *Op.Cit,* pp. 103-105.

25. Weinhold, J. (2017). *Op.Cit.*

CHAPTER THREE

26. van der Kolk, B. , McFarlane, A. & Weisaeth, L. (1996). *Traumatic stress: The overwhelming experience on mind, body and society.* New York: Guilford, p. 4.

27. Porges, S. (2003). Social engagement and attachment: A phylogenetic perspective. In J. A. King, C. F. Ferris & I. I. Lederhendler (Eds.) *The roots of mental illness in children.* New York: New York Academy of Sciences.

28. Roque L1, Veríssimo M, Oliveira TF, Oliveira RF, (2012). Attachment security and HPA axis reactivity to positive and challenging emotional situations in child-mother dyads in naturalistic settings. *Developmental psychobiology.* May;54(4):401-11. doi: 10.1002/dev.20598. Epub 2011 Aug 23.

29. Weinhold, J. & Weinhold, B. (2011). *Op. Cit.*, p. 160.

30. Schore, A. (2004, August 30). "Raising baby: What you need to know." *Psychology Today.* Retrieved December 10, 2017 from https://www.psychologytoday.com/articles/200007/raising-baby-what-you-need-know.

31. Ibid.

32. Niehoff, D. (2002). *The biology of violence: How understanding the brain, behavior, and environment can break the vicious cycle of aggression.* New York: The Free Press.

33. Goleman, D. (1996). *Emotional intelligence.* New York: Bantam, p. 50.

34. van der Kolk, B. (1988). The trauma spectrum: The interaction of biological and social events in the genesis of the trauma response. *Journal of Traumatic Stress.* 1(3), pp. 273–290.

35. Wilson, J. L. (2001). *Adrenal Fatigue: The 21st Century Stress Syndrome.* Petaluma, CA: Smart Publications.

36. Zodkoy, S. (2014). *Misdiagnosed: The Adrenal Fatigue Link.* Waitsfield, VT: Babypie Publishing.

37. Kolk, B. , McFarlane, A. & Weisaeth, L. (1996). *Traumatic stress: The overwhelming experience on mind, body and society.* New York: Guilford, pp. 369–370.

38. Ibid. p. 371.

39. Cole, P. & Putnam, F. (April 1992). Effect of incest on self and social functioning: A developmental psychopathology perspective. *Journal of Consulting and Clinical Psychology,* Vol. 60(2), pp. 174-184.

40. Scaer, R. (2001). The Neurophysiology of dissociation & chronic disease. *Applied Psychophysiology and Biofeedback,* 26(1), p. 73.

41. *The Adverse Childhood Experiences Study.* http://www.acestudy.org. Retrieved August 29. 2015.

42. Violato, C. & Russell, C (1994, July 1). *Effects of non-maternal care on child development: A meta-analysis of published research.* Poster session presented at the 55th Annual Convention of the Canadian Psychological Association, Penticon, B. C. Canada.

43. Bureau of Labor Statistics. (2008). Employment characteristics of families summary, Washington, D. C.: U. S. Department of Labor.

44. Schore, A. (2003a). *Affect regulation and disorders of the self.* New York: W. W. Norton, p. 77.

45. Kammerman, S. B. (2000). From maternity to parental leave policies: Women's health, employment and child and family well-being. *The Journal of the American Women's Medical Association,* 55, p. 97.

46. Waldfogel, J. (2001). *What children need: (The family and public policy).* Cambridge, MA: President and Fellows of Harvard University. p. 29.

47. Nelson C. & Luciana, M. (Eds.). (2008). *Handbook of developmental cognitive neuroscience.* Cambridge, MA: MIT Press, p. 73.

CHAPTER FOUR

48. Weinhold, J. & Weinhold, B. (2010). *Healing developmental trauma: A systems approach to counseling individuals, couples and families.* Denver: Love Publishing.

49. Wylie, Mary Sykes (2010). "The Long Shadow of Trauma," *Psychotherapy Networker,* March/April.

50. van der Kolk, B., quoted in "The Long Shadow of Trauma," *Psychotherapy Networker,* March/April.

51. Stolbach, B. 2007. "Developmental trauma disorder: A new diagnosis for children affected by complex trauma. *International Society for the Study of Trauma and Dissociation News*, Vol. 25 No.6, pp. 4-6

52. Wylie, Mary Sykes (2013). "Developmental trauma disorder: Distinguishing, diagnosing and the DSM." *Psychotherapy Networker*. Retrieved December 10, 2017 from https://www.psychotherapynetworker.org/blog/details/35/developmental-trauma-disorder-distinguishing-diagnosing

53. Ibid, p. 9.

54. Schore, A. (2012). *Emotional revolution in a cognitive world*. Retrieved December 1, 2017 from https://www.tendingsouls.com/2012/08/08/emotional-revolution-in-a-cognitive-world/.

55. Ryan, R (2007). "A new look and approach for two reemerging fields," *Motivation and emotion: 31:1-3*.

56. Wylie, Mary Sykes (2011). "The attuned therapist: Does attachment theory really matter?" *Psychotherapy Networker*, March/April.

57. Weinhold, J. (2018). *LOVEvolution: A heart-centered approach for healing developmental trauma*. Colorado Springs, CO: CICRCL Press.

58. Siegel, D. (2012). *The developing mind: How relationships and the brain interact to shape who we are*. New York: Guilford Press, p. 74.

59. van der Kolk, B. (2014). "Psychotherapy in the spotlight." *Psychotherapy Networker*. Retrieved December 1, 2017 from https://www.psychotherapynetworker.org/blog/details/360/bessel-van-der-kolk-takes-on-the-new-york-times.

60. Van der Kolk, B., quoted in Wylie, Mary Sykes (2010). "The Long Shadow of Trauma," Psychotherapy Networker, March/April, p. 9

61. Ibid, p. 10.

CHAPTER FIVE

62. Siegel, Dan (2012). *The Developing Mind*, New York: Guilford Press, p. 91.

63. Weinhold, B. and Weinhold. J. (2010). *Conflict resolution: The partnership way, 2ⁿᵈ Edition*. Denver, CO: Love Publishing.

64. Ainsworth, M. & Bell, S. (1970). Attachment, exploration, and separation: Illustrated by the behavior of one-year-olds in a strange situation. Child Development, 41, 49-67.

65. Main, M. & Solomon, J. (1986). "Discovery of a new, insecure-disorganized/disoriented attachment pattern." In M. Yogman & T. B. Brazelton (Eds.), *Affective development in infancy*. Norwood, NJ: Ablex, pp. 95–124.

66. Main, M. (1995). "Recent studies in attachment: Overview with selected implications for clinical social work." In S. Goldberg, R. Muir, & J. Kerr (Eds.), *Attachment theory* (pp. 407-474). Hillsdale, NJ: The Analytic Press.

67. Belsky, J. (2005). "The developmental and evolutionary psychology of intergenerational transmission of attachment." In C. S. Carter, L. Ahnert, K. E. Grossman, S. B.

Hardy, M. E. Lamb, S. W. Porges, & N. Sachser (Eds.), *Attachment and bonding: A new synthesis* (pp. 169-198). Cambridge, MA: The MIT Press.

68. Main, M. (1995). Attachment: Overview, with implications for clinical work. In S Goldberg, R. Muir & J. Kerr (Eds.) *Attachment theory: Social, developmental, and clinical perspectives* (pp. 407-474. Hillsdale, NJ: Analytic Press.

69. Siegel, D. (2012). *The Developing Mind, 2nd Ed.* New York: Guilford Press, p. 100.

70. Mahler, M., Pine, F. & Bergman, F. (1975). *Psychological birth or the human infant: Symbiosis and individuation.* New York: Basic Books.

CHAPTER SIX

71. Weinhold, J. (2018). *Op.Cit.*, p. 44-46.

72. Klaus, M. (1995). *Importance of post-natal relationships.* Speech given at the 7th International Congress of the Association for Pre-natal and Perinatal   Psychology and Health.

73. Gutmann G. (1987). Blocked atlantal nerve syndrome in infants and small children. Originally published in *Manuelle Medizine*, Springer-Verlag. English translation published in *International Review of Chiropractic*, July/Aug 1990.

74. Schore, A. (1999). *Affect regulation and the origin of the self: The neurobiology of emotional development.* Hillsdale, NJ: Lawrence Erlbaum Associates, Inc.

75. Schore, A. (2003a). *Affect regulation and disorders of the self.* New York: Norton.

76. Schore, A. (2003b). *Affect regulation and the repair of the self.* New York: Norton. p. 40.

77. Yamada, et al. (2000). "A milestone for normal development of the infantile brain detected by functional MRI." *Neurology*, 55, 218-223.

78. Lipari, J. (2000). Cited in *Psychology Today*, Raising baby: What you need to know. July/August issue.

79. Hess, E. H. (1975a). "The role of pupil size in communication. *Scientific American*, 233, pp. 110-119.

80. Schore, A. (2003a). *Affect regulation and disorders of the self.* New York: W. W. Norton, p. 41.

81. Schore, A. (2003b). *Affect regulation and the repair of the self.* New York: W. W. Norton, p. 122.

82. Schore, A. (2003a), *Op. Cit,*, p. 122.

83. Schore, A. (2003a), *Op. Cit.*, p. 122.

84. Schore, A. (1996). "The experience-dependent maturation of a regulatory system in the orbital prefrontal cortex and the origin of developmental psychopathology." *Development and Psychopathology*, 8, p. 60.

85. Hofer, M.A. (1990). "Early symbiotic processes: Hard evidence from a soft place." In A. Glick and S. Bone (Eds.), *Pleasure beyond the pleasure principle.* New Haven: Yale University Press, p. 71.

86. Schore, A. cited in Lipari, J. (2004). "Raising baby: What you need to know," *Psychology Today*. www.psychologytoday.com.

87. Schore, A. (2003a). *Op Cit.*, p. 265.

88. Schore, (2004). *Op Cit.*

89. Crenshaw, T. (1997). *The alchemy of love and lust*. New York: Pocket Books, p. 106.

90. Ibid., p. 106.

91. Last, W. (2007), "Sexual energy in health and spirituality," *Nexus Magazine*, Vol. 14:3, May-June, p. 25.

92. Crenshaw, T. (1997). *Op. Cit.*, p. 106.

93. Alexandra, P. (2015). *Intergenerational cycles of trauma and violence: An attachment and family systems perspective*. New York: Norton.

94. Ibid, p. 46.

95. Ibid, p. 46.

96. Main, M. (1995). Attachment: Overview, with implications for clinical work. In S Goldberg, R. Muir & J. Kerr (Eds.) *Attachment theory: Social, developmental, and clinical perspectives* (pp. 407-474. Hillsdale, NJ: Analytic Press.

97. Weinhold, B. & Weinhold, J. (2008a). *Breaking Free of the Co-dependency Trap*. Novato, CA: New World Library, pp. 8–9.

98. Cook, Blaustein, Spinazzola, & van der Kolk (2003).). Complex trauma in children and adolescents. Durham, NC: White paper from the National Child Traumatic Stress Network Complex Trauma Task Force.

CHAPTER SEVEN

99. Weinhold, J. (2018). *Op.Cit.*, pp. 64-67.

100. Mahler, M. (1968). *On human symbiosis and the vicissitudes of individuation*. New York: International University Press.

101. Ibid.

102. Weinhold, B. (2014). *The male mother*. Colorado Springs, CO: CICRCL Press, pp. 119-123

103. Weinhold, B. & Weinhold, J. (2017). *Breaking free of the drama triangle and victim consciousness*. Colorado Springs, CO: CICRCL Press.

104. Alexander, P. (2015). *Op. Cit.*, p. 46

105. Shemmings, D. and Shemmings, Y. (2011). *Understanding Disorganized Attachment*. London: Jessica Kingsley Publishers, p. 35.

CHAPTER EIGHT

106. Weinhold, B. and Weinhold. J. (2010). *Conflict resolution: The partnership way 2nd Edition*. Denver, CO: Love Publishing.

107. Lipton, B. (2005). *The biology of belief.* Santa Rosa, CA: Mountain of Love/Elite Books. pp. 197-198.

108. Ibid.

109. Lipton, B. (2005). *Op. Cit.*, p. 67-73.

110. Weinhold, J. (2017). *Op Cit..*, pp. 265-266.

111. Epel, E. et. al. (2009). "Can meditation slow rate of cellular aging? Cognitive stress, mindfulness, and telomeres." Ann N Y Acad Sci. 2009 Aug; 1172:34-53. doi: 10.1111/j.1749-6632.2009.04414.x.

112. Schore, A. (2003a). *Affect regulation and the repair of the self.* New York: W. W. Norton. p. 40.

113. Perry, B; (1996). "Incubated in terror: Neurodevelopmental factors in the cycle of violence." In J. Osofsy (Ed.). *Children, youth and violence: Searching for solutions.* New York: Guilford Press.

114. Schore, A. (1996). "The experience-dependent maturation of a regulatory system in the orbital prefrontal cortex and the origin of psychopathology." *Development and Psychopathology*, 8, 60, p. 40.

115. Schore, A. (2003a). *Op. Cit.*, p. 92.

116. Schore, A. (2004). Cited in Lipari, J. "Raising baby: What you need to know." *Psychology Today.* (www.psychologytoday.com).

117. Weinhold, J. (2017). *Op. Cit*, p. 13.

118. Goerner, S. (1995). "Chaos, evolution, and deep ecology." In R. Robertson & A. Combs (Eds.), *Chaos theory in psychology and the life sciences.* Mahwah, NJ: Eribaum. pp. 17–38.

119. For a more detailed analysis, please consult Schore, 2003a, pp. 92–95.

120. Weinhold, B. & Weinhold, J. (2009). *Conflict resolution: The partnership way 2nd Ed.* Denver, CO: Love Publishing Co. p. 70.

CHAPTER NINE

121. Weinhold, J. (2017). *Op. Cit.*, p. 261.

122. Lipton, B. (2005). *The biology of belief.* pp. 67-69. Santa Rosa, CA: Mountain of Love/Elite Books.

123. Peckham, H. (2013).epigenetics: the dogma-defying discovery that genes learn from experience. *International Journal of Neuropsychotherapy*, 1, 9-20.

124. Peckham, H. ().epigenetics: the dogma-defying discovery that genes learn from experience. *International Journal of Neuropsychotherapy*, 1, 9-20.

125. Starvation effects handed down for generations, *Science News*, July 31, 2015. http://www.sciencedaily.com/releases/2015/07/150731105240.htm.

126. Siegel, D. (2012). *The developing mind: How relationships and the brain interact to shape who we are, 2nd Edition.* New York: Guilford Press.

127. Blackburn, E. H., & Epel, E. S. (2012). Telomeres and adversity: Too toxic to ignore. *Nature, 490.* 169-171.

128. Epel, E. et. Al. (2015). The science of presence: A central mediator of the interpersonal benefits of mindfulness. In *Handbook of mindfulness theory, research and practice*, Edited by Brown, K., Creswell, J.D., and Ryan, R. New York: Guilford Press.

129. Steele, H. & Steele, M. (2008). *Clinical applications of the adult attachment interview.* New York: Guilford Press.

130. Siegel, D. (2012). *Op. Cit.*, p. ix.

CHAPTER TEN

131. Wallin, D. (2012). "We are the tools of our trade: How the therapist's own attachment patterns shape therapy. Retrieved December 3, 2017 from http://www.psychoanalyticevents.com/we-are-the-tools-of-our-trade-how-the-therapists-own-attachment-patterns-shape-therapy-david-wallin-phd/.

132. Weinhold, J. & Weinhold, B. (2011). *Op. Cit.*

133. Weinhold, J. (2017). *Op. Cit.*, p. 261.

134. Find Perelandra homeopathic products at http://www.perelandra-ltd.com.

135. Seligman, M. (1998). Building human strength: Psychology's forgotten mission. *APA Monitor*, 29(1).

136. Weinhold, B. & Weinhold, J. (2017). *Betrayal and the path of the heart.* Colorado Springs, CO: CICRCL Press.

CHAPTER ELEVEN

137. Weinhold, B. & Weinhold, J. (2017). *Op Cit.*, p. 219.

138. Weinhold, J. & Weinhold, B. (2011). *Op. Cit.*, pp.345-348.

CHAPTER TWELVE

139. Weinhold, B. and Weinhold. J. (2010). *Op. Cit.*, p. 174.

140. Weinhold, B. & Fenell, D. (2003). *Counseling Families.* Denver, CO: Love Publishing.

141. Minuchin, S. (1974). *Families and family therapy techniques.* Cambridge, MA: Harvard University, Moreno Archives.

142. Haley, (1971). *Changing families: A family reader.* New York: Grune & Stratton.

143. deMause, L. (1982). *Foundations of psychohistory.* New York: Creative Roots, p.135.

144. Weinhold, B. (2014). *Breaking Free: How To Identify and Change Your Addictive Family Patterns.* Colorado Springs, CO: CICRCL Press.

145. Weinhold, J. & Weinhold, B. (2011). *Healing developmental trauma.* Denver, CO: Love Publishing co. pp. 266-267.

146. Ibid, pp. 376-379.

CHAPTER THIRTEEN

147. Bernstein, P. *Family ties, corporate bonds*. (1985). New York: Henry Holt, p. 176.

148. Weinhold, B & Weinhold, J. (2011). *Conflict resolution: The partnership way*. Denver, CO: Love Publishing Co. p. 235.

149. Bolton, R. (1070). *People skills*. New York: Simon & Schuster.

150. Bernstein, P. (1985). *Op. Cit.*

151. Litvak, E. (1961). Models of bureaucracy which permit conflict. *American Journal of Sociology*, 67:177-184.

152. Likert, R. & Likert, J. (1961). *New ways of managing conflict*. New York: McGraw-Hill.

153. Jongeward, D. (1973). *Everybody wins: Transactional analysis applied to organizations*. Menlo Park, CA: Addison-Wesley. p. 6.

154. Schein, E. ((1969). *Process consultation: Its role in organizational development*. Reading, MK: Addison-Wesley.

CHAPTER FOURTEEN

155. Frankl, V. (1963). *Man's search for meaning*. New York: Washington Square Press.

156. Updegraff, J., Silver, R., & Holman, E. (2008). "Searching for and Finding Meaning in Collective Trauma: Results From a National Longitudinal Study of the 9/11 Terrorist Attacks," *Journal of Personal and Social Psychology*. September, 95(3); 709-722.

157. Ibid.

158. Frankl, V. (1963). *Op. Cit.*

159. Yalom, Irvin D. (1980). *Existential psychotherapy*. New York: Basic Books.

160. Siegel, D. (2010). *Mindsight: The new science of personal transformation*. New York: Bantam Books.

161. Siegel, D. (2010). p. 170.

162. Kaplan, C., Kaplan, N., & Main, M. (1985). *The adult attachment interview*. Unpublished manuscript, UC-Berkeley.

163. Wylie, M. S. & Turner, L. (2010). The attuned therapist. *Psychotherapy Networker*, March issue, p.4.

164. Jung quoted in Anthony Stevens, *Jung* (Oxford 1994) p. 110.

165. Carey, B. (2011). "Expert on mental illness reveals her own fight." *The New York Times*. June 23.

166. Diamond, S. (2011). "Jung and Linehan as wounded healers," *Psychology Today*, December issue. Retrieved December 5, 2017 from https://www.psychologytoday.com/blog/evil-deeds/201112/linehan-and-jung-wounded-healers.

167. Weinhold, J. (2014). *Con job: How to break free of con artists, sociopaths & predators*. Colorado Springs: CICRCL Press.

168. Smith, R. (1996). *The wounded Jung*. Northwestern University Press, p. 177.

169. Jung, C. G. (1993). *The practice of psychotherapy*. Princeton University Press, p. 172.

170. Levy P. (2010). *The wounded healer, Part 1*. Retrieved December 6, 2017 from http://www.awakeninthedream.com/wordpress/the-wounded-healer-part-1/.

171. Campbell, J. (1949). *The Hero with a Thousand Faces*. Princeton: Princeton University Press, p.23.

172. Morath, J. et. Al. (2014). "Effects of psychotherapy on DNA strand break accumulation originating from traumatic stress," *Pub Med., Psychosom.* 2014;83(5):289-97. doi: 10.1159/000362739. Epub 2014 Aug 6. Retrieved December 6, 2017 from https://www.ncbi.nlm.nih.gov/pubmed/25116690.

173. Siegel, D. (2012). *The mindful therapist*. New York: Norton, p. 32.

174. Author unknown.

CHAPTER FIFTEEN

175. Adapted from PBS Online's "Timeline: Treatments for Mental Illness". Retrieved 27 June 2012.

176. "A Brief History of Counseling and Therapy," Retrieved December 7, 2017 from http://changingminds.org/disciplines/counseling/history.htm.

177. A remark made by Bessel van der Kolk at a conference in Denver, CO in November 2014.

178. Shedler, J. Where is the evidence for 'evidence based' therapy? *The Journal of Therapies in Primary Care*. Vol. 4, 2015 pp. 47 - 59.

179. Buss, K., Warren, J., and Horton E. (March 2015). Trauma and Treatment in Early Childhood: A Review of the Historical and Emerging Literature for Counselors. http://tpcjournal.nbcc.org/trauma-and-treatment-in-early-childhood-a-review-of-the-historical-and-emerging-literature-for-counselors/ Retrieved August 4, 2015.

180. (2017). "Trauma and Violence," SAMHSA, Rockville, MD. Retrieved August 22, 2015 from https://www.samhsa.gov/trauma-violence.

181. (2017). "Trauma Informed Care," National Council for Behavioral Health, Washington, DC. Retrieved August 23, 2015 from http://www.thenationalcouncil.org/topics/trauma-informed-care/.

182. Retrieved December 8, 2017 from http://www.thenationalcouncil.org/topics/trauma-informed-care/

183. Ibid.

APPENDIX

SELF-INVENTORIES AND AWARENESS EXERCISES

SELF-QUIZ: HOW MUCH HIDDEN DEVELOPMENTAL TRAUMA DO YOU HAVE?

Barry K. Weinhold. PhD

Directions: Read the statements below and use 1-4 to indicate in the blank your self-assessment of each item: 1= mostly not true, 2=occasionally true, 3= usually true and 4=almost always true.

_____ 1. I have trouble feeling close to the people I care about.

_____ 2. I feel other people are more in charge of my life than I am.

_____ 3. I seem reluctant to try new things.

_____ 4. I have trouble keeping my weight down.

_____ 5. I am easily bored with what I am doing.

_____ 6. I have trouble accepting help from others even when I need it.

_____ 7. I work best when I am under a lot of pressure.

_____ 8. I have trouble admitting my mistakes.

_____ 9. I tend to forget or not keep agreements I make.

_____ 10. I have trouble handling my time and money effectively.

_____ 11. I use intimidation or manipulation to settle my conflicts.

_____ 12. I feel personally attacked when someone has a conflict with me.

_____ 13. I have a difficult time giving and receiving compliments.

_____ 14. I have a short fuse when I feel frustrated with myself or others.

_____ 15. I tend to blame others for causing the problems I have.

_____ 16. I feel like I have a huge empty place inside of me.

_____ 17. It is hard for me to have positive thoughts about my future.

_____ 18. Inside I feel like a tightly coiled spring.

_____ 19. When I get anxious I tend to eat or drink too much.

_____ 20. I feel empty and alone.

_____ 21. I tend to question the motives of others.

_____ 22. I feel unloved by others.

_____ 23. I have a hard time defining what I want of need.

_____ 24. When I get into a conflict somebody else gets his or her way.

_____ 25. I tend to overreact to certain people and/or situations that bug me.

_____ 26. I feel like I am on an emotional roller coaster.

_____ 27. I have trouble sticking with any spiritual practices I start.

_____ 28. Important people in my life have abandoned me emotionally or physically.

_____ 29. have trouble concentrating on what I am doing.

_____ 30. When I think about my childhood, I draw a big blank.

_____ 31. I have trouble experiencing the intimacy I want in my relationships.

_____ 32. I have trouble falling asleep and staying asleep.

_____ 33. I tend to "walk on eggs" around certain people or situations.

_____ 34. I avoid places or situations that remind me of experiences from my past.

_____ 35. I have recurring bad dreams about what happened to me in the past.

_____ 36. My thoughts seem to have a life of their own.

_____ 37. I have trouble paying attention to what others are saying.

_____ 38. I tend to avoid situations and people that could cause me conflict.

_____ 39. I experience big gaps in my memory about my childhood.

_____ 40. I have a hard time knowing what I am feeling inside.

_____ **Total Score**

Interpretation:

If your score was between:

40 - 80 = Some evidence of hidden developmental traumas causing your
freaked out reactions.

81 –120 = Moderate evidence of hidden developmental traumas causing
your freaked out reaction.

121-160 = Strong evidence of hidden developmental traumas causing your
freaked out reactions.

Further analysis:

Look at the content of items where you scored 3-4. These might provide
clues to possible unhealed developmental trauma that is causing you to freak
out in your relationships.

81 –120 = Moderate evidence of hidden developmental traumas causing
your freaked out reaction.

121-160 = Strong evidence of hidden developmental traumas causing your
freaked out reactions.

Further analysis:

Look at the content of items where you scored 3-4. These might provide
clues to possible unhealed developmental trauma that is causing you to freak
out in your relationships.

ADVERSE CHILDHOOD NEGLECT INVENTORY

Barry K. Weinhold, PhD

In the first year of your life specifically and generally prior to your
18th birthday:

1. Were you placed in childcare or with someone other than a primary
    caregiver before you were one month old?
    Not Applicable___ If Yes, enter 1 ___

2. Did you spend less than 20 hours a week being cared for by your
    mother during your first year of life?
    Not Applicable___ If Yes, enter 1 ___

3. As an infant, were you allowed to cry yourself asleep at night without
    your parent(s) attempting to comfort you?
    Not Applicable___ If Yes, enter 1 ___

4. Did you feel afraid of your mother or other adult caregivers?
   Not Applicable___ If Yes, enter 1 ___

5. Was your mother or another primary caregiver chronically depressed?
   Not Applicable___ If Yes, enter 1 ___

6. Did your mother or other primary adult caregiver suffer from substance abuse?
   Not Applicable___ If Yes, enter 1 ___

7. Did your mother or any other primary caregiver fail to tell you that they loved you?
   Not Applicable___ If Yes, enter 1 ___

8. Did your mother or other primary adult caregiver avoid hugging you, picking you up or making eye contact with you?
   Not Applicable___ If Yes, enter 1 ___

9. Were you separated from your mother for more than a week for any reason in your first year of life?
   Not Applicable___ If Yes, enter 1 ___

10. Did your primary caregivers leave you with strangers or other non-bonded caregivers for more than one week before your first birthday?
    Not Applicable___ If Yes, enter 1 ___

11. Were you told directly or indirectly that your parents were too overwhelmed to care for you?
    Not Applicable___ If Yes, enter 1 ___

12. Did your parents fail to make your home environment safe leading to accidents?
    Not Applicable___ If Yes, enter 1 ___

13. Were you told or treated by either of your parents to "be seen and not heard?"
    Not Applicable___ If Yes, enter 1 ___

14. Did you frequently move when you were very young?
    Not Applicable___ If Yes, enter 1 ___

15. Was your mother cold toward you when you were a child?
    Not Applicable___ If Yes, enter 1 ___

16. As a child, did you feel your parents didn't understand your needs?
    Not Applicable___ If Yes, enter 1 ___

17. Did you feel unwanted by your parents?
    Not Applicable__ If Yes, enter 1 __

18. Were you unplanned by your parents?
    Not Applicable__ If Yes, enter 1 __

19. Did you have frequent illnesses when you were under a year of age (colic, ear infections, etc.)?
    Not Applicable__ If Yes, enter 1 __

20. Even though you weren't adopted, did you feel you were "adopted" when you were growing up in your family?
    Not Applicable__ If Yes, enter 1 __

21. Was your mother under 19 years of age when you were born?
    Not Applicable__ If Yes, enter 1 __

22. Were you a "play-pen" baby?
    Not Applicable__ If Yes, enter 1 __

23. Did you believe that there was something fundamentally wrong with you because of the way you thought or behaved?
    Not Applicable__ If Yes, enter 1 __

24. Were you "parentized" or put in an inappropriate parenting role when you were very young?
    Not Applicable__ If Yes, enter 1 __

25. Did your parents fail to provide proper medical care for you?
    Not Applicable__ If Yes, enter 1 __

26. id your parents fail to teach you or require you to develop proper personal hygiene habits?
    Not Applicable__ If Yes, enter 1 __

27. Were you left unsupervised for long periods of time?
    Not Applicable__ If Yes, enter 1 __

28. Were you left in the care of someone who was significantly impaired or of questionable character?
    Not Applicable__ If Yes, enter 1 __

29. Were you placed in dangerous situations or with dangerous people?
    Not Applicable__ If Yes, enter 1 __

30. Were you verbally abused and your parent(s) did nothing to protect you?
    Not Applicable__ If Yes, enter 1 __

31. Were you sexually abused and your parent(s) did nothing to protect you?
    Not Applicable__ If Yes, enter 1 __

32. Were you physically abused and your parent(s) did nothing to protect you?
    Not Applicable__ If Yes, enter 1 __

33. Were you emotionally abused and your parent(s) did nothing to protect you.
    Not Applicable__ If Yes, enter 1 __

34. Did your parents fail to make sure you got to school on time?
    Not Applicable__ If Yes, enter 1 __

35. Did your parents fail to make sure you completed your homework?
    Not Applicable__ If Yes, enter 1 __

36. Did my parents fail to provide proper nutrition for me?
    Not Applicable__ If Yes, enter 1 __

37. Did your parents fail to provide proper or clean clothing for you?
    Not Applicable__ If Yes, enter 1 __

38. Did you have siblings who were less than one year older than you?
    Not Applicable__ If Yes, enter 1 __

39. Were you a "latch key" child who had no one there when you came home from school?
    Not Applicable__ If Yes, enter 1 __

40. Did your parents compare you unfavorably to your siblings?
    Not Applicable__ If Yes, enter 1 __

Scoring: Count the number of items where you answered, "Yes."

Interpretation:
If you had five or more yes's, you likely had developmental traumas in your childhood caused by neglect. The higher number of "yeses," the more severe the developmental traumas were in your childhood.

SELF-QUIZ: THE TWO LISTS

Barry K. Weinhold, Ph.D. & Janae B. Weinhold, Ph.D.

Use this exercise to identify any aspects of unhealed developmental trauma you may still have. Fill out the charts using information from your childhood related to your interactions with your mother or your father. When filling out List #1, include those things you believe would have made your life not only different, but also probably easier. When filling out List #2, include those things you believe hurtful or even harmful to you, and still affect you somewhat today.

List #1. Look back to your childhood prior to age 18 and list of all the things that you wish your mother or father had done for you or said to you while you were growing up. These are the things that you believe, had you gotten them, would make your adult life easier. These are the things you feel may have held you back. For example, "I wish my parents had told me directly that they loved me" or "I wish they had given me birthday parties and helped me celebrate my birthday." Place these items on the mother or father list, as appropriate, under List #1 in the first column: "What I Wanted That I Did Not Get" (From My Mother/ or My Father).

List #2. Look back to your childhood and list all of the things you can remember that you wish had not been done or said to you while you were growing up. This list represents the things that hurt or damaged you in some important way and interfered with your adult life. For example, "I wish they hadn't humiliated me when I got pregnant in high school" or "I wish they hadn't punished me by calling me names and hitting me." Place these items on the mother or father list, as appropriate, under List #2 in the second column, all that you can remember that fits with: "What I Got That I Did Not Want" (From My Mother or My Father).

If you had a primary caregiver in addition to or in place of one or both of your parents, cite these experiences as well. Write just enough to help you identify relevant experiences, such as, "The time my baby sitter yelled at me when I got hurt in the second grade." At the end of this exercise, you will find an explanation for the meaning of each list.

MOTHER

List #1 "What I Wanted That I Did Not Get"	List #2 "What I Got That I Did Not Want"

List #1 "What I Wanted That I Did Not Get"	List #2 "What I Got That I Did Not Want"

FATHER

List #1 "What I Wanted That I Did Not Get"	List #2 "What I Got That I Did Not Want"

List #1: "What I Wanted That I Did Not Get". Anything that appears on this list is related to unhealed developmental trauma that took place in the codependent stage of development (0 to 8-9 months), which indicates that you may still have unmet needs from your early childhood development. These unmet needs are usually caused by incidents indicating a lack of emotional support and neglected needs for bonding and closeness.

The items on this list are needs that you unconsciously fantasize about getting met in your adult relationships, without having to ask for them. You may try to manipulate or control others in order to get them. Initially, the hope may be that you will find someone who will function as the "perfect parent" you never had who now can fill your unmet needs for intimacy and connection. This kind of unconscious expectation now usually leads to big disappointment. People also use codependent language or victim body language to attract rescuers who will give them what they need.

Use List #1 to identify where you can get each need met now. Beside each item, place the name of a person who could help you meet this need. Perhaps you still feel angry and resentful toward your mother or father and fantasize that someday they will offer you what you need without your requesting it. Grudges and illusions can cause a kind of terminal stuckness, which is defined as waiting for somebody else to change so you can feel better.

Maybe you fear asking for what you want because you might be refused or rejected. Indirect strategies usually don't work. They just keep you locked in anger, resentment, and rejection and feeling hopeless, helpless, and victimized. You need to be willing to ask for what you want and need 100% of the time in order to heal the effects of these early traumas. You can't stay angry and grow up at the same time. You will have to choose one or the other.

List #2: "What I Got That I Did Not Want". These items are related to unhealed developmental trauma that occurred in the counter-dependent stage of development (9 months to 3 years). The items on this list come from experiencing things that were hurtful and/or harmful to you while you were growing up and not receiving support for your feelings.

These emotional wounds make it difficult to be close to other people. People with these early developmental traumas tend to avoid eye contact, do not approach others, or define themselves as different from others. They believe, "I have built a wall around me and I'm not going to let you see who I really am."

Alternatively, they might believe, "I'm not going to let you get close to me because I don't want to get hurt again." They engage in defensive behaviors that hide their vulnerability. The dilemma is that people must face the risk of being hurt again in order to get their needs met.

If you have many items in List #2, you have probably erected barriers to prevent closeness and protect yourself from being hurt. This puts you in a bind. You may want to get close so that you can get your needs met but, because of fear-related defenses, you refuse to take the risk.

Instead, you might try to make people feel guilty or ashamed in order to get them to meet your needs without having to take the risk to ask them directly for help. To break through this, you must penetrate your defenses in order to receive what you need. The first step may be admitting to yourself that you have needs that are not being met and then take the risk to ask others to help you meet those needs.

BREAKING FREE OF YOUR PERSONAL LAW

Barry K. Weinhold. Ph.D.

Here you identify the the bottom-line most negative beliefs or thoughts about yourself that feed self-hatred. They usually show up in the self-talk that you engage in when you make a mistake or do something that doesn't turn out the way you want. It could also show up when you feel guilty for something you did or said or didn't do or say.

1) Write down exactly what you say to yourself when this happens.
2) Working with your partner your job is to convince him/her that what you wrote down is true.
3) Your partner's role is to listen to you and ask any questions to help clarify what you mean and then to rate you from 1-100 on how convinced they are they what you told them is true. Give them an actual percentage
4) This time you need to try to convince your partner that this is not true of you and again partners need to rate how convincing you are that this is true. Again give them a percentage.
5) Then look at the two percentages and subtract the higher one from the lower one to get your actual score.
6) This represents how difficult it will be to change your belief.
7) Switch roles and repeat this process.

Here you are dealing with your the bottom-line most negative beliefs or thoughts about yourself. These are the basis of self-hatred. This usually shows up in the self-talk that you engage in when you make a mistake or do something that doesn't turn out the way you want. It could also show up when you feel guilty for something you did or said or didn't do or say.

8) Write down exactly what you say to yourself when this happens.
9) Working with your partner your job is to convince him/her that what you wrote down is true.
10) Your partner's role is to listen to you and ask any questions to help clarify what you mean and then to rate you from 1-100 on how convinced they are they what you told them is true. Give them an actual percentage
11) This time you need to try to convince your partner that this is not true of you and again partners need to rate how convincing you are that this is true. Again give them a percentage.
12) Then look at the two percentages and subtract the higher one from the lower one to get your actual score.
13) This represents how difficult it will be to change your belief.
14) Switch roles and repeat this process.

SELF-QUIZ: WAS YOUR FAMILY OF ORIGIN A SOURCE OF HIDDEN DEVELOPMENTAL TRAUMAS?

Barry K. Weinhold. Ph.D.

Directions: Using the following 25 characteristics of dysfunctional families, rate your own family of origin. In the blank before each item, place a number from 1 through 5. 1 = Not present at all; 2 = Present to a small degree; 3 = Present sometimes; 4 = Present most of the time; 5 = Present all of the time.

_____ 1. The family promotes competition rather than cooperation. This means that children are compared with each other and sibling rivalry is actually promoted.

_____ 2. There is a misuse of parental power. Parents may use their power to threaten, intimidate, control, and subjugate their children to obey their will. This usually involves a deliberate, but often unconscious, attempt to break the will of the child, often while the child is still an infant. It is often justified as "necessary for their own good."

_____ 3. There is no respect for the basic human rights of children or women. Women and children are treated like chattel or property, without basic human rights. Children are expected to be seen and not heard and have no needs or wants of their own.

_____ 4. There are rigid, compulsive rules. There is an attempt to over-control or over-regulate the behavior of family members through rigidly enforced rules. Reasons for rules are usually not provided and obedience is mandatory.

_____ 5. There are rigid gender roles. The boys or men are supposed to follow their traditional roles and the girls or women theirs. No exceptions are allowed. People tend to interact with each other through their roles rather than through their individual interests and needs.

_____ 6. There is no sharing of housework or household chores. Women and girls are expected to handle the household chores; the boys and men are exempt from these duties. Boys growing up in this type of family often expect to be waited on by their spouses when they get married.

_____ 7. There are no joint family activities planned. This type of family is very fragmented, and there are no structures or planned activities, such as family outings, that promote unity and family bonding.

_____ 8. The economic condition of the family is kept secret from family members. In these families, children are not told about the family's income and little or no financial responsibility is shared appropriately with other family members.

_____ 9. There is no respect for personal privacy. Children do not have their own personal space or property. Toys, clothing, bedrooms, furniture, and personal items belong to the family not individuals. Parents do not respect their children's needs for privacy or boundaries.

_____ 10. There is no shared decision making in the family. The head of the household makes all the major decisions, and other family members have very little say in these decisions.

_____ 11. There is no shared parenting. Almost all parenting is done by one parent, usually the mother. The father is absent or not involved in the day-to-day parenting, and perhaps is only involved occasionally in disciplining the children.

_____ 12. There is no support for the expression of feelings. Family members are taught to hide their feelings or are punished for their attempts to express normal feelings such as anger, sadness, fear, or even joy.

_____ 13. The main forms of discipline utilized are spanking, threats, or shaming. The level of physical or emotional violence is high in these families. Usually there is abuse of alcohol or drugs by one or both parents.

_____ 14. Win–lose conflict resolution methods are utilized. Whenever there is a conflict, someone wins and someone loses, instead of finding a solution where both parties can win. Partnership resolutions require a set of problem-solving skills that most parents don't have.

_____ 15. No one admits making a mistake or apologizes for their actions. Parents are always right in these families, and they present themselves as infallible. If they make a mistake, they try to hide it or explain it away instead of owning it and apologizing to those who were affected by the mistake.

_____ 16. Problems are blamed on others. There is a defensiveness in the family; when something bad happens, there is a quick attempt to blame it on someone else. There is no personal accountability or responsibility for one's own actions.

_____ 17. There is resistance to outsiders. There is a "we versus them" attitude toward anyone outside the family. The family is not opened to guests coming in or to sharing with others outside the family.

_____ 18. Loyalty to the family is seen as a duty. Children are expected to defend the family against outside criticism, even when the family is in the wrong. Protecting the family name is overemphasized.

_____ 19. There is resistance to change. Even though the family has obvious dysfunctional elements, there is strong resistance to changing them. There seems to be a fear that any change may bring about something worse. Sometimes people have lived for generations with these dysfunctional elements and have become comfortable with their "familiarity." To change them means going into unfamiliar territory.

_____ 20. There is no family unity. In this type of family, "two against one" triangles develop to create some unity or safety. There is often a lot of indirect communication where one person may communicate to another through a third person.

_____ 21. There is no protection from abusive acts. In this type of family, every conflict is swept under the rug. Children may be emotionally, physically, or sexually abused by one or both parents, and the other parent does nothing to protect the child from this abuse. This can also be true in sibling abuse, where an older sibling abuses a younger one and nothing is done by either parent to stop the abuse or protect the younger child.

_____ 22. Conflicts in the family are often ignored. In this type of family, every conflict is swept under the rug rather than resolved effectively. This often causes a heavy, oppressive family atmosphere in which there is conflict in the air and no one is talking about it.

_____ 23. There are a large number of family secrets. Almost every family has some secret they don't want people outside the family to know. The children are admonished not to reveal these secrets. However, in many instances the children are not told these secrets and the presence of these secrets colors relationships among family members. Often some members know the secret and others don't, creating "unholy alliances" in the family.

_____ 24. There is little joy or laughter in the family. In these families, parents often feel overburdened or overwhelmed by the job of parenting, so they can't have fun or allow laughter in the family. In some families, the only laughter that is permitted is when someone is teased or made the butt of a joke. This is a dysfunctional form of humor.

_____ 25. The children are unplanned or unwanted. More than 50% of all children born in this country are either unplanned or unwanted. Children often know they are unplanned or unwanted, even though no one ever tells them. An illegitimate birth is often kept as a family secret.

_____ **Total Score**

Scoring and Interpretation:

Add the numbers in the left-hand column to record the total score of how you perceive the level of dysfunction present in your family of origin. Below is a suggested interpretation of your overall rating.

If your score was between:

25- 50 = There was almost no evidence of hidden developmental traumas present in your family of origin that could cause you to reenact them in your present life situation.

51-75 = There is some evidence of hidden developmental trauma present in your family of origin that could cause you to reenact them in your present life situation.

76–125 = There is considerable evidence of hidden developmental trauma present in your family of origin that could cause you to reenact them in your present life situation.

Caution: Too rosy a picture of your family of origin could indicate some denial of these hidden developmental traumas and their possible effects on your tendency to reenact them reenact them in your present life situation.

SELF-QUIZ: FAMILY PATTERNS INVENTORY

Barry K. Weinhold, Ph.D.

Directions: In the blank before each item, place a number from 1 through 4 that indicates how true it is for you. 1 = Almost Never. 2 = Occasionally. 3 = Usually. 4 = Almost Always.

_____ 1. My current relationship conflicts remind me of conflicts I had as a child.

_____ 2. My partner says or does some things that irritate me and remind me of the way my parents treated me.

_____ 3. My partner disapproves of some things I say or do just the way my parents did.

_____ 4. I criticize myself and others the way I was criticized as a child.

_____ 5. Even though I don't want to, I find myself saying and doing things that hurt my children or partner the same way people hurt me while I was growing up.

_____ 6. I get upset at myself, I say some of the same critical things to myself that my parents or others said to me when I was a child.

_____ 7. The way my partner relates to me reminds me of the way my parents related to me when I was a child.

_____ 8. I find myself acting weak and helpless so others will feel sorry for me or help me out.

_____ 9. I can see similarities between the kinds of intimate relationships I now have and the relationship my parents had or still have with each other.

_____ 10. I tend to feel uneasy when everything seems to be going well in my relationships.

_____ 11. When I have conflicts with others, I tend to focus on what they did to cause the conflict.

_____ 12. I tend to give more than I receive in my relationships.

_____ 13. I have trouble enjoying sex the way I would like.

_____ 14. I am afraid to be "too successful."

_____ 15. I don't like to take risks and prefer to stay with what is familiar.

_____ 16. I feel my intimate partners treats me unfairly.

_____ 17. When asked, I have trouble thinking about or listing positive traits about myself.

_____ 18. I cannot express my feelings the way I would like.

_____ 19. I encounter people who tend to treat me like my parents treated me.

_____ 20. I feel controlled by the expectations of others.

_____ **Total Score**

Scoring and Interpretation:

Add the numbers in the column to the left of the statements to get your total score. Use the following guidelines to help you interpret the possible meaning of your score.

If your score was between:

20–40 = A few family patterns are likely sources of your present reactions.

41–60 = Many family patterns are the likely sources of your present reactions.

61–80 = Almost all of your reactions have their source in unprocessed family patterns.

SELF-QUIZ: FAMILY STRESSORS THAT CAN CAUSE DEVELOPMENTAL TRAUMAS

Barry K. Weinhold, Ph.D.

Directions: Place a check mark next to each of the questions that indicate that this problem was present in your family of origin. In this activity, you are only to determine the presence or absence of the problem and not the degree to which the problem might have been present.

Two-Career Families

_____ 1. Did both of your parents work or spend considerable time away from the home while you were growing up?

_____ 2. Did you come home from school to an empty house or without a parent there to greet you?

_____ 3. Did the absence of one or both of your parents cause you any problems while you were growing up?

_____ 4. Did you receive less care than you needed from your parents because one or both were working or away from your home a considerable amount of time?

Marital Dysfunction

_____ 5. Was there marital discord present between your parents while you were growing up?

_____ 6. Were you forced to take sides in any marital disputes?

_____ 7. Did the marital discord in your family lead to divorce or legal separation?

_____ 8. Did you feel that any of your important needs were neglected as a result of marital discord?

Single-Parent Families

_____ 9. Did you spend some time growing up in a single-parent family?

_____ 10. Did you spend some time growing up in a stepfamily?

_____ 11. Did you feel in the middle between divorced or separated parents?

Drug and Alcohol Abuse

_____ 12. Was abuse of drugs or alcohol present in your family of origin?

_____ 13. Did you develop codependent or counter-dependent behaviors as a result of growing up in your family?

_____ 14. Were there other addictions (food, work, sex, etc.)present in your family of origin?

School-Related Problems

_____ 15. Did you have difficulties in school?

_____ 16. Did you need more support from the school or your parents to cope with your problems?

_____ 17. Was your self-esteem adversely affected by school-related problems?

Child Management Problems

_____ 18. Did your parents have difficulty disciplining you effectively as a child?

_____ 19. Were you a family scapegoat who was blamed for problems that were not of your making?

_____ 20. Did you rebel against parental authority?

_____ 21. Did you try to take care of your parents by not causing them any problems?

Adolescent Depression and Suicide

_____ 22. Were you depressed for extended periods of time as an adolescent?

_____ 23. Did you ever contemplate or attempt suicide?

_____ 24. Did you ever feel that you were unable to live up to parental expectations?

_____ 25. Was either of your parents depressed or suicidal while you were growing up?

Adult Children Leaving Home

_____ 26. Was your departure from home in late adolescence full of conflict?

_____ 27. Did your parents make it difficult for you to leave home?

_____ 28. Did you ever return to live with your parents after you had been on your own?

Grandparents Live with Family

_____ 29. Did one or more of your grandparents have to live with your family while you were growing up?

_____ 30. Did problems over the care of your grandparents cause discord in your family while you were growing up?

SELF-QUIZ: HOW FAMILY-RELATED STRESSORS CAUSE DEVELOPMENTAL TRAUMA

Barry K. Weinhold, Ph.D.

This self-quiz asks you to focus on the effects the problems in the previous list had on your Tendency to freak out. Think about how they affected your thoughts, feelings, values, beliefs, and behaviors. Go back to the items you checked in the previous quiz on "What Family-Related Problems Were Present in Your Family of Origin?" and, on a separate sheet of paper, list the possible effect you think these problems had on you. On a separate sheet of paper, answer the following questions:

1. What are possible effects of these problems on my present tendency to reenact my Developmental Traumas?
2. What are the possible effects of these problems on why I reenact my Developmental traumas?
3. What are the possible effects of these problems on my values?
4. What are the possible effects of these problems on my beliefs?

SELF-INVENTORY: THE OPENNESS TO CHANGE INVENTORY

Barry K. Weinhold, PhD

Directions: Place a check in the column that best represents your experiences of living within your organizational culture. 1= Almost Never; 2= Occasionally; 3= Usually; and 4= Almost Always.

_____ 1. The salary/wages I receive are fair for the work I provide.
_____ 2. The benefits I receive meet my health care needs and other important needs.
_____ 3. I trust that those who supervise me have my best interests at heart.
_____ 4. My superiors listen to me and respect me as a person.
_____ 5. When I have a problem or need, I know my superiors respond seriously and effectively to my request for assistance.

_____ 6. I have sufficient time to develop relationships with my coworkers.

_____ 7. My superiors encourage me to contribute any new ideas I might have.

_____ 8. There are few rules in this organization that restrict my freedom.

_____ 9. I am consulted on decisions that affect me directly.

_____ 10. Information and important decisions are shared in face-to-face meetings in which I feel free to express my opinions and feelings.

_____ 11. Important information and decisions are communicated in memos, policy letters, telephone calls, faxes or e-mail messages so I have a record of them.

_____ 12. When I want an answer to something, I know who I need to check with for an answer.

_____ 13. I am encouraged to "wear as many hats" as the situation calls for.

_____ 14. I am free to change what I am doing in response to my needs or the needs of mycustomers, clients, and coworkers.

_____ 15. If I perform above my expected level, my superiors will praise me.

_____ 16. Managers, supervisors, and employees work together toward common goals and objectives.

_____ 17. I have the power to make the decisions that affect me most directly.

_____ 18. My superiors support and/or reward my efforts toward personal growth and mastery.

_____ 19. I have input into all procedures and schedules that are followed in this organization.

_____ 20. The goals and purposes of this organization are determined through input from all those involved in the organization.

_____ 21. When I have a conflict with a supervisor or administrator, I anticipate an equitable resolution.

_____ 22. Theopportunityexistsinthisorganizationforpeopletotakecooperative and collective action to reach their goals and objectives.

_____ 23. The basic attitude of "everyone is only looking out
for themselves, not looking out for each other" is
actively discouraged.

_____ 24. A top priority of this organization is the personal growth and
development of each employee.

_____ **Total Score**

Scoring and Interpretation:

This inventory yields four sub-scores and a total organizational score. The scoring procedures to obtain each sub-score are explained below, along with an interpretation of each sub-score and the total relationship score.

Codependent Stage (Items 1– 6) Add the numbers preceding these items to get the: Sub-score _____

Counter-dependent Stage (Items 7–12) Add the numbers preceding these items to get the: Sub-score _____

Independent Stage (Items 13–18) Add the numbers preceding these items to get the: Sub-score _____

Interdependent Stage (Items 19–24) Add the numbers preceding these items to get the: Sub-score: _____

_____ **Total Organizational Score**
   (Add the four sub-scores to get a total organizational score.)

Interpretation of sub-scores: Check your sub-scores for each of the four stages and refer to the following interpretation.

21–24 = Most major developmental processes have been completed in this organization at this stage of development.

15–21 = A few major incomplete developmental processes may be present in this organization. (Check the lowest of the four sub-scores.)

11–15 = Clear evidence exists of the presence of major incomplete developmental processes in this organization. (Check the lowest of the four sub-scores to locate the incomplete processes.)

6–10 = Major reorganization of some of the basic structure of the organization may be necessary. Essential developmental processes have not been completed at this stage of development.

Interpretation of The Total Organizational Score:

83–96 = Most major developmental processes have been completed in this organization.

68–82 = A few major incomplete developmental processes may be present in this organization. (Check the lowest of the four sub-scores.)

43 – 68 = Clear evidence exists of the presence of major incomplete developmental processes in this organization. (Check the lowest of the four sub-scores to locate the incomplete processes that need to be addressed.)

24 - 42 = Major reorganization of some of the basic structure and processes of this organization may be necessary.

SELF-INVENTORY: IDENTIFYING INTERGENERATIONAL FAMILY PATTERNS IN ORGANIZATIONS

Directions: In the blank before each item, place a number from 1 through 4 to indicate how true each statement is for you in your workplace. 1 = Almost Never; 2 = Occasionally; 3 = Usually, and 4 = Almost Always.

_____ 1. My feelings about my boss remind me of those I had with a parent when I was growing up.

_____ 2. My boss says or does things that irritate me and remind me of ways that my parents treated me.

_____ 3. My boss disapproves of things I say or do just the way my parents did.

_____ 4. I criticize myself and others the way I was criticized as a child.

_____ 5. Even though I don't want to, I find myself saying and doing things that my coworkers the same way people hurt me while I was growing up.

_____ 6. When I get upset at myself at work, I say some of the same critical things to myself that my parents or others said to me when I was a child.

_____ 7. The way my boss relates to me reminds me of the way my parents related to me when I was a child.

_____ 8. I find myself acting weak and helpless so others at work will feel sorry for me or help me out.

_____ 9. IcanseesimilaritiesbetweenthewayIrelatetomycolleaguesandtheway I related to my siblings.

_____ 10. I tend to feel uneasy when everything seems to be going well at work.

_____ 11. When I have conflicts with others at work, I tend to focus on what they did to cause the conflict.

_____ 12. I feel underpaid and unappreciated at work.

_____ 13. I feel so stressed by my job that I have no energy for play or exercise.

_____ 14. I am afraid to appear too successful at work.

_____ 15. I avoid taking risks at work and prefer to do what others expect of me.

_____ 16. I sacrifice myself and/or my family life for the sake of the company.

_____ 17. When asked, I have trouble thinking about or listing positive traits about my work responsibilities.

_____ 18. I cannot express my feelings the way I would like while at work.

_____ 19. I encounter people at work who tend to treat me like my parents treated me.

_____ 20. I feel controlled by the expectations of people at work.

_____ **Total Score**
(Add the numbers in the column to get your total score.)

Scoring and Interpretation:
Use the following guidelines to help you interpret the possible meaning of your score.

If your score was between:
20–40 = A few family patterns are likely sources of your present work conflicts.
41–60 = Many family patterns are likely sources of your present work conflicts.
61–80 = Almost all of your present work conflicts have their sources in unprocessed family patterns.

Review each item on which you answered 3 (Usually) or 4 (Almost Always). These items can offer clues to your family patterns that may be present in any of your current work conflicts. For example, if you answered 4 (Almost Always) to "I feel that I give more to my work than I receive back," explore the possibility that you were "parentized" in your family of origin and required to take care of others more than yourself. This might create work situations in which you feel angry, unappreciated, and resentful. If this is true, it is important to begin redirecting your anger toward family-of-origin members who expected you to deny your needs. Then learn effective ways to get your needs met in your current work relationships.

INDEX

H

I

J

L

Made in the USA
Columbia, SC
03 October 2018